Organizational Literacy
for Educators

◆ ◆ ◆

TOPICS IN EDUCATIONAL LEADERSHIP

Larry W. Hughes, Series Editor

Organizational Literacy
for Educators

◆ ◆ ◆

Jason Earle
John Carroll University
Sharon D. Kruse
University of Akron

 LAWRENCE ERLBAUM ASSOCIATES, PUBLISHERS
1999   Mahwah, New Jersey   London

Lawrence Erlbaum Associates, Inc., Publishers
10 Industrial Avenue
Mahwah, New Jersey 07430-2262

Cover design by Kathryn Houghtaling Lacey

Library of Congress Cataloging-in-Publication Data

Earle, Jason.
    Organizational literacy for educators / Jason Earle,
Sharon D. Kruse.
        p. cm. — (Topics in educational leadership)
    Includes bibliographical references (p   ).
    ISBN 0-8058-2639-4 (pbk.)
    1. School management and organization—Social as-
pects—United States. 2. Organizational sociol-
ogy—United States. 3. Educational sociology—United
States. 4. Educational equalization—United States. I.
Kruse, Sharon D. II. Title. III. Series.
LB2806.E27 1999
371.2'00973—dc21   98-29684
                                                                CIP

Books published by Lawrence Erlbaum Associates are printed
on acid-free paper, and their bindings are chosen for strength
and durability.

Printed in the United States of America
10 9 8 7 6 5 4 3

Contents

◆ ◆ ◆

Preface

◆ ◆ ◆

A series of shared experiences in our academic and professional lives provided the foundation for this book. As teachers of seemingly different subject areas (Sharon teaches educational administration and qualitative research methods, and Jason teaches foundations of education courses), we kept finding reason to discuss the need for a text that would provide students an introductory understanding of the social patterns that shaped schooling. It seemed, as we discussed issues related to school structure with our students, that they had little experience with social theories, especially those of a critical nature. This lack of exposure and awareness of how the larger systems of schooling operated seemed to undermine even the best of our students' efforts to create meaningful and lasting school reform. In some ways this was not surprising. The literature suggests that educators acquire the necessary knowledge to conduct their work in classrooms, but receive little information, if any, about how to operate successfully in the wider school organization (Blase, 1984, 1985; Kuzmic, 1993). Our own teacher and administrator preparation programs were not very different from those described in the literature. Our undergraduates focused on learning the basics of curriculum and instruction; our graduate students often were so deeply entrenched in the idea that their classrooms operated as islands of protection within a sea of potentially hostile colleagues, parents, and administrators that they often could not imagine systems of education from any other metaphor.

We initially decided to write this book in order to have the kind of text we wanted to use in our own classes. We wanted to explore the variety of ideas present in the sociological, historical, administrative, and school-change literatures to provide other metaphors for schools and educators. Additionally, we wanted to focus on issues of inequality and inequity in schools. The end result was that our book was informed by four important ideas. The first idea was that although every educator and school is unique, there are common social patterns that structure the way teachers, students, and administrators interact with each other. Unfortunately, U.S. culture, with its inordinate emphasis on individualism, makes it difficult to perceive these patterns. Educators, however, can develop the skills to recognize these patterns, skills we refer to as *organizational literacy*.

Second, organizational literacy should be applicable to real school settings. In this spirit, cases and exercises in the chapters help educators analyze their own schools. Also, each chapter features an extended narrative, based on case data, that demonstrates how a teacher might use the knowledge from the chapter to initiate change. Each chapter ends with a practice case, followed by exercises, allowing the student to practice the ideas presented in each chapter. Finally, each chapter offers a concluding exercise, in which students are encouraged to explore how the various theoretical ideas are present in their own school settings.

Third, understanding school organizations requires knowing about the historical and social contexts in which school organizations are embedded. As a consequence, the book combines literature from educational leadership with the social and historical foundations of education. We believe these areas compliment each other and deserve to be integrated into one text. Finally, academic textbooks should be interesting and readable. We made a sustained effort to write in an accessible manner and to include instructional features that would be appealing. For example, each chapter presents a different theory about school organizations, but does so through the use of narratives and cases that illustrate how the theory actually looks in practice. Additionally, the book assumes little prior experience with theories about school organizations. This book can be read without the necessity of a substantial background in the social sciences. Therefore, although the book is designed as an introductory text for graduate students, it may be used by advanced undergraduates and groups such as site-based management teams and district professional development committees.

Each of the chapters in the book is devoted to cultivating organizational literacy. Chapter 1 provides an introduction to the concept of organizational literacy and an overview of several social patterns common to schools in the United States. The subsequent chapters focus on each of the patterns. Chapter 2 discusses bureaucratic social patterns, which are characterized by a fixed division of labor, a hierarchy of offices, explicit rules, and specialized job training. We explore how these patterns of bureaucracy have affected schools and the work accomplished within them. Chapter 3 emphasizes political social patterns. Politics in schools often focuses on power and scarcity of resources. In chapter 3, we discuss the arenas in which power is exercised and its affects on those who work and learn in schools. Chapter 4 describes communal social patterns. Although the political chapters focus, to some extent, on a system of a more competitive nature, this chapter focuses on another form of school organization, that of a community. We suggest that a theory that embraces an ethic of care may offer educators a viable alternative metaphor. Chapters 5, 6, and 7 focus on patterns of inequality based on social class, race, and gender. Each of these chapters describes a variety of often unexamined social patterns that affect how students experience the practices of schooling. Each offers, as well, a message of hope for how schools can knowingly begin conversations to mitigate the influences of inequity based in differences in social class, race, and gender. Chapter 8 provides some concluding thoughts focused on the complexity of school change and how the ideas in this book can help others to create school organizations of promise and optimism. Finally, additional practice cases that can further improve organizational literacy are provided in chapter 9. These cases are designed for use in class discussions or as analysis cases for students to examine as final, on-going, individual, or group projects.

ACKNOWLEDGMENTS

We acknowledge the contributions of the reviewers for this manuscript: George Crawford, University of Kansas—Lawrence; Larry W. Hughes, University of Houston; Alan K. Gaynor, Boston University; and Nina Bascia, University of Toronto. Their careful reading and insightful comments helped us write a more thoughtful manuscript. We thank Naomi Silverman, our editor at Lawrence Erlbaum Associates, for her receptivity to the book we wanted to write and providing the encouragement we needed to complete it. Additionally, we thank our colleagues at John Carroll University and the University of Akron for their support. Finally, we acknowledge Taylor Kruse, whose patience during the process of writing this book surpassed that of any mortal 11-year-old.

—*Jason Earle*
—*Sharon D. Kruse*

1

Organizational Literacy and Social Patterns

◆◆◆

Educational scholar Blase (1984, 1985) coined the term *organizational literacy* to describe the type of education that would better prepare individuals to deal with a significant characteristic of schools that is often overlooked. Schools are made up of social patterns, regularities in how teachers, students, and administrators interact with each other everyday. Blase (1984) captured some of this when discussing the ineffectiveness of personal problem solving to grapple with systemic obstacles:

> Many of the problems stemming from arrangements deeply rooted in the social and economic organization (of schools) may exert a powerful effect on personal life but be impervious to personal efforts to change them. ... Coping failures, therefore, do not necessarily reflect the shortcomings of individuals; in a real sense they may represent the failure of social systems in which individuals are enmeshed. (p. 173)

When Blase spoke of a social system, he was referring to recurring patterns of action, shared amongst people, that literally sustain schools over many generations and across the United States. Implicitly, he is also communicating that these patterns can be identified and understood.

People often regard literacy as developing the ability to interpret and read texts; printed materials of various sorts. However, a number of scholars have begun to argue that the patterns constituting social life can be thought of as texts that need to be read and interpreted (Fiske, 1989; Geertz, 1983; Greene, 1997). And just as individuals have to develop the literacy to read printed texts, so too do they have to acquire the literacy to read social texts. Hopefully, this book will teach the skills and knowledge needed for reading and interpreting the patterns that constitute the social texts in school organizations. Additionally, we hope to enhance educators' abilities to be reflective and critical about school organizations, supporting efforts to change schools for the betterment of students and staff.

1

INDIVIDUALISM VERSUS SOCIAL PATTERNS IN THE UNITED STATES

A meaningful place to start is to explain why those who spend their lives in schools often do not recognize social patterns. An important reason is that over the course of U.S. history, social patterns have been controversial (Bellah, Madsen, Sullivan, Swidler, & Tipton, 1991; Carroll & Noble, 1989). They remain so to this day. Despite the growing social interdependence brought by urbanization and industrialization in the 20th century, many Americans still like to view themselves, in the 19th-century manner, as rugged individualists (Wills, 1997). We wish to be separate from the pushes and pulls of social influence in the present and from the past. As one noted scholar wrote, the typical American sees him or herself as, "an individual emancipated from history ... an individual standing alone, self-reliant and self-propelling, ready to confront whatever awaits him with the aid of his own uniqueness and inherent resources" (Lewis, 1955, p. 5). Acknowledging and accepting social patterns threatens this sense of individuality. We struggle to get out from under the control of any social experience that constrains our sense of freedom. Some writers have characterized this exaggerated emphasis on individualism as a kind of innocence (Lewis, 1955; Wills, 1989). Innocence has its virtues, but it also has important drawbacks. One is that social patterns become impossible to talk about because the official story of U.S. life suggests they do not exist and, if they do, they have little significance. For educators, this is quite a bind. We are forced to overlook the existence of social regularities that significantly affect our daily work life.

SOCIALIZATION AND SOCIAL PATTERNS

A first step in making sense of social patterns in schools means acknowledging and understanding socialization, the process by which all of us learn these patterns and, literally, make them a part of our identity (Berger & Berger, 1979). Eminent social thinker Mead suggested that identity actually develops through patterned interaction with others (Berger & Berger, 1979). During the first stage of socialization, children begin to imitate the way significant people in their lives like mothers, fathers, and siblings act toward them. The developing child will role-play the way one person acts, and then another. Through this process, children come to internalize the patterned responses of those around them. However, as each of these role-playing sessions focuses for a short time on just one person, there is no unified pattern of expectations by which the child stands in relationship to many people simultaneously, as in a school organization.

Later, during what Mead (Berger & Berger, 1979; Karp & Yoels, 1993) called the game stage of socialization, children learn to interact with many people at the same time during group activities such as hopscotch or baseball. To successfully sustain a game of hopscotch or baseball, individuals must be able to coordinate their actions in relation to the roles others perform around them. They must also understand and act according to a body of rules that fellow participants agree will organize what is done together. From these game experiences, developing individuals eventually internalize a variety of patterned responses and expectations that enable them to operate in a range of group settings. It is individuals' internalization of different social patterns over their life span that enables them to organize in recurrent ways in relationship to one another in schools.

Additionally, Mead (Berger & Berger, 1979) thought it was important that socialization not be viewed solely as aiding the maintenance of social patterns. He distinguished between two parts of the self, the "I" and the "me." The "I" is the unique part of each and every one of us, the idiosyncratic and spontaneous awareness present in every aspect of our lives. The "me" is the part of the self that internalizes social patterns over the course of socialization. The "me" sustains group social interaction. Some also refer to the "me" as a person's social identity.

DOMINANT SOCIAL PATTERNS
AND SOCIAL IDENTITY

Different societies, by virtue of their more common social patterns, create a more typical or dominant social identity (Berger & Berger, 1979; Robertson, 1992). In the United States, dominant social identities have varied over time as the country has moved through different historical periods, generating new social patterns to handle contemporary problems and changing circumstances (Rotundo, 1993). However, older social patterns and their matching social identities do not completely fade away over time (Amato, 1982; Gross, 1992). They often remain, although, frequently in an altered form (Carroll & Noble, 1989). Consequently, all of us participate in a variety of historically grounded social patterns (Buell, 1994). In fact, one of the things that makes this current period in the United States so difficult for educators is that there are so many social patterns struggling for dominance, pulling us in contradictory directions. However, clearly, as is described later in this chapter, some social patterns and identities are still more dominant than others.

What follows is a discussion of some of the important social patterns and identities that U.S. educators continue to bring to their daily lives in schools: communal, individualistic, bureaucratic, and political. Indication of dominant social identities during different historical periods, does not suggest that other types of social identities did and do not exist. We discuss this issue when focusing on the problems associated with class, gender, and racial identity. Also, the importance of the "I," the idiosyncratic and highly personal identity possessed by each one of us, is vital to remember.

Communal Patterns and Social Identity

In some ways it is odd that educators do not recognize social patterns because, historically, schools have played an important role in socializing students into the dominant social identity. This was certainly the case in colonial New England (Cremin, 1970). Socializing agencies such as schools, and especially family and church, helped children internalize the communal patterns of New England village life. For members of this society, there was a sense of physical and social closeness (Rotundo, 1993). The villages were small and all the inhabitants knew one another's names and communicated on a daily basis in face-to-face conversations. The villagers also shared common religious beliefs and a common way of life organized around farming. Villagers often shared kinship ties as well. Community members were judged not on individual achievements but on the basis of their "public usefulness" and contribution to village life as a whole. An important related value was the notion of *duty*. This was a sense of obligation that tied each member of the village in a reciprocal relationship to others in the village. The ideal person was "pleasant, mild-mannered, and devoted to the good of the community" (Rotundo, 1993, p. 13).

Rather than looking forward, community members looked to the past as a model to promote stability and ward off innovation and change (Brown, 1976). The past for most indicated a mixture of rich and poor people in the community. Consequently, the communities were hierarchically organized with poor people, considered lower in social rank, expected to demonstrate deference to the wealthier people. Patriarchy or male-rule in all spheres (home, work, church, government, and school) played an important role in establishing and maintaining this social ranking system. However, there were changes taking place as the country moved toward independence and began the next century in 1800 (Appleby, 1992).

Individualistic Patterns and Social Identity

In the first decades of the 19th century, a social identity that stood in opposition to the communal past began to dominate. It emphasized the individual who operated based on his own self-interest, rather than deferring to social betters (Brown, 1976). He picked his own goals and calculated the means to achieve those goals. Consequently, he was forward-looking, energetic, and he optimistically believed in his ability to improve his own life and those of his children through social mobility. The new and developing public education system in the 19th century helped to promote this focus on individual development (Kaestle, 1983). The extension of voting rights from White male property owners to all White males in many new states seemed to encourage this individualism as well (Carroll & Noble, 1989). As is apparent, however, this new individualistic social pattern was very much granted to males rather than females, and Whites as opposed to people of color.

With confidence in his "capacity to improve the natural and social environments" (Brown, 1976, p. 95) and unfettered by communal bonds, individualistic man struck out for what he regarded as the open lands of, first, the midwest and, then, the far west. This emphasis on geographic mobility coupled with the vastness of the continent fostered a sense that this individualistic social identity was open to anyone willing to take the initiative and risk (Carroll & Noble, 1989). The possibilities for social mobility and progress seemed unlimited. The authority and traditions of the past were thought to be left behind.

Individual initiative and risk were also fostered by a new developing approach to the economy—capitalism (Appleby, 1992). Communal man had farmed just enough to sustain his family year in and year out (Brown, 1976). Moving into the end of the 18th century and the beginning of the 19th, farmers grew crops to feed their families but also cultivated extra that could be taken to the market and sold to generate additional money (Hofstadter, 1955). This money could be poured back into the family farm and even more crops could be sold at the end of the next harvest. It also became apparent that there were quicker, more efficient ways to plant, cultivate, and harvest. Different processes or pieces of technology could be planned for and used to significantly increase productivity. Time honored ways of cultivation were left behind by individuals in the rush to compete with other farmers to be the most productive, efficient, and, consequently, the most profitable. This same commercial ethic was adopted by small business owners over the course of the 19th century.

However, communal social patterns continued to exist, albeit in a diluted form, promoted by proximity, kinship ties, and shared religion (Weibe, 1967). In fact, communalism played an important part in organizing the small towns and villages that dotted the 19th century landscape of the midwest and far west (Wills, 1989). Not surprisingly, 19th century rural schools encouraged individual development, but they also continued to support communal social patterns (Finkelstein, 1979). However, large changes were taking place in the 19th century, altering individualistic and communal social patterns (Presthus, 1979; Weibe, 1967).

Bureaucratic Patterns and Social Identity

Early factories that manufactured such things as clocks and shoes during the first decades of the 19th century offered an alternative to making money through the individualistic commercialism of farmers and small business owners (Carroll & Noble, 1989). Factories organized many people to collectively produce items more quickly and in greater quantity than individual craft artisans. This was the beginning stage of a social pattern that would expand exponentially in the second half of the 19th century.

Starting during the Civil War and its aftermath railroads grew significantly, laying track that joined the country from coast to coast. As a consequence, regional businesses could sell their wares across the country and enlarge their potential markets and profits. Many businesses grew in size to tap these possibilities (Carroll & Noble, 1989). However, these larger companies could no longer be efficiently operated through an owner personally supervising a dozen family members and apprentices. With hundreds of employees, sometimes even more, to be coordinated and operations stretching over vast geographic space, a new form of coordination developed to enable these large groups of people to accomplish shared outcomes. Bureaucratic social patterns admirably performed this collective task.

Bureaucracy organized people based on having each employee perform a specialized job function, follow impersonal rules, and work in a ranking of authority not unlike the military with its different levels of command from general to colonel, to major, to captain, and on down (Carroll & Noble, 1989). This eventually became the dominant way of organizing every sector of U.S. society: business, labor, communications, entertainment, and government. Schools, as a part of the growing government sector, also came to be organized in this manner and helped to socialize individual students into a social identity adapted to this form of social life (Spring, 1972).

Exacerbating this trend was the development of enormous businesses called corporations that bought up smaller, competing firms and consolidated them under one ownership (Presthus, 1979). Bureaucratic social patterns enabled corporations to effectively coordinate these new sprawling, consolidated operations. It also helped corporations remove their competition and dominate various market sectors. Small businesses could not compete with the volume, speed, and lower prices offered by corporations. By 1934, the 200 largest corporations came to control half the country's national industrial wealth. Similarly, in many different industries such as automobile production three or four giant corporations came to dominate about 50% of all production. The consequences of corporate, bureaucratic growth had enormous significance for individualistic social patterns. By 1970, less than 10% of the population worked for themselves. The majority of Americans were working in large bureaucratic settings. The words of oil magnate, John D. Rockefeller, in 1870 seemed to be prophetic for the 20th century. He wrote, "The day of [corporations] is here to stay. Individualism has gone, never to return" (Rockefeller, cited in Carroll & Noble, 1989, p. 261).

Also contributing to the decline of early 19th-century individualistic social patterns was the growth and coordination of densely inhabited urban environments. In 1890, only 30% of the 63 million Americans lived in cities (Cremin, 1988). By 1920, a little more than half of the 106 million population had come to reside in urban areas. By 1950 "almost two-thirds of a population of 151 million lived in the cities, and in 1980 some three-fourths of a population of 227 million lived in cities" (p. 4). To administer all the needs and requirements of this often chaotic city life, state and local governments developed large bureaucracies. By 1975, 10 million people worked for state and local government bureaucracies. Paralleling this growth, by 1979 nearly 3 million people worked for the federal government. Henceforth, in the 20th century, city, state, federal, and corporate bureaucracies would come to "provide the environment in which most of us spend our lives" (Presthus, 1979, p. 10).

The final blow to early 19th-century individualistic social patterns was the exhaustion of the midwest and far west frontier. As reported by the census of 1890, the land formerly available to anyone willing to pull up stakes and leave was gone (Noble, Horowitz, & Carroll, 1980). However, despite the depletion of the frontier and the massive bureaucratic social reality, the image of early 19th-century individualism continued, as noted at the beginning of this chapter, to be the way Americans commonly viewed themselves in the 20th century (Wills, 1997). The notion of the individual finding a place of his or her own on the western frontier was transferred and revitalized to fit the new bureaucratic social reality (Noble, 1980). The individual would now seek mobility in the endless opportunities offered by the jobs and rungs of the corporate bureaucratic world. However, although significantly altered and eviscerated by bureaucracy and the growing impersonality of city life, some communal social patterns continued to be touted and sustained (Brinkely, 1982, 1998; Carroll, 1982; Gerstle, 1989). During World War II and its aftermath, new social patterns would add yet another social identity to this mix.

Political Patterns and Social Identity

Early 19th-century celebrants of individualistic patterns believed that if everyone pursued their own self-interest, this would "automatically work for the welfare of the community" (Noble, 1985, p. 87). There would be no conflict between the differing desires of individuals because there was enough geographic abundance to ensure prosperity for all Americans. Consequently, there was a kind of natural harmony between Americans based on their shared experience as small landowners. When the land was gone by 1890 and large corporate bureaucracies dominated the landscape, many Americans revitalized this belief in a natural harmony by arguing that corporate bureaucracies would generate unending amounts of wealth (Noble, 1980). There would be more than enough created by industrialization to go around for everyone. Also, by working in an interdependent setting like a bureaucracy, people would learn the importance of cooperation. Consequently, in a corporate bureaucratic world there would be "a perfect partnership of all citizens and all values" (Noble, 1985, p. 39). Again, this meant a natural harmony amongst Americans.

This emphasis on natural harmony to some extent assumed shared Anglo-Protestant values (Noble, Horowitz, & Carroll, 1980). Until the time of the Civil War most of the country's inhabitants consisted of White northern European Protestants. However, in the last third of the 19th century and the first six decades of the 20th, the large immigration of southern and eastern Europeans, the aggressive expansion of the United States into the international marketplace, involvement in World War I and II, and the civil rights movement forced Anglo-Protestants and other Americans to cope with a country and world made up of many different groups who did not always share exactly the same values.

By the 1960s, the United States was finally groping toward recognizing political or pluralistic social patterns. An important piece of this growing acceptance of pluralism was acknowledging that in addition to harmony, human societies were also subject to inevitable conflicts (Dahl, 1967). This new belief argued that individuals and groups differed with regard to their goals, values, and interests. Conflicts were the natural consequences of difference. However, with conflict as a regular feature of social life, there must also be "individuals or groups with enough authority or power to secure—if need be to compel—a settlement" (p. 7) when disagreements arose. Inevitably this meant a need to exercise power to ensure the creation of a working consensus and also to keep any one group's interests from dominating all others. Americans had come to initially accept political social patterns that had long existed but had been delegitimated due to an enormous emphasis on harmony and homogeneity in the country.

Schools played a role in socializing students into these new pluralistic political patterns. During the 1960s and 1970s—with parents wishing to have more influence on schools, taxpayers wanting to reform school finance, minorities seeking desegregation and equality of educational opportunity, the courts extending the legal doctrine of individual rights to students, the increasing power of teacher organizations, and the growing influence of federal and state authorities—schools were inundated by political patterns (Wirt & Kirst, 1982). The aforementioned groups were competing in schools to achieve their differing goals and interests. As a result, conflict and the exercise of power came to be intermingled with the older communal, individualistic, and bureaucratic patterns in schools.

Our more typical individualistic way of perceiving U.S. society hides the complexity of the social patterns and history just discussed. More importantly for educators, this individualism makes it very difficult to read the complicated social texts in school organizations. It also obscures the connections between our schools and the wider society. And, finally, our individualistic view shields us from making sense of the problems in the United States and its schools related to issues of social class, race, and gender.

PROBLEMS WITH THE DOMINANT
SOCIAL PATTERNS AND IDENTITIES

The United States has prided itself on offering equality to all of its citizens. However, historically and currently we are still struggling to achieve this ideal (Takaki, 1993). Some groups have been excluded from full participation in the educational, economic, social, and political domains of the United States and, as a result, inequitable social patterns and subordinate social identities have been created and sustained in addition to those previously discussed. These inequitable patterns and subordinate identities are based on social class, race, and gender.

Social Class

The individualistic social patterns that have dominated U.S. consciousness since their ascendance in the early 19th century were initially created in England to support the "tight-knit middle class aristocracy of powerful merchants and landowners" (Noble, 1965, p. 8) against the monarch James II. However, from that point forward, including their transplantation to America, individualistic social patterns have maintained an association with the middle class and a certain level of prosperity (Bercovitch, 1993). Additionally, by virtue of making a relatively comfortable middle class the standard for individualism in the United States, the poor have been viewed as subordinate in many areas of U.S. life. For example, after America achieved its independence from England, the Founding Fathers were concerned with defining citizenship in such a way as to only encourage "the worthy part of mankind" to settle in the country (Takaki, 1993, p. 79). The Naturalization Act passed by Congress in 1790 developed a probationary period so the desirability of new immigrants could be assessed. Through this measure, Congress hoped to exclude paupers from living in America. Up until the 1820s, allowing only property owners, ostensible members of the middle class, to vote in elections also marginalized the poor.

Even during the ascendance of individualistic social patterns in the early 19th century, people with some previous wealth seemed to benefit the most from the new opportunity in the cities and rural areas of America (Carroll & Noble, 1989). And this relatively well-to-do group was the most likely to publicly applaud the new individualistic social patterns. Those with less financial resources faced a more grim economic and social reality. The port towns of the northeast during the 1840s swelled with poor people who lacked the money to be geographically mobile and purchase their own land. There, many of the urban poor remained the rest of their lives "amid industrial poverty, sporadic unemployment, and limited opportunity" (p. 158). Hierarchies based on class also developed in the expanding western territories. "[E]arly arrivals seized the best lands and the main chance, and thus became an entrenched elite. Late arrivals confronted a social hierarchy not dissimilar from that of the eastern states" (p. 156).

The growing urban poor of the northeast, in fact, became an important factor in the creation of the U.S. public school system (Kaestle, 1983). Early Americans had assumed that with vast amounts of frontier lands, each citizen would have land of his own (Noble, 1980). They believed that property ownership would naturally serve to initiate people into individualistic social patterns by teaching people about autonomy, self-reliance, and responsibility. The gathering of the poor in cities during the 1830s and 1840s signaled that vast numbers of people would never have the character-building experience of land ownership. Consequently, government-sponsored schools were necessary to ensure the poor learned how to be moral and respect property in the manner of the individualistic, middle-class property owners.

In the bureaucratic and political patterns of the 20th century, the poor continued to be excluded. Whether intended to or not, a disproportionate number of poor children are tracked into vocational programs and less rigorous academic classes (Oakes, 1985). This sorting process substantially lowers the probability that students from poor backgrounds will have the same job opportunities in their futures as middle and upper class children. A similar social class issue is exemplified in the current problems with school finance. Schools situated in poor communities have less local property wealth to generate tax money for their schools. Consequently, poor children have less in the way of advanced educational programs, equipment, technology, textbooks, and school buildings than their peers in wealthy districts (Kozol, 1991). Middle- and upper class communities have been reluctant to alter existing patterns of school finance.

Race

White Europeans exploring the North and South American continents during the 16th centuries ranked the new cultures they encountered by how closely their religion and way of life resembled Christian Europe (Takaki, 1993). White European Christians regarded themselves as civilized. Those who differed substantially were viewed as uncivilized, closer to the animal kingdom than the world of human beings. For example, early English settlers of colonial America likened Native Americans to "'cruel beasts,' who possessed 'a more natural brutishness' than wild animals" (p. 35). These views allowed the colonists and, later, 19th-century Americans to subordinate Native Americans, taking their lands and frequently their lives. The Native American settlements of the midwest and the far west became open lands for the taking by virtue of Whites' belief in the inherent superiority of their individualistic social patterns. Henceforth, individualistic social patterns would maintain some linkage with White racial identity as well as a connection to the middle class.

When Africans were forcibly brought to the colonies, similar forms of exclusion were applied to them. Benjamin Franklin spoke for many of the English colonists when he asked, "Why increase the Sons of Africa, by Planting them in America, where we have so fair an opportunity, by excluding all Blacks and Tawnys [i.e., Asians], of increasing the lovely White ... ?" (Takaki, 1993, p. 79). These beliefs were formalized when Congress passed the Naturalization Act of 1790, which excluded all non-Whites from citizenship in the United States (Franklin, 1976). The institution of slavery in much of the south clearly embodied convictions regarding White racial superiority. However, even free Blacks in the north during a significant portion of the 19th century were not allowed to vote.

These forms of subordination were extended to the peoples of Asian descent as well in the latter half of the 19th century and the first half of the 20th (Takaki, 1993). White Americans during the latter half of the 19th century regarded Asians entering the country with the same suspicions and prejudices heaped on African and Native Americans. President Rutherford Hayes warned Whites about the Chinese invasion, because "[o]ur experience in dealing with the weaker races—the Negroes and Indians ...—is not encouraging" (p. 206). Building on this sentiment, Congress passed legislation in 1882 prohibiting Chinese immigration into the United States. Japanese Americans were driven from their homes and way of life during World War II and placed in internment camps. Although many had spent most or all their lives in America, their racial background made them suspect to many Whites in the country.

Schools in the 19th century socialized students into the social patterns that supported these racial inequities (Spring, 1997). In the north, African Americans were generally segregated in schools separate from Whites. These schools were also afforded far fewer resources. Once public schooling began to develop in the south, African Americans were segregated in underfunded schools as well. Native and Asian American students also suffered racially based indignities from schools in the 19th century.

Although there has been a positive transformation in patterns of racial inequality since 1960 (Omi & Winant, 1994), our schools still struggle toward the ideal of racial equality. Non-White students continue to be excluded academically and socially based on whether they exhibit White individualistic social patterns (Fordham, 1988/1993). Bureaucratic social patterns still seem to divide students based on race. White students dominate the upper college preparatory curriculum tracks in high schools; students of color remain the disproportionate inhabitants of the vocational and remedial curriculum tracks (Bennett deMarrais & LeCompte, 1995).

Gender

From the beginnings of the colonial period, male domination or patriarchy was a key social pattern that created women's subordinate social identity in the wider community (Brown, 1976). As one influential Protestant theologian remarked, "Let the women be satisfied with her state of subjection, and not take it amiss that she is made inferior to the more distinguished sex" (Calvin, cited in Evans, 1989, p. 22). Additionally, based on the customs of English common law that the colonists brought with them to the Americas, women had no independent legal standing. Therefore, they could not own property, sign contracts, or control wages they had earned. All of these, as did even a woman's person, came under the rule of the husband or father.

These gendered social patterns influenced women's continuing exclusion during the revolutionary period in America (Evans, 1989). American revolutionaries made a clear distinction between the public and the private sphere. The public sphere consisted of the formal and informal meetings where financially independent individuals gathered to discuss the political decisions that would shape and control the local, state, and national way of life. This was the arena solely of men. The private sphere, of less importance than the public, was the arena of women. Here in the domestic realm of the household, women attended to feeding their families and nurturing the development of their children. This division was reinforced for a long period of time by granting only men the right to vote.

During the early 19th century, this split between the public and private was altered to some extent when it encountered the ascendant individualistic social patterns of the period (Rotundo, 1993). The world of work was added to the public sphere of men. Based on the new individualistic social patterns, men stepped out on their own to compete aggressively in the work world for upward mobility and money to support the family. Women were assigned complete control over the domestic sphere or home, where they served as beacons of purity and morality for their husbands and children. Henceforth in the United States, individualistic social patterns would have some linkage with males as opposed to females. Also, as men came to work in the large bureaucracies of the 20th century, given the view of men as the wage earners for the family, the bureaucratic social identity came to be associated with males rather than females.

The subordination of females into different spheres than men was also reinforced in the developing urban public schools of the 19th century (Tyack & Hansot, 1992); "[W]omen practically monopolized the lower grades, while men worked in the higher grades and as managers" (p. 84). The educational nurturing of younger children in the lower grades was viewed as an extension of a women's domestic role in the home. Men, with their supposedly superior intellectual and managerial abilities, were thought to be better suited to the more academically oriented upper grades and the leadership roles such as principal and superintendent. In the beginning of the 20th century, the school curriculum also played a role in socializing women into domestic roles and men into the world of work. Female students were tracked into home economics classes to improve their work in the home and their role as mothers. Men were sorted into the vocational classes or college preparatory classes that would eventually prepare them for the competitive world of work.

Currently, research indicates that schools still sustain inequitable social patterns for females (Bennet deMarrais & LeCompte, 1995). Males dominate administrative positions in schools, communicating that "men hold positions of authority and power in society while women play subordinate roles, having control over the children in their classrooms" (p. 266). In textbooks, women are frequently ignored or assigned to domestic roles rather than active roles in the world of work. Females are discouraged from taking advanced science, math, and computer classes because these subject areas are frequently deemed a male domain. Male students are frequently reinforced for being academically assertive in the classroom, whereas females are socialized to remain passive and quiet.

Again, our typical individualistic view of America and its schools hides these inequitable social patterns. This makes it hard for us as educators to understand how best to cope with these social texts as they manifest themselves in our classrooms and corridors. We believe that the organizational literacy required to read these inequitable social patterns might enable us to better serve all the children in our schools.

SOCIAL PATTERNS AND THE ORGANIZATION OF THE BOOK

Each of the next seven chapters focuses on the different social patterns and problems discussed already. The chapter on bureaucratic social patterns explains how individuals are assigned to specific roles in school organizations. Each role is regulated according to explicit rules so that the collective job of educating children is conducted efficiently and predictably day in and day out. Bureaucratic patterns tend to organize the relationships between staff and students hierarchically; they are also based on a technical orientation, finding the best means possible to accomplish desired educational outcomes.

The chapter on political social patterns highlights the use of conflict and power to influence what happens in schools. Political patterns tend to become more prominent during periods of change when the traditional ways of doing things and the past distribution of important resources are altered. In such situations, individuals and groups jockey for control and seek new alliances in the hopes of achieving their goals or supporting key value orientations. With the recent political and economic transformation to the country, schools have increasingly been the site of political social patterns. This can potentially make schools dynamic and innovative places to work and learn, as well as stressful, difficult places.

There has been a resurgence of interest recently in the positive qualities associated with communal patterns in American society (Bellah et al., 1991; Carroll, 1982). The chapter on communal social patterns focuses on how schools have begun to put more emphasis on this as well, stressing the importance of the implicit and explicit bonds that provide a sense of belonging. These social patterns can foster unity and interdependence among people who spend considerable time together. Many educators, through a good deal of effort and time, develop shared beliefs, language, and knowledge that enables the staff to work together more effectively to educate students. Communal patterns put an emphasis on the professional side of schooling and the affective side of education.

As noted previously, inequitable social patterns continue to play a role in structuring relationships in U.S. schools. Scholars have interpreted and explained these patterns in a number of ways. This book draws on critical and feminist approaches for understanding patterns of inequality. The chapters on critical approaches place an emphasis on the importance of recognizing how the economic system in the United States plays an important role in creating inequality for students. Feminist approaches sensitize us to the way gender roles structure patterns of inequality. Both approaches aspire to help educators reduce the social inequality in schools.

Each of the chapters just sketched has a number of instructional features to assist the understanding of the social patterns. The chapters open with a narrative that exemplifies some of the important aspects of each pattern. A brief history is provided that explains how and why the social pattern developed. The key components of each pattern are discussed. Where appropriate, a current reform initiative that embodies the social pattern is identified and analyzed. Each chapter also provides an overview of the benefits and limitations of each pattern.

We very much wanted to create a book that helped people apply what they learned. We feel strongly that being able to put knowledge into action is a key part of developing a sense of empowerment. Because of this, each chapter has additional instructional features. An extended practice case provides an opportunity to identify the social patterns as they exhibit themselves in a school. Another narrative models how a teacher might apply her understanding of a particular social pattern to successfully bring about change. At the conclusion of the chapter, additional activities encourage the application of organizational literacy to the educator's own school. Finally, there are extra cases in chapter 9 to provide more practice interpreting the social texts in school organizations.

A FINAL NOTE

As educators, we are clear that each individual is unique, as is each school by virtue of being staffed by a group of unique individuals. However, we are also clear that as educators we play a part in social patterns that enable school organizations to exist year after year. The process of socialization ensures that this is true for all educators. Having the organizational literacy to read these social patterns and understand them provides the opportunity to escape from the innocence of seeing all problems as personally or individually based. Additionally, organizational literacy can afford us a more informed, critical perspective as to whether we should maintain, alter, transform, or completely reject a particular social pattern. Hopefully, this will empower us to participate more thoughtfully in schools and serve our students and colleagues in potentially new and beneficial ways.

RECOMMENDED READINGS

Bellah, R., Madsen, R., Sullivan, W., Swidler, A., & Tipton, S. (1991). *The good society*. New York: Knopf. This is a very readable book that discusses the problems associated with the United States' emphasis on individualism. It also provides a very helpful overview of the social patterns common to different institutions in the country.

Carroll, P., & Noble, D. W. (1989). *The free and the unfree: A new history of the United States* (Rev. Ed.). New York: Penguin. A very accessible and informative history of the country. It emphasizes the rise of individualism in the United States and the subsequent problems it posed for many social groups in this country. This was one of the first comprehensive histories of the United States to focus on the dynamic relationship between leadership groups and those excluded from positions of power.

Evans, S. (1989). *Born for liberty: A history of women in America.* New York: The Free Press. An exceptionally readable history that focuses on the changing role and power of women in the United States.

Spring, J. (1996). *The American school, 1642–1996* (3rd ed.). New York: McGraw-Hill. Spring offers a comprehensive history of education in the United States. He also provides very clear discussions regarding the relationship of schooling historically to patterns of inequality in America.

Takaki, R. (1993). *A different mirror: A multicultural history of America.* Boston: Back Bay Books. Another very readable history of the United States that emphasizes the multicultural nature of the United States from its very beginnings.

2

Bureaucratic Social Patterns and Schools

◆ ◆ ◆

People who study school organizations often refer to them as *bureaucracies*. In popular parlance, many people associate this term with excessive fussiness about rules or the frustrations of red tape. For scholars, bureaucracy means something different. It characterizes the social patterns that organize what people do together in schools. Bureaucratic patterns set some social boundaries on what we can and cannot do as teachers and administrators. Understanding these patterns offers an initial form of organizational literacy for reading the recurrent social interaction in schools. Consider the teacher and school district illustrated here.

"Mrs. Holton, how do we get an A on the test tomorrow?"

Kenisha Holton smiled and responded more patiently to this question than she had her first 3 years at Theodore Metcalf Junior High. It still bugged her a bit that students worried more about their grades than they did about actually knowing history. "If you go over your notes and the text and faithfully respond to what's on the study guide, you'll do well on the test." Even though her evaluations the first 3 years had indicated she would clearly get tenure, she stood before these students more confident and at ease now that the tenure decision, however taken for granted, was past. Along with this, some new inner voice informed her that teaching was more than just a job.

"I am a teacher," she told herself with a combination of surprise and pride. Teaching took up a big piece of her life. It was clearly a primary occupational identity for her now. When she first started teaching, she entertained thoughts of writing short stories during her free time. Over the last 3 years there had been a minimum of free time. As it was she struggled to balance the demands of teaching with the time and care her husband and daughter needed.

The bell rang and Kenisha said, "Okay everyone. Study hard. I'll see you tomorrow." She made a last minute check to see that everything she needed for tomorrow's classes was all set. She saw Hal Lassowtiz, the other seventh-grade social studies teacher, coming out of his class across the hall, "Are your kids ready for the test?" she asked him. "I think so," he replied. "Let's compare notes after you score the tests."

Kenisha smiled and nodded in agreement. She headed for the first of two after-school meetings.

Kenisha's first meeting was with Allen Bester, the school psychologist. One of her students, Eric Sales, continued to have difficulty learning things most of her students rarely struggled with. She and Allen met for 20 minutes and worried over the grades, achievement test scores, intelligence assessments, and teachers' notes in Eric's file. Eric was clearly having some problems, but neither Kenisha or Allen were certain about the cause. They agreed that a talk with Eric's parents and possibly further testing might be in order.

From there, Kenisha went to a meeting of the building testing committee. Helen Washington, her principal, had asked her to be a part of a building team that would play a role in organizing and administering the state's new ninth-grade proficiency exams the following spring. She was flattered by Helen's request, given her relative lack of experience with standardized testing, and pleased to have a chance to draw on the new knowledge she had learned about testing in her graduate classes. She remained skeptical about the practicality of this knowledge, but some of it made sense. She entered the teachers' lounge and greeted the three other teachers on the committee, one of the building counselors, and Helen.

Helen opened the meeting by discussing some of the key rules and policies that Superintendent Meyers and the district testing director had presented to a meeting of the principals the previous week. Helen stressed the importance of the committees and the rest of Metcalf Junior High's teachers' and students' cooperation with these rules and policies to ensure the successful administration of the state exam and its validity. Kenisha smiled at hearing the word "validity." Her measurement professor had talked about validity at the beginning of the semester. She began to take some notes as Helen continued to discuss other aspects of the proficiency exam.

This narrative about Kenisha probably feels somewhat familiar because each of the participants and structures have counterparts in school districts across the country. Surprisingly, however, much of what we take for granted in this narrative did not exist in early U.S. schools. Consider the case of a 19th-century teacher, Lucia B. Downing (1951/1981). Downing started teaching in Vermont in 1882. At the age of 13, barely finished with her own elementary schooling, she applied to a local doctor for a teaching certificate. "In our little town, the duties of a school superintendent were not burdensome, nor the position lucrative, and for many years our superintendent was the village doctor.... The doctor could easily combine the two occupations ... " (p. 28). The doctor gave her a series of relatively easy questions to answer. After writing for a while, she handed in her work and a week later she received a teaching certificate in the mail. Not long afterward, Downing began teaching students all by herself in a one-room school. Frequently, she ran out of things to do with the children during the school day:

> I still wonder how I put in the time. I did not knit or crochet, for I had heard of teachers who made trouble for themselves by so doing. I was not skillful at drawing, and I couldn't sing much, being like the old woman who knew just two tunes—"Old Hundred" and "Doxology" and when each pupil had read and ciphered and spelled and passed the water and recessed and recessed and passed the water and spelled and had a lesson in geography and read and spelled, there was usually an hour before I dared dismiss them. (p. 33)

Downing's experience was not atypical of other teachers during the 19th century (Hoffman, 1981; Tyack, 1974). These schools and teachers had an informality and an individualistic style that Kenisha and her colleagues would have found odd. There was little or no supervision by other educators such as a superintendent or a principal to ensure that proper teaching was going on or that curriculum guides were being followed. Teachers had little, if any, education in the best ways to teach or the different aspects of the curriculum. What knowledge teachers possessed regarding curriculum and instruction they absorbed from their own experience as students in a one-room school. For that matter, there was no explicit curriculum to follow. Students brought whatever textbooks happened to be hanging around the home to use at school. There was nothing like a policy and procedure manual to offer general guidelines for teachers, let alone students. Additionally, because the school was largely under the control of the local community, rather than the weak and distant state governments, teachers kept their jobs from term to term—there were frequently two, winter and spring—on the whim of the local farmers. If you governed well, by which they meant you kept the students in line physically, morally, and a wee bit academically, you were hired to teach another term. If not, they hired someone else in your place. Local school boards often hired relatives to teach in their schools because it meant extra income for the family (Fuller, 1982).

This informality pervaded the country's other institutions during the 19th century as well. Historian Weibe (1967) described the United States during this period as a mass of small, rural towns and villages, each held together by shared Protestant religious beliefs, personal relationships, and customs handed down from the past. Individualism and casual cooperation between community members were sufficient to successfully perform the tasks of daily living such as farming, religion, governing, and, of course, schooling the young. Similar arrangements organized daily life in urban areas as well (Tyack, 1974).

Enormous changes to the country from 1876 to 1920 began to alter this informal, individualistic approach to social organization (Tyack, 1974; Weibe, 1967). The populations of cities rose substantially as waves of southern and eastern Europeans immigrated to the United States. Rural Americans also moved to cities when agricultural work declined in the countryside. Large factories sprang up in these growing urban areas and became the dominant means for producing and distributing economic goods for the country as well as its largest employers. Due to the increased complexity of this emerging urban industrial society, the country's leadership groups argued that new methods for organizing people in work and public service settings such as schools, police, and fire fighting were required (Tyack, 1974; Wiebe, 1967). The new methods, they believed, needed to be more deliberate and formalized than the haphazard ones of small town America.

THE FEATURES OF BUREAUCRATIC
SOCIAL PATTERNS

Weber (1864–1920), a German sociologist, lived during the same period that this transition was occurring in the United States (Coser, 1977). Many European countries had already been through the same transformation. Weber wrote extensively about this phenomena in an attempt to explain and make sense of it. Among other things, he stressed the importance of rationalization and bureaucracy (Weber, 1968). Rationalization meant "the systematic and logical application of formal rules and procedures" (Karp & Yoels, 1993, p. 202) for organizing social life. Weber believed rationalization would play a growing role in modern life because it provided an important benefit. Rationalization organized people based on the optimal means for solving problems, rather than on mercurial personal emotions or limiting traditions from the past (Ritzer, 1993). For Weber, the embodiment of rationalization and one of the problem-solving structures par excellence was what he termed *bureaucracy*. Although he had doubts about some of the long-term consequences of bureaucracies, Weber saw them as the optimal means for coordinating large numbers of people to accomplish collective goals. Bureaucracies achieved this through the deliberate use of six features (Weber, 1968):

- A division of labor.
- A hierarchy of offices.
- An explicit set of rules.
- Thorough training in a field of specialization.
- A job as one's primary activity.
- Written documents or files.

It was to these six features that U.S. business, government, and educational leaders in the latter part of the 19th century turned to create order and efficiency. Educational leaders were particularly dazzled by the possibilities offered by this new form of organizing people. "The division of labor in the factory, the punctuality of the railroad, the chain of command and coordination in modern businesses—these aroused a sense of wonder and excitement in men and women seeking to systematize the schools" (Tyack, 1974, p. 28). In the words of Tyack (1974), educational leaders during this period tried to create the one best system of urban public schools by implementing bureaucratic patterns. Schools like the one in which Kenisha works still bear the legacy of educational leaders at the turn of the century who attempted to rationalize the educational process through bureaucracy. To better understand what significance this has for interpreting what goes on in our schools today, consider each of the six features of a bureaucracy.

Fixed Division of Labor

In the early 19th century, there was no formal division of students into different rooms based on age or ability level, or separate teachers assigned to each age group. A teacher such as Downing would teach a variety of subjects to children with a wide range of ability levels all in the same room. For example, a Rhode Island Grammar School in 1840 had 228 students in one room (Spring, 1997). In addition, students might range in age from 3 to 20. School leaders during the middle of the 19th century argued for changing this by using the graded school organization. This Prussian-borrowed model grouped students of a similar age or attainment level into one classroom and assigned a teacher who focused solely on that group. In short, schools began to develop a division of labor. This has been one the dominant features of U.S. schools ever since.

A division of labor breaks the work of the organization into separate jobs. Each job has a very specific set of tasks clearly differentiated from the others. For example, in an elementary school the work is separated into a kindergarten teaching job, a first-grade teaching job, a second-grade teaching job, a third-grade teaching job, and so forth. Students, depending on their age, are separated into a kindergarten student job, a first-grade student job, a second-grade student job, and so forth. In a high school, the work is separated into an English teacher job, science teacher job, social studies teacher job, math teacher job, and so forth. Individual adults and children are assigned to each of the specific teacher and student jobs in a school, performing the tasks required on a regular basis. Larger organizations might have several people or a whole department performing the same type of job. For example, in a large junior high, like the one employing Kenisha, there are several seventh-grade social studies teachers.

Hierarchy of Offices

The county superintendent discussed in the story about Downing represents an initial attempt by 19th-century reformers to create a hierarchy of offices. Superintendents were positioned above teachers and charged with the task of maintaining a uniform quality of education in a particular geographic area. In actual practice, each teacher, within the bounds suggested by the community, pretty much did as he or she pleased. With the development of the graded school and the increased complexity of urban schooling in general, reformers argued for positions that would provide general supervision and control of the whole. Reformers campaigned for principal positions at the building level and superintendent positions at the city, district, and county levels to serve in this capacity.

Those seeking these changes articulated a number of reasons to justify the new administrative positions. They feared that individuals performing a specific job would focus only on their own work, ignoring how they effected the overarching goals of the organization. Reformers insisted that a supervisory position invested with the authority to monitor and coordinate the workers would help everyone contribute toward a shared outcome. Supervision would also help maintain a uniform level of quality.

This can be seen in the earlier example of Kenisha's school. If the proficiency exam is to be carried out properly throughout the district and in each building, Superintendent Meyer and principals such as Helen must coordinate the efforts of their whole staff. This same orientation informs the daily work of each school in the district. In an elementary school, the first-grade teacher supervises his or her 25 students as they perform their jobs. The teacher helps them individually and collectively to progress as a group toward the second grade. The principal supervises the kindergarten teachers, the first-grade teachers, second-grade teachers, and so forth to ensure that the whole school operates smoothly, with students progressing through each grade and eventually graduating. In a large high school, the U.S. history teacher oversees his or her 30 students each period as they work at their student jobs. The chairperson of the social studies department ensures that all the textbook orders, classroom materials, and special events are taken care of for the teachers in his or her department. The principal of the high school makes certain that each department chair and all the teachers help students master their academic work so they can graduate.

An Explicit Set of Rules

Downing's deliberation about how to spend her time each day probably indicated that few explicit rules existed about how to perform her job. Part of the evolution of U.S. public schooling system from the 19th to the 20th century was a growing emphasis on explicit rules and guidelines for each job in the school: administrator, teachers, and students. For example, in the narrative about Kenisha there were rules to guide the administration of the proficiency exam. Rules existed that indicated how teachers should conduct the exam. There were rules that governed how students should take the exam. There were even rules for the superintendent and principals. Most schools and other bureaucratic organizations have rules about the general functioning of each job that, of course, have nothing to do with state proficiency exams. These rules are often written up in job descriptions or handbooks and distributed to members of the organization. Additionally, there are rules that apply to nearly all the employees in an organization: designated times when all building staff have to show up for work, when they can leave, and when report cards should be completed.

A key feature of the explicit rules in a bureaucracy is their impersonality. The rules are meant to be followed by everyone in the school. No matter which individual fills the first-grade teaching job, the same rules would apply. This provides continuity from one person to the next. Each individual might perform the job a bit differently, but a general level of performance can be counted on from day to day. This also means, regardless of the different individuals filling all the different jobs, the school would essentially function the same way, day in and day out. In this way, the rules also help coordinate the work of organization members, adding to the smooth operation of the school. The end result of following both individual job rules and the general organizational rules is that the work of principals, bus drivers, office personnel, teachers, custodians, and cafeteria workers links together and consistently contributes to furthering the collective goal of educating and graduating students each year.

Thorough Training in a Field of Specialization

Clearly, Downing, the teacher from the one-room school in the 19th century, had a limited amount of knowledge about curriculum, teaching, and a range of other schooling matters. Not surprisingly, compared to teachers today, she received a very limited preparation for her job. Most Americans during the 19th century did not believe that teaching required much specialized knowledge. This changed as people began to recognize the benefits of what Weber (1968) called *technical knowledge*. For Weber, technical knowledge consisted of the information that provided the best means possible for accomplishing a job. He believed that technical knowledge was critical for the success of bureaucracies because it enabled individuals and, consequently, bureaucracies as a whole to operate far more efficiently than other organizations. Therefore, each job holder in a bureaucracy had to possess a body of technical knowledge. This knowledge was to be attained from both a specialized, thorough training and by performing the same job year in and year out.

Increasingly, as many nations moved from the 19th to the 20th century, scientific research became the dominant means of generating technical knowledge. In parallel with this trend, public servants such as teachers were seen to be competent and well trained by virtue of their mastery of scientifically generated knowledge. And as the university became the dominant home of scientific research, a university-based education became the appropriate vehicle for teacher preparation. Currently, a university education is still the official legitimate way to provide teachers the technical knowledge to fill their positions.

This current definition of technical knowledge means that a teaching job cannot be performed by someone right off the street. Technical knowledge presumes that individuals such as Kenisha have a thorough, specialized training to perform their jobs as teacher. In fact, most of the positions in schools now can only be filled with individuals who have a thorough, specialized training in their fields. This means that school organizations, like other bureaucracies, will probably run more efficiently and effectively.

A Job as One's Primary Activity

The local doctor in Downing's village doubled as the school superintendent. As Downing wrote, there was little work or money involved with being a superintendent, so performing both jobs did not pose a problem. This was true of a number of public service occupations in the early 19th century such as teaching, police work, and fire fighting (Tyack, 1974; Tyack & Hansot, 1982). Individuals might volunteer as police officers and firefighters in their spare time. Similarly, early 19th-century lawyers, professors, and ministers doubled as educational reformers, textbooks writers, and teachers. When cities grew larger and more complex, it became difficult to handle everyday police, fire, and educational problems with part-time volunteers. Increasingly, urban citizens turned over these tasks to full-time specialists. These new specialists devoted their lives to careers in these areas.

A similar process took place in Kenisha's life. Early on, she had hoped to teach and write short stories. Over the course of her first 3 years on the job, it became apparent that teaching well required lots of time. Between teaching and her family, there was little time left to write. Weber (1968) argued that a bureaucracy like Kenisha's school would operate more effectively than a one-room school overseen by a part-time village doctor because Metcalf would be staffed by people, like Kenisha, who devoted their primary vocational efforts to their jobs. This would ensure a commitment to their jobs and the ongoing development of even more expertise.

Written Documents or Files

Weber (1968) believed that written documents or files enabled the bureaucratic organization to better manage its activities than older approaches that relied on human memory and oral culture. Oral culture is a phrase that scholars use to refer to groups of people who do not organize their lives predominantly through written language. The long-lasting nature of written records offered a number of benefits over oral culture. Files could be reviewed at any time. Patterns might be apparent from careful study of the documents. Written files would also provide continuity from day to day, offering stability and order to the organization.

Many of these benefits are apparent in Kenisha's work with the school psychologist. By reviewing a student's file, they had more information by which to help him with his learning problems. They will in turn probably add information to his file that other staff in the school district will be able to use. Student files also help the school monitor its success at educating hundreds of children each year. Without the files it would be difficult to establish educational continuity from one school year to the next. The files also provide clear documentation by which parents, tax-payers, and state officials may monitor the educational continuity and progress of schools.

Similarly, files help track the accomplishments of teachers. The principal, Helen Washington, did not have to rely on her memory in deciding whether to tenure Kenisha. Helen reviewed the file and saw that she had evaluated Kenisha positively during each year of her probationary period. The decision was based on information provided by the permanent files in the main office of Metcalf Junior High.

Each of these bureaucratic features do not stand isolated and apart from the others. They operate as a system of interrelated features that work together to create a more effective organization overall (Scott, 1992). Kenisha's school, Theodore Metcalf Junior High, would be recognizable to Weber. He would probably argue that it was a more effective organization than its historical precursors by virtue of its division of labor, hierarchy of offices, explicit rules, thoroughly trained and career-oriented staff, and written files.

GOALS

Those building on Weber's scholarly foundation have argued that goals are also an important part of a bureaucratic organization (Abrahamsson, 1993). In our earlier discussion of Weber, we discussed that rationalization involved the selection of the optimal means for achieving particular goals, and desired outcomes. At the time, that may have seemed obvious. However, historically speaking, the importance of explicit educational goals for schools is some-thing new. Downing and the village doctor/superintendent might have been hard pressed to articulate specific short- and long-range education goals. Due to a combination of factors, there was not much emphasis placed on written, formalized goals in the local rural schools that dominated 19th-cen-tury America. Schooling generally reinforced the community's values and students came away with a smattering of readin,' writin,' and figurin'. This usually met the educational needs of most villages and towns.

The development of the U.S. public school system in the 19th century changed that considerably. Before 1830, there were local community schools but there was no public school system (Spring, 1997). Prior to this

time, Americans had been reluctant to have centralized government authorities regulate schools to accomplish shared public goals. Each local community school pretty much did as it pleased. However, between 1830 and
1860, many U.S. leaders and reformers believed that a uniform public school
system would create national unity and order (Kaestle, 1983). From this belief sprang the Common School, the country's first attempt at standardizing
America's schools. The Common School reformers constructed a set of educational goals to create similar schools in each local community and in each
state of the country. Disseminating these goals to every community and
state would socialize U.S. children into a common public experience.

Schools such as Theodore Metcalf Junior High have inherited this legacy
of explicit goal development from past educational reformers. Goals serve a
number of purposes. For example, curriculum goals set by state, district, and
building leaders offer an important means for directing and coordinating the
efforts of all school and district personnel toward common, shared ends. If
district and building administrators effectively communicate these goals,
everyone in a school or district will share a similar conception of the goal.
This will enable individual teachers such as Kenisha to regulate themselves
individually and in relationship to others in the organization toward successful achievement of the goal. If state leaders effectively communicate
their goals, individual districts will be more able to regulate themselves toward achieving a shared state goal. In many regards the state proficiency ex-
aminations discussed earlier are designed to provide a shared public goal
that the state school system as an entity will accomplish. Many current state
governments, similar to early Common School reformers, hope every school
district will achieve standardized, uniform goals.

VERTICAL COORDINATION AND AUTHORITY

After reading the previous discussion, some people may experience misgiv-
ings about bureaucracies because they centralize much of the authority and
power with those at higher levels of the organization, administrators and
state officials. Weber would affirm that bureaucracies do this. Contemporary organization theorists sometimes refer to this use of authority in organizations as vertical coordination (Bolman & Deal, 1991). *Vertical
coordination* involves people at higher levels of the organization such as principals, superintendents, and state officials coordinating and controlling the
actions of people at lower levels of the organization, such as teachers. This is

accomplished through investing authority in the different hierarchical levels of offices and the rules.

Drawing on our initial narrative about Kenisha, we can see that the state officials, via the legal authority invested in their positions, can require that Superintendent Meyer administer the proficiency examination in his district. Superintendent Meyer, by virtue of the district's rules and the authority in his position, can legally require Helen and other principals in the district to administer the state proficiency exam in each of their buildings. Helen, in turn, can ask the same from her staff. Kenisha and the other teachers can insist that their students take the exam. Vertical coordination starts at the top and works its way to the bottom of the organization.

Anyone along the way can certainly refuse to comply with their superior if certain policies and rules that protect subordinates are ignored. A supervisor's request can be arbitrary and irrational and can legally be grieved to a higher office in the school or the district. However, even though many things in schools happen by virtue of teachers' individual initiative, legally principals and superintendents do have the authority to require that teachers perform certain tasks. In the same way, teachers have the legal authority to direct students, in particular limits, to perform educational tasks.

Compared to the relationships in 19th-century schools, this is a significant change in how educators and students currently relate to one another. Teachers come together to work in the same building by virtue of technical knowledge, not because they initially selected each other as friends and acquaintances. Families in the community send their children to schools to be supervised by technically competent strangers and impersonal rules because the state government has legally certified that each of these strangers has the specialized knowledge to work with their children. The state legally compels families to have their children spend a certain number of years in school. This is not to say that these arrangements preclude the development of friendship between staff in schools and the community or that people in schools are not operating based on caring motives. Rather, we are coming back to a point made earlier: Bureaucratic patterns organize our relationships to one another based on hierarchy and specialized knowledge. This creates limits on what we can and cannot do as members of a school organization. Historically, the time when people pretty much did as they pleased, individually and as communities, has altered considerably in the last century and a half. Why did we allow this to happen?

Weber (1968) argued that we as teachers, individual citizens, and parents accept and voluntarily go along with the authority of hierarchically superordinate offices (such as state governments, superintendents, principals, and teachers) and rules because like other nations in the world during the 19th and 20th centuries, we have gone through the modernization process. This means that collectively we have increasingly come to accept legal authority as the legitimate form of domination, rather than traditional and charismatic authority. By domination Weber meant "the probability that certain specific commands (or all commands) will be obeyed by a given group of persons" (pp. I, 212). We have come to increasingly obey commands given by designated legal authorities rather than traditional or charismatic authorities.

Kenisha obeys Helen and Helen obeys the superintendent because they are professionally trained, certified by the state, hired on their technical merits, and rules say this is how it should be. Legal authority invests rules and those elevated into positions by virtue of the rules to issue commands that we must follow. Weber argued that over time, we came to accept this process of allocating authority as being more rational than the two other forms of authority. A set of hierarchical positions of authority and impersonal rules were thought to provide a more deliberate and systematic way of organizing people to achieve valued outcomes. Positions and rules can be subjected to critical scrutiny and altered to achieve the best results.

With traditional authority, obedience is based on the way things have always been done in the past. This makes it difficult to create something new if the need arises. Also, historically, a ruling elite such as an aristocracy continued to exercise authority because they had always done so in the past. This did not allow people who had the talent and technical knowledge to assume leadership roles. We obey a charismatic authority when we follow a leader because of her or his special religious revelations, heroism, or exemplary character. For Weber, the process of modernization involved the growing acceptance of legal authority and the decline of traditional and charismatic authority in all avenues of life, including education. In this country, as soon as we started to create a uniform public education system by having the state government step in to organize the individual local community schools, we made a significant step toward adopting legal authority as the legitimate form of domination in education.

LATERAL COORDINATION

Vertical coordination is not the only strategy available nor the one most commonly used for controlling and coordinating the work in schools.

Although the authority of the principal and the superintendent legally enable them to make particular demands of teachers, using vertical coordination as the sole means of controlling people may not always be effective. Educators and their leaders depend to a great degree on lateral coordination. Lateral coordination works through committees and meetings. It often involves more informal communication between individuals who work on a similar level of the organization. For example, Kenisha met with the school psychologist to help a student who is struggling. This was not accomplished through a rule or by a higher authority. Kenisha and the psychologist pooled their technical knowledge to work together in the best interest of the student.

Similarly, Kenisha is working with three other teachers and a building counselor on the building testing committee. The committee will assist the principal in having Metcalf Junior High successfully administer the proficiency exam. Committee members will pool their technical skills to coordinate the exam. Helen seeks to persuade and gain the cooperation of Kenisha and the rest of the committee and they will in turn work with other teachers to help administer the test to their students. Helen could potentially order the teachers to do the test with their students. But the task is complex and more likely to be successfully completed if Helen enlists the help of four other people. And by gaining their voluntary cooperation, the job will be accomplished more efficaciously than it would by a direct use of her authority.

BUREAUCRATIC PATTERNS AND REFORM

The features of bureaucracy have come to play a considerable role in current school reforms focused on issues of accountability and standards. For example, consider a recent reform called High Expectations Learning Process for Standard-Driven Units of Study (HELPS; Rothman, 1996). HELPS was developed by the National Alliance for Restructuring Education and lays out several steps that schools and districts can follow to better align their instructional and assessment practices with state and national academic standards. The steps are identifying standards, developing ideas for a culminating event, aligning the culminating event to the standards, identifying the blocks, creating rubrics, and developing instructional activities. According to HELPS' promoters, these steps will aid educators in improving student mastery of academic standards.

In the first step, teachers look at the standards created by national, state, and district leadership groups. From this review of standards, teachers develop a list of standards they want their students to display. Once the standards are set, teachers then create possible culminating events. These could be a product the student creates or a public performance for teachers and other students. The next task for teachers is to make sure the culminating event requires students to demonstrate attainment of one of the standards reviewed earlier. Teachers then develop blocks, the individual lessons that will incrementally build the students' knowledge and skill toward the final culminating event. Scoring guides are developed to provide teachers and students with criteria for assessing successful performance after each block and after the culminating activity. Once the blocks and scoring rubrics are in place, teachers create instructional activities to facilitate students acquiring the knowledge and skills in each block.

Principals and district administrative staff also play important roles in the process (Rothman, 1996). District staff is supposed to provide each school with the necessary resources of time and information to carry out the HELPS process. They monitor the progress of each school—elementary, middle, and secondary—as they work to achieve student mastery of key standards. Principals in the HELPS model supervise their teachers as they implement the steps. Principals ensure that teachers follow the model and successfully align the different standards with their culminating activities. They also monitor teachers' progressive efforts to help students toward the culminating activities. Principals and other administrators also use a tool developed by the National Alliance to manage student records and track student performance.

HELPS consists of many of the features of a bureaucracy. There is a division of labor. Different aspects of the work are assigned to district administrators, principals, teachers, and students. Supervisory work is performed by those in hierarchical positions above others: district staff over schools, principals over teachers, teachers over students. There are general rules that apply impersonally to all. The national, state, and district standards are viewed as authoritatively binding on all public education personnel. The steps are also seen as a set of guidelines to be followed by everyone. Everyone is provided with the necessary technical information to enable them to perform their appropriate job in the HELPS model. Files filled with student data on successful mastery of the standards serve as permanent records of the process. If everyone in a school district performs their job as the HELPS model suggests, it is believed schools will better enable students to attain many more of the state, national, and district standards than before. And, by virtue of the results being placed in student files, the success or lack of success will be easily and obviously calculable. HELPS represents a systematic and deliberate attempt to have schools work in an efficient and predictable manner—what we have come to call a bureaucracy.

BUREAUCRATIC SOCIAL PATTERNS AND TEACHER-INITIATED CHANGE

Knowledge of bureaucratic social patterns can also provide assistance in directing teacher-initiated change efforts. As an example of this, we discuss how Bob Wildman, a high school biology teacher, applied his knowledge of bureaucratic patterns to make changes in his classes and school district.

Bob became interested in the benefits of educational computing during the process of teaching his biology class. He started working with computers by finding software that complemented different topics in the curriculum. He found that students were often more engaged and efficient in their learning when using computers. In addition, student scores went up in topic areas such as genetics. In the past, his students had often struggled with genetics.

Bob's colleagues heard about his efforts and sought his help in learning computer basics and tracking down appropriate software for their classes. Increasingly, Bob spent a lot of his time assisting teachers in the building and the rest of the district. He enjoyed this work. He felt that technology had made a large difference in his classroom and had the potential to do the same in the district. Bob considered initiating a district wide program to use computers and other technology more systematically. He also contemplated serving as the coordinator of this program.

Bob knew from past experience in the district that following what he called the chain of command was important if his idea was to succeed. He first spoke to his principal, Don La Rocca, to get his input and blessing before approaching the district staff. Don thought Bob's ideas were quite good but that he would first have to be professionally trained in the use of educational technology before he would be taken seriously at the district level. Don also indicated that currently the management of technology in the district was handled by the director of curriculum.

Bob took Don's advice and enrolled in a master's program in educational computing at a nearby university. Once he had a year's worth of courses under his belt and was well on his way to gaining a second master's degree, Bob approached Linda Curran, the district's director of curriculum. Linda had doubts about the use of computers for regular classroom instruction. However, there were a number of pressing problems the district had, such as finding efficient and effective ways to remediate elementary students who did poorly on basic reading and math skill tests. The students needed more intensive practice and to have their progress or lack thereof carefully tracked. Linda, although ultimately responsible for technology in the district, did not have the time to specialize in the educational computing. Linda challenged Bob to identify computer solutions for these problems and demonstrate that he had the necessary technical skills to have computers make a direct impact on student achievement district wide.

Bob surveyed a range of software solutions and discovered that there was something called computer-managed reading instruction software. He investigated this software further and then suggested to Linda that it might be piloted at one elementary school to see if it worked. The software was purchased and Bob worked to inservice the teachers who volunteered to have their students work with the software in the school's computer lab. Students who used the new software improved their basic reading skills as measured by a number of assessments. In addition, having the students work with the software periodically proved to be relatively easy to manage. The software kept records of student progress that were easily accessed by the teachers and principal. As a follow-up to the pilot, Bob and Linda successfully wrote a grant to the state. The grant helped fund the use of computers to enhance basic reading and math skills in the district. It also helped support a half-time computer coordinator to coordinate this effort. Bob started to split his time between teaching biology and working on the district's educational technology plan and curriculum.

In this teacher-initiated change, a number of bureaucratic features are apparent. Bob could not act as an independent entrepreneur to develop a district technology plan. He had to win the approval of individuals in hierarchical positions above him, the principal and the director of curriculum. Technical knowledge was viewed as a prerequisite for Bob to be able to legitimately perform a particular function in the district. There was a division of labor; the management of technology was regulated by a particular office in the district, the director of curriculum. Bob and his computer-managed reading software solution were considered valuable only in so far as they contributed to organization goals such as student achievement. An important factor in the success of the software was the record keeping function that kept track of student progress. The information from the software could also be easily stored in students files.

This narrative is not meant to indicate how all teacher-initiated change might be accomplished, but rather suggests that possessing organizational literacy about bureaucratic patterns might provide some useful ways to approach teacher-initiated change.

THE BENEFITS OF BUREAUCRATIC
SOCIAL PATTERNS

What is it about bureaucratic social patterns that makes them, according to Weber, the optimal means for coordinating the work of many people? We have hinted at a number of the benefits provided by bureaucratizing schools. Now we discuss these issues more explicitly. Bureaucratic organizations like schools are thought to provide three benefits: control, efficiency, and predictability (Ritzer, 1993). These three benefits as a consequence make possible another benefit, a high degree of calculability.

Compared to the performance of machines, human behavior has significant elements of uncertainty. You can never completely predict what people will do. Each of the features previously discussed—division of labor, hierarchy of offices, rules, thoroughly trained staff, career orientation, files, and explicit goals—plays a role in reducing uncertainty. Spelling out the specific duties each person should perform, providing a supervisor to oversee the work of others, and detailing rules to guide action provides control over the different aspects of an organization's ongoing operation. Hence, the different features of a bureaucracy provide school administrators the tools to carefully control the work of employees and successfully educate children in cities the size of New York and Chicago.

As a consequence of having more control over each function performed in a large organization, bureaucracies can typically boast greater efficiency than other forms of collectively organized behavior (Weber, 1968). For example, as already argued, bureaucracies have historically been an important means for this country to accomplish its public goals, particularly with the large influx of people in the latter part of the 19th century and the early part of the 20th (Weibe, 1967). Public schools had difficulty educating the growing numbers of students in the late 19th century. Public schools as bureaucracies offered the controls that enabled the increasing numbers of children to be educated as efficiently as possible year after year (Tyack, 1974).

Bureaucracies offer predictability (Ritzer, 1993) The different features, when combined, seem to deliver results that can be counted on repeatedly. For example, by performing the same job every day, an individual becomes a highly skilled specialist at executing one piece of the organization's work. That individual can be counted on to generally provide a consistently high performance compared to someone who might perform the job occasionally. If supervisors monitor and coordinate employee work each day, we come to expect that routinely the organization will function better than it would without supervision. If explicit rules for individual and collective performance exist and are understood by everyone, we also come to look forward to regular progress toward various organizational goals. By embodying the different features of a bureaucracy, most schools have been able to predictably educate millions of children each year.

Calculability is a derivative of the word calculate, meaning to compute through the use of mathematics. Calculability became an issue for organizations in this country with the rise of capitalism as an economic system. In capitalism, people produce goods and services for the purposes of accumulating profit. Profit can be reinvested in a business to enable even more production and sales and, consequently, more profit. Exact and systematic mathematical calculations are required to determine whether a business is making a profit. Weber (1968) argued that capitalistic businesses turned increasingly to the use of bureaucracy because as a form of organizing, it helped facilitate calculability. It did this by offering a more precise control of time, money, labor, and profit. Bureaucratic control of each organization element helped the capitalist to calculate the total resources that could be spent and still generate profit.

Calculability to some extent offers similar things to schools. Having each element of the school organization carefully controlled and regulated enables school officials to track very carefully the educational progress, grades, and scores of thousands of students each year. Grades and scores on tests become a means of assessing the profitability, if you will, of schools as organizations. Grades and scores also become the means to determine if different elements of the organization such as teachers or principals or departments, are functioning effectively. Plans to improve the performance of the overall organization or individual pieces can be developed based on the calculation of grades and scores on tests.

THE LIMITATIONS OF BUREAUCRATIC
SOCIAL PATTERNS

All of this may suggest that bureaucratic social patterns create a kind of people machine that moves along in a smooth, orderly, and effective fashion. Teachers perform their individuals jobs so that students learn the necessary knowledge and skills. Principals monitor teachers to ensure teachers individually and collectively work toward a common goal of educating students. Superintendents supervise the buildings in their district and state officials oversee the different districts. All parts of the organization would appear to function quite well together. Unfortunately, schools as bureaucracies do not work quite as the theory suggests. In fact, the rest of this book is about the problems with viewing schools solely as bureaucracies. At this point, however, we would like to emphasize three particular problems: loose coupling, technical ties, and ideal types (Morgan, 1986; Weick, 1976).

Loose Coupling

Weber's notion of bureaucracy assumes that the couplings between different jobs in the organization at the same level and between different levels of the organization are connected tightly and responsively. *Couplings* are the links that join different jobs and different levels of the organization together so that all the things individuals do contribute to the ongoing achievement of the organization's common goals. For example, in the narrative about Metcalf Junior High, Helen asked Kenisha, a building counselor, and several other teachers to comprise the building testing committee. Because of the couplings between supervisor and subordinate, Kenisha and the others showed up at the meeting at the appointed time. They were legally obligated to respond to Helen's authority as principal. Similarly, Helen is coupled to the superintendent, who gave instructions about administering the proficiency exam, which Helen followed. A different form of coupling, but nonetheless still a form of it, linked the work of Kenisha and the other history teacher. They both planned to administer tests the next day as part of their shared efforts at having students move through the seventh grade social studies curriculum. They coordinate their work together as specialists who have similar jobs in the school to promote their students' academic achievement. Similarly, Kenisha and the school psychologist harmoniously meshed their work together to achieve the common goal of helping a student. The bureaucratic model assumes that the couplings between people at the same level and different levels are tight and responsive.

Some organization theorists argue that many aspects of an organization are loosely coupled (Weick, 1976). There is not a tight, responsive coupling between supervisor and subordinate. Neither is there a strong coupling between individuals at the same level of an organization. As discussed in the first chapter, Americans tend to put an emphasis on the individual (Bellah, Madsen, Sullivan, Swidler, & Tipton, 1985; Carroll & Noble, 1989; Karl, 1983). As a culture, we resist the limits that bureaucracy places on individual discretion (Karl, 1983). This thinking has carried over into our schools. Even though bureaucratic patterns shape the general character of schools, educators often retain an older American emphasis on individual choice and decision making.

This individualism often results in weak couplings between educators at different hierarchical levels and at the same level.

Another factor that plays a role in promoting loose coupling is the placement of teachers in individual classrooms (Bennett deMarrais & LeCompte, 1995). Generally working apart from the other adults in the organization makes it difficult to communicate and interact with people other than students. Also, in traditional bureaucracies, supervisors and managers directly observe and coordinate the actions of subordinates on a regular basis. Principals typically do not observe or directly supervise teachers' work nearly as frequently. These features loosen the coupling between teachers and between administrators and teachers. It also loosens the coupling between the individual and the larger organization.

Technical Ties

In organizations coordinated through bureaucratic patterns, people relate to one another based on their command of technical expertise. Some scholars have argued that this kind of technically oriented relationship does not satisfy basic human needs for a sense of belonging and community (Kruse, 1995). Growing numbers of people insist that bureaucratic patterns result in work settings that are cold, impersonal, and alienating (Yankelovich, 1981). Recent school reform efforts reflect these concerns (Abas, 1997). There is a new importance being placed on communal patterns in schools (Louis & Kruse, 1995). This issue is developed in more depth in the chapter on communal patterns.

Ideal Types

Finally, Weber developed the notion of bureaucracy as an abstract, analytic construct to understand large-scale changes to the social organization of modern societies (Coser, 1977). Weber called this type of abstract, analytic construct an *ideal type*. Bureaucracy, as an ideal type, helps us explore a wide range of organizations, comparing their differences and similarities. However, Weber did not believe that a specific organization would necessarily have all the features suggested by the bureaucratic ideal. An organization might have one, two, five, or none. Hence, a certain amount of caution must be used in applying Weber's notion of bureaucracy to a specific school. We must be sure that when we identify one of the bureaucratic features in a school, we do not simply assume the obvious existence of the other features. Bureaucratic patterns certainly allow us to better understand the large-scale historical changes that influenced how public schools are generally organized. However, carelessly applying bureaucracy as an analytic tool to a particular school could be misleading.

SUMMARY

In this chapter, we described the important role that bureaucratic social patterns played in the development of contemporary school organizations. Bureaucratic social patterns consist of a range of features: division of labor, hierarchy of offices, explicit rules, specialized training, a job as one's life work, and written documentation or files. We also discussed the importance of goals. All these features work to help the vertical and lateral coordination of bureaucracies such as schools. By using bureaucratic social patterns, schools are believed to be offering more control, predictability, efficiency, and calculability in the efforts to educate children. However, critics argue that schools are actually more loosely coupled than traditional bureaucracies and the emphasis that bureaucratic patterns place on a technical orientation to relationships can create schools with an atmosphere that is impersonal and alienating.

PRACTICE CASE—SCHOOL CHANGE
AT HOWARD ELEMENTARY

Following the publication of A Nation At Risk (National Commission on Excellence in Education, 1983), in 1983, public schools underwent a decade of unprecedented reform (Louis & Kruse, 1995). Principals and teachers clamored for creative and innovative ways to teach children and to organize the work life of teachers (Newmann & Associates, 1996). Reforms sprang up to address the enduring isolation teachers felt in their previous, formalized roles. Included in this wave of reform were innovations focused on instructional technique—cooperative learning and inquiry-based classrooms. Curriculum innovations were popular as well—manipulative-based mathematics, whole language, and problem solving as a distinct, teachable skill, to name a few.

Innovations also included a reconfiguration of teachers' work; from largely isolated and separate individuals working with their kids in their classrooms to teachers who were expected to regularly seek the assistance and support of their colleagues. Teaching teams sprang up nationwide.

Although the advent of teaching teams was centered largely in middle schools, many elementary and high schools tried similar approaches. The traditional model of organizing schools was challenged as well. Site-based management, building leadership teams, and district-level restructuring councils were formed in many schools across the country and Canada. The administrative power that had once rested in the hands of one person, the principal, now was to be shared among the teaching staff and, in many cases, parents, community members, and students. The following case describes one such attempt to transform a traditionally organized school into one that shares the role of managing the school and the responsibility that goes with this new role.

Howard Elementary School is a growing suburban school nestled in a valley that divides two larger industrial centers. After construction of the school in 1975, Howard enjoyed stability in both its teaching ranks and its administrative team. Unlike the schools in the districts that neighbored the Howard attendance area, teachers often stayed their entire careers in the district. Many lived within the boundaries of the school district and enjoyed coming to work with their own children, who were enrolled in a colleague's class just down the hall. Parents were supportive of the school and the faculty were often treated to appreciation lunches and classroom and playground equipment purchased from money raised by varied fund-raising efforts sponsored by the parent–teacher association.

Stability was a hallmark of the Howard administrative team as well. Although the school was more than 20 years old, surprisingly little turnover had occurred in its administrative ranks. The building was opened under the direction of a well-loved man who had retired from the district about 5 years before. Mr. Smith was known for his ability to handle any situation with thoughtful confidence. Teachers both trusted and respected Mr. Smith's decision-making abilities. He was an easy man to work for because he remembered his own years in the classroom and often shared personal stories of his own professional growth. Additionally, he was quick to praise good instruction when he observed it and was often seen walking the halls of Howard Elementary, dropping into classes and leaving behind encouraging notes.

The current principal was a woman in her 40s who had left teaching to take the offer of a principalship when Mr. Smith retired. Her appointment was no surprise to the staff because Ms. Jackson had interned under Mr. Smith when she had returned to graduate school to obtain her master's degree and administrative credential. In the years since her internship, Mr. Smith had allowed Ms. Jackson to continue her apprenticeship by often leaving her in charge of the building when he was asked to attend meetings downtown at the district offices. He would also consult Ms. Jackson when he was interested in the opinions of the faculty before acting on issues related to student discipline rules and curriculum issues. She had been groomed for the position by Mr. Smith and still consulted him when she felt unsure about a particular task or decision.

In the 5 years since becoming principal, Ms. Jackson had steered the faculty through a series of textbook adoptions, a controversial health education program adoption, and most recently, a burst of attendance that left classrooms filled to capacity. Following the influx of more than 100 new students, bringing the attendance to more than 750 students, the position of assistant principal was created to help handle the growing administrative concerns. Discipline was turned over almost entirely to the new assistant principal. Although Mr. Jones was not a Howard veteran, he appeared to fit in well with the rest of the teaching staff and enjoyed the mentoring Ms. Jackson provided.

The teachers believed they benefited from the careful leadership of Ms. Jackson and Mr. Jones. Faculty meetings were brief, cheerful affairs marked by little discussion and lots of treats. As was the tradition when Mr. Smith ran the weekly meetings, Ms. Jackson began with a short teaching excellence story, usually from one of her many walks around the building in the past week. The teacher whose efforts were the focus of staff attention would then receive a lottery ticket as a reward. Although no one had ever won more than $20 in the 10-year period that this ceremony had been occurring, it was a highlight of the morning meeting for the teaching staff. Following this warm-up, Ms. Jackson would move swiftly to the issues of the meeting. She would start with the superintendent's report and end with upcoming important dates and events at Howard. Discussion was limited to questions of clarification rather than in-depth discussion. Once informed, the teaching staff would return to their classrooms as the busses began to arrive. Teachers commented on how they liked this division of labor; they believed it left them able to attend to teaching and removed from the politics that often characterized other faculties in the district. Additionally, teachers liked Ms. Jackson's ability to "keep the information to a minimum. She doesn't waste our time with the details of decisions, she makes them and then tells us what to do."

The national press to reform schooling had not missed the teachers at Howard School. The teachers had eagerly attended classes in new instructional techniques and curriculum. In fact, many grade-level teachers now planned lessons together and had even experimented with some teaming for science and social studies. Usually those efforts resulted in a division of the tasks related to the creation of a large, unit-culminating event such as an international feast or a science fair. One teacher would order the supplies for the event, another would create the letter for parents to explain the task, and another would teach the project to the assembled classes. Teachers reported that they enjoyed these opportunities—"It's so much easier to do large events like this with the help of your friends"—and the new events quickly became traditions younger students would look forward to doing when they reached that particular grade level. Teachers had also informally begun to meet and discuss their teaching. A few had also tried some peer coaching ideas, watching each other teach and offering suggestions for improvement.

This practice had several unintended consequences for faculty. A few were gaining a reputation as whole-language experts and were enjoying a new role as informal coaches for teachers newer to these ideas. Other faculty had experienced great success with pairing science activities with mathematics lessons because their efforts at planning interdisciplinary units had been both fun and had resulted in a class picture in the local paper. Others felt that the level of excitement for teaching and using new ideas had blossomed at Howard. Ms. Jackson was beginning to jokingly complain that the numbers of lottery tickets she was having to purchase was rising to unaffordable levels.

So when Ms. Jackson announced to the staff that Howard had been chosen to pilot a district plan for site-based management, the faculty quickly agreed to the idea. Ms. Jackson described the idea behind site-based management as one in which "power is shared among the teachers, administration, and, hopefully at a later date, parents." She added that, "By sharing the decision-making power at the school it is hoped that teachers would feel more investment and have more understanding of those aspects of the school organization." She finished by announcing that following the training she was to finish at the end of the month she would invite the staff to nominate faculty members to participate on a management council. From there she envisioned the faculty having open discussions about what kinds of issues the management council should address.

As Ms. Jackson progressed in the weekly district-level inservice, she would occasionally update the staff on the ideas she was learning. One idea she was particularly excited about was the f creation of an additional council of team leaders who would guide the decision-making processes of the school related to curriculum. She explained that the grade-level innovations the faculty had already begun could serve as the template for the curriculum council meetings, "Only here we'd all be talking rather than just grade-level folks."

She asked the teachers to think about who would like to participate. Teachers began to talk among themselves about who might want such an extra-curricular task. A few counted themselves out immediately—one woman felt that her child-care situation did not lend itself to more out-of-school time and a few other teachers thought they were already stressed by taking graduate classes at night for their master's degree. However, all agreed it was an important opportunity for the right person.

After a month of speculation, Ms. Jackson finally announced that she was opening both the management council and the curriculum council to nominations. She explained further that she felt the nomination process should be a "closed affair to assure the elections were handled fairly." Although some teachers agreed this was a good idea, others were beginning to wonder just when they would actually begin to become part of this new process. To them it seemed like business as usual. A vocal fourth-grade teacher publicly began to question the superintendent's decision to train the principals rather than all the faculty members who were to participate in the process. She stated, "It seems uneven, like she still has all the power. We don't even know what's expected when and if we do get on a council.

While the staff wondered about who was to participate and what they would do when chosen, the assistant principal wondered where he stood as this new school organization took form. Currently, he had almost complete power over discipline and its related duties—playground, busses, and lunchroom. In every discussion with the principal, he had been assured that he would have a role but what the role would encompass was left unclear. He feared that with the creation of a management council that made decisions related to discipline and "who knows what else" his position would become unnecessary or driven by the whims of a council about which he knew little. The shift to new roles and responsibilities at Howard was beginning to confuse and anger some members of the staff.

Finally, the fourth-grade teacher who had been vocal about her concerns decided to talk directly with Ms. Jackson. She made an appointment to see the principal during her preparation period the following day. Nervously, she entered the office armed with a carefully written list of her concerns. She began with a question directed at the purposes of the two new councils and ended with a question directed at how much power each council would ultimately hold. Ms. Jackson admitted that, being new to this herself, she did not have exact ideas about how the councils would operate. She thought council meetings would provide smaller numbers of the staff more opportunity to meet face to face and discuss the management and curriculum concerns of Howard. They agreed that the faculty's concerns could be handled by an open meeting in which "the faculty would have the opportunity to air their worries and the new organizational structure could be discussed." After discussing how such a meeting might progress, it was agreed they would cochair the meeting in an effort to begin implementing a new approach to how the school was organized.

EXERCISES

1.   Using this case as your data bank, identify the features of the formal organization—hierarchy, division of labor, and organizational rules—that are present at the beginning of the case. Contrast it with the new structures that were created as part of the site-based management project. In what ways are these structures similar? In what ways are they different? Under which system would you prefer to work? Why?

2. Interview a teacher or administrator. Describe how they experience the features of the formal organization—hierarchy, division of labor, and organizational rules—in their daily work life. Which do they find act as facilitators to doing their job well? Which do they find act as barriers to doing their job well?

3. Consider an organization you have worked in. Pictorially represent the division of labor and hierarchy of office that characterizes that organization. Be sure to start from the top of the organization and include all the levels of labor that exist. If possible, identify each layer by defining the formal and informal rules that govern the tasks completed at each level.

4. Site-based management has experienced both success and failure across the nation. Successful site-based schools are credited with creating a school climate that empowers teachers, creating a sense of efficacy in the work of teaching, and that extends the responsibilities of teachers beyond that of their own classroom, thus creating a community of teachers who feel responsible for the teaching and learning of all members of the school organization. Teachers from these schools report that, "Site-based management has drawn us closer together. We're more interested in the things that other teachers do and we can learn so much from each other."

Teachers from schools that have struggled with site-based management report that the amount of time spent on the process of decision making often interferes with their classroom duties and is too time consuming for the kinds of decisions that left for the faculty to decide. In the words of one high school teacher, "The principal claims we are site-based but in reality we aren't. I mean he still makes all the big decisions like scheduling and we're left deciding on how much time the kids need to pass in the halls."

Do you think teachers benefit from input into the decision-making processes of schools or do you think site-based management is a distraction from the primary task of teaching? Explain your thinking.

READING YOUR OWN SCHOOL

Consider your own school. How are the ideas and concepts presented in this chapter present in your work setting? How might these ideas help you to make sense of your school and the events that occur there? List five examples of how you see these concepts in practice at your school; examples might include the actions of administration, staff, faculty, students, or parents; or specific issues or events such as a curriculum adoption or annual school celebration. Link each event to an idea or concept presented in this chapter. Do you think these actions or events facilitate student growth and learning, faculty and staff efficacy and sense of well being? Or do these actions or events create barriers to student growth and learning, faculty and staff efficacy and sense of well being? Finally, how could you use these ideas to initiate positive change within your school setting?

RECOMMENDED READINGS

Ritzer, G. (1993). *The McDonaldization of society.* Thousand Oaks, CA: Pine Forge Press. This book gives an easy-to-read introduction to Weber's theory of rationalization. Ritzer also offers a wonderful discussion of how this process has affected many other aspects of modern life.

Scott, W. R. (1989). *Organizations: Rational, natural, and open.* Englewood Cliffs, NJ: Prentice-Hall. Scott's book is an exceptionally well organized and clearly written introduction to organizational theory. He provides a very useful overview of bureaucracy and other approaches to understanding organizations.

Tyack, D. (1974). *The one best system: A history of urban education.* Cambridge, MA: Harvard University Press. Tyack provides a very readable history that describes the incorporation of bureaucratic social patterns into the public schools in the late 19th century and early 20th. He also offers a commendable look at the politics that surrounded this transformation.

Weber, M. (1968). *Economy and society* (3 vols.) New York: Beminster. Volume I of this massive work provides an important introduction to Weber's views of bureaucracy and its place in modern society.

3

Political Social Patterns
and Schools

◆◆◆

Historically, educators have believed that schools are not and should not be involved in politics (Wirt & Kirst, 1982). Since the mid-1970s, however, a number of scholars have begun to demonstrate that schools, like other U.S. institutions, are influenced by and engaged in politics. In fact, many scholars suggest that, contrary to the orderliness suggested by the bureaucratic model, schools operate like small political systems (Ball, 1987; Blase, 1991a; Hoyle, 1986). This focus on political social patterns offers another form of organizational literacy for understanding the recurrent relations that organize what we do with one another in schools, how it is we act together. Consider the teacher and school illustrated here.

Lou Tanaka thought that compared to most third-grade students at Kennedy Elementary, Kelly Hatch was not really applying herself in spelling. Kelly was an interesting student. She had close to the highest grade in Lou's class in science, math, and social studies, but she was performing near the bottom of the class in spelling. She qualified for the district's gifted program and for special tutoring due to her difficulty with spelling and written communication. Although Lou recognized Kelly had some special problems, he also noticed that Kelly had developed a number of avoidance strategies that contributed to her lack of success on weekly spelling tests. She constantly drew pictures during spelling practice of what looked like dresses he had seen on his daughter's Barbie doll. Kelly's drawing also seemed to attract the interest of other girls near her so that they strayed off task also.

Kelly thought spelling was boring. The spelling workbook had long lists of silly words she did not care about and spelling practice consisted of repeatedly writing these lists. Besides being bored, Kelly knew she had messy penmanship compared to her friends. She was also embarrassed by how long it took her to learn the words everyone else seemed to spell so easily. She often wondered why spelling could not be more like making doll clothing. She loved designing and making doll clothes, and she was quite good at it. In fact, she had won a statewide competition in her age group for fashion design. She did not see

46

why Lou got impatient with her and made her stop sketching outfits in class. Kelly thought that was a much better use of her time. She was glad her parents had set up a conference with Lou for the next day.

There was clearly tension in the room as Lou sat across from Kelly's parents. Earlier in the year, Kelly's parents, very powerful lawyers in town, had convinced the tutoring staff, based on the results of several psychological and academic assessments, that Kelly should not receive a grade for spelling. This had been incorporated into Kelly's individual education plan (IEP). Kelly knew that no matter how poorly she did in spelling she would not receive a grade. Lou felt confident that if Kelly was more accountable during spelling time, she would do much better. Lou also very much supported the district's very explicit policy on academic excellence. There was a very strict grading scale even in the primary elementary grades. Consequently, he had continued to assign grades to her weekly spelling tests and had given her a spelling grade on her report card. In Lou's honest professional judgment, Kelly would not learn how to spell properly unless she was pushed a little more.

Mr. and Mrs. Hatch had overlooked the grades on Kelly's weekly spelling tests because they thought Lou just wanted to communicate a clear understanding of her progress. They were quite angry, however, when they found a spelling grade on Kelly's report card in November. A lot of time had gone into securing an IEP that was best suited to Kelly's particular learning needs. During her first 3 years of schooling, Kelly's teachers were unwilling to acknowledge that a girl as bright as she might have a learning disability related to spelling. The testing had supported what the Hatches had suspected all along and they moved determinedly to have the school get extra help for Kelly and to adjust her IEP accordingly. Lou had clearly stepped on their child's legal rights under the new IEP and they quickly set up a conference with him. During the conference, they told him in very clear language that they expected the IEP to be honored unless they were contacted and allowed to discuss changes.

Lou was frustrated. Kelly was not going to progress much now unless he spent a considerable amount of one-to-one time with her. However, the likelihood of that seemed small. With the importance of the new district competency exams, Lou was forced to cover material much more quickly to ensure that all the material on the exam was taught. Making this situation even worse, a large number of families with third-grade children had moved into his school's attendance area this year and swelled the size of all the three third-grade classes. Contrary to the good faith agreement between the teachers and the school board to cap classes at an enrollment of 25, the teacher to student ratio had risen to 35:1.

Lou had very little time these days for one-on-one work with students. In fact, he and his fellow third-grade teachers had joined together to speak with the principal, Mr. Doll, about hiring another third-grade teacher. Mr. Doll, who most of the teachers viewed as an effective administrator, listened closely to them. Lou had a reputation in the building for being a very hard-working teacher, so Mr. Doll listened with sincere attention to their problem with class size and soon after the meeting discussed the issue with the superintendent, Dr. Rand. However, so far Mr. Doll had not gotten back to the teachers after their discussion. Unbeknownst to the third-grade teachers, two other problems had arisen at Kennedy Elementary that required immediate attention and a considerable amount of Mr. Doll's time. Lou and the other third-grade teachers grew frustrated that Mr. Doll had not gotten back to them. They began to quietly encourage their students' parents to write letters to Mr. Doll, complaining about class size.

In the conference with Kelly's parents, Lou apologized for misunderstanding the IEP. He had thought that as a teacher he had some professional leeway in deciding when the use of grades might be appropriate. His thinking was that getting an actual grade would motivate Kelly to work harder. He had not in any way wanted to infringe on Kelly's legal rights. Lou also expressed his frustration with having 35 students and how it kept him from spending one-on-one time with Kelly. The Hatches were upset to learn that their daughter and other third-grade children were in such overcrowded classrooms. They quickly agreed to write a letter to Mr. Doll about the situation in the third-grade classes. However, after the conference was over, they thought it might expedite matters if a letter was sent to Dr. Rand, the superintendent, and the school board as well as to Mr. Doll. The Hatches had close friends on the school board and they had a good working relationship with Dr. Rand from other community activities.

Dr. Rand was surprised as she stared at the letter from the Hatches and chagrined when she noticed that the school board had also received a copy. She had just come from very contentious salary negotiations with the cafeteria workers and an earlier meeting about budget cuts to the districts' athletic programs. She quickly called Mr. Doll at Kennedy Elementary to find out how the Hatches got involved with all this. Mr. Doll explained that Lou, along with the other third-grade teachers, had begun to complain to parents about class size and asked them to write letters to him. The Hatches had apparently taken it on themselves to write to Dr. Rand and to the board.

Dr. Rand had planned to bring the third-grade situation at Kennedy Elementary to the board's attention at the meeting the following month. In fact, she was in the process of working out a plan to make a three fourths-time teaching aide available for the Kennedy third-grade teachers. Now the Hatches, two of the community's most prominent residents, had made it look to the board as if she was not on top of an important problem in the district. She quickly worked to speed up the placement of the new three fourths-time teaching aide and wrote a letter of response to the Hatches. A copy of the response was also sent to the board. Finally, Dr. Rand asked for a meeting to be set up with the third-grade teachers and herself and Mr. Doll.

Lou had never met Dr. Rand in person, but this meeting had convinced him that despite her small stature she was unquestionably formidable. Dr. Rand had started out by acknowledging the problem with class size and how the new three fourths-time teaching aide would work. Lou and his colleagues were happy about this news, but Dr. Rand quickly shifted tone. She grew quite stern and the room got quiet as she warned them never, ever to bring the school's dirty laundry to the parents' attention again without talking with Mr. Doll or herself first. Mr. Doll chimed in with, "Problems are to be handled in-house first, last, and always." Mr. Doll assured them that this incident would be remembered when future special requests for various things crossed his desk.

This case highlights some of the political aspects of schools. Many people associate politics with the running of the government and the election of candidates for national, state, and local offices. However, this is only a small part of what constitutes political activity (Gamson, 1968). Concepts typically associated with government politics such as conflict and power can usefully be employed to make sense of what goes on daily in schools (Ball, 1987; Blase, 1991a; Hoyle, 1986). Political patterns are not an unusual experience in schools, but are an integral part of the organization. However, it has been a long process by which political patterns have come to be seen as significant and potentially even a beneficial phenomena in the United States (Hofstadter, 1969) and its schools (Wirt & Kirst, 1982).

THE GROWING ACCEPTANCE OF CONFLICT, POWER, AND PLURALISM

During and after the Revolutionary War, the country's new citizens drew on the legacy of English political traditions that emphasized everyone working toward a "comprehensive unity or harmony" (Hofstadter, 1969, p. ix). This did not mean a "total agreement of all ... on all matters of policy ... but only a desire for ... [a] general oneness of spirit" (p. ix). Because of this emphasis on harmony, early inhabitants of the United States "did not usually see conflict as functional to society" (p. ix). This meant that individuals or groups who expressed opposition and created conflict (such as political parties) were viewed as divisive and dangerous. Despite the actual development of political parties and other sanctioned forms of opposition, many in the United States up until World War II retained a distrust of conflict and continued to stress the importance of a unified America (Noble, 1985). The notion of the United States as a melting pot was an extension of this belief. Southern and eastern European immigrants coming to this country from 1880 to 1920 were required to loose their old world identities so as to maintain a harmonious Anglo-Protestant country (Noble, Carroll, & Horowitz, 1980).

Following World War II, the country developed a growing acceptance of pluralism (Carroll & Noble, 1989). Pluralism suggested that the United States, like the international community of which it was a part, was made up different religious, ethnic, social, economic, and political groups. There was a general American Way, shared beliefs that most Americans subscribed to (Herzberg, 1955), but there were also a variety of discordant values, beliefs, and interests. These differences invariably led to conflict (Dahl, 1967), which now began to be more accepted as a natural part of a diverse society. What harmony existed was a provisional one, developed through the compromises and negotiations between different groups at a particular time. Conflict also came to be acknowledged as important during the turbulence of the 1960s.

Additionally, for the new advocates of pluralism, the meaning of power was transformed. *Power* is a common term in politics. However, its exact meaning among scholars is still widely debated. A reasonable starting point is to consider power as "[t]he ability to make people ... do what they would not otherwise have done" (Allison, 1996, p. 396). The new acceptance of pluralism helped to legitimate the use of power in a country that had long viewed it with a good deal of suspicion.

The rhetoric of Americanism during and after the Revolutionary War period stressed that all citizens were created equal and that individual liberty was inviolate (Kazin, 1995). The country strove to root out any lingering traces of the kind of power formerly exercised by the English monarchy and aristocracy. This meant constantly being on guard against the possibility that a small group of elites would rise up, centralize control of the country in their own hands, and rule over the people like the monarchs and aristocrats of the past.

Power was thus viewed as an illegitimate force, something sought after and used by various corrupt elites during the country's history. For example, according to the followers of Jefferson, the elite were a:

> pro-British cabal of merchants, landholders, and conservative clerics; for Jacksonians, a "money power" directed by well-born cosmopolitans. For activists in the new Republican Party of the 1850s, it was the "slave power" of the South that throttled civil liberties. (Kazin, 1995, p. 16)

Many Americans continued their suspicions that the use of power was linked to the machinations of scheming elites well into the 20th century. This changed to a considerable degree during the combined efforts of the allies in World War II to topple fascism. The ample command of the federal government exercised by Franklin Roosevelt to curb the Great Depression also changed people's attitudes. Growing numbers of Americans came to believe that power had some legitimate uses. Power residing in a governing force could be used responsibly to maintain democracy and liberty by stopping the complete domination of one group over all the others (Noble, 1985). Power could also be a legitimate means for managing the allocation of scarce resources (Malen, 1994).

Resources is another key term in politics. Individuals and groups have conflicts over values and prized material and symbolic resources. Prized material resources in an organization can be things such as money, time, promotions, supplies, and positions. Symbolic resources can be things that signify status or reputation in an organization such an office with a window, parking spot locations, and being sought after by administrators for ideas and opinions. There are typically not as many resources as there are individuals and groups who want them. Hence, conflicts arise over who gets what. Power residing in a governing force came to be seen as a legitimate means for equitably allocating various resources among the different competing individuals and groups; ideally, a governing power would distribute resources so that the best interest of the community as a whole was maintained (Dahl, 1967). Power also came to be viewed as a legitimate means for a group or individual to ensure it acquired needed resources from a governing force (Gamson, 1968).

Thinking of schools as places where power was dispensed and employed developed in response to changes during the 1960 and 1970s (Wirt & Kirst, 1982). It was during this period that schools became the site of dramatic public conflicts. Parent groups increasingly sought more influence on school policies and practices. Opposing taxpayer groups struggled over issues of local and state school finance. A range of minority groups rightly contested the segregated nature of public schools. They argued successfully for desegregation and equality of educational opportunity. Several important legal decisions extended the doctrine of individual rights to school students. This increased the power of students relative to the power that school authorities wielded in the past. Teacher associations and unions gained more power to influence schools, especially regarding better work conditions, salaries, and benefits. State and federal governments increasingly encroached on the local control of districts, requiring particular kinds of programs, curriculum, guidelines, and forms from schools.

From these historical developments, school organizations have come to be viewed as having political patterns and, consequently, caught up with conflict, power, and resources (Ball, 1987; Blase, 1991a; Hoyle, 1986). This is still a relatively new way to understand schools and there continues to be disagreement among scholars about terminology and focus (Malen, 1994). However, there are some areas of agreement. Just like the rest of society, schools are made up of a range of individuals and groups: teachers, administrators, students, cafeteria workers, custodians, and secretaries. These individuals and groups frequently share values and resources to enable the ongoing operation of the school, but because of their diverse values and the scarcity of resources, there is also inevitably conflict in schools. However, this "does not mean that … [schools are] torn apart by ceaseless conflict" (Baldridge, cited in Ball, 1987, p. 20). "Much of what goes on in schools, on a day-to-day basis is not marked by dispute or strife" (p. 19). Yet, this does not mean that conflict can be ignored as inconsequential. Conflict is present and it can be potentially healthy, helping to "revitalize an otherwise stagnant system" (Baldridge, cited in Ball, 1987, p. 20).

Teachers, students, parents, principals, and district personnel use power to advance particular value stances and to gain important material and symbolic resources for themselves. These political struggles in a school take place in what are referred to as arenas (Malen, 1994; Mazzoni, 1991). There are several important arenas in schools: teacher–student arena, faculty arena, teacher–principal arena, and school–parent arena. Some of the characteristic political patterns within each arena are discussed next.

TEACHER–STUDENT ARENA

Power, conflicts, and resources can be seen in Lou's interactions with Kelly. The teacher is having a conflict over values with Kelly. He places a value on Kelly learning spelling. Kelly places a low value on spelling, preferring to design doll clothing. As the teacher, Lou is the governing force within the classroom. He has the power to use a resource such as time to help his third graders learn knowledge and skills such as spelling. As the governing force, he also has the power to use another key resource, grades, to help students learn. Due to the overcrowding in the classroom and the need to move through lots of content in preparation for district competency tests, Lou has a limited amount of time to deal with students who have difficulty learning or to deal with a variety of off-task behavior. Additionally, the district's strict grading scale means a limited number of students will get high grades. Along with these other factors, Lou believes it is wrong to lie to children about their actual progress and skills level by giving everyone a high grade. He also believes it is not fair to give everyone an "A"; this is especially unfair for those children whose skill level and efforts enabled them to genuinely earn an "A." Consequently, time and grades are scarce resources. Students compete with each other in Lou's classroom for finite amounts of his time and a finite number of good grades. Given the teacher's limited time for helping Kelly, he attempts to use his power to allocate average or low grades to increase her motivation to learn spelling. Lou's ability to maximize the academic accomplishments of Kelly and as many students as possible depends on making good political decisions regarding the use of power, conflict, and scarce resources.

Research suggests that politics plays a considerable part in other classrooms as well. Blase (1991c) has long studied the political patterns in schools, particularly from the perspective of teachers. Through investigating the teacher–student arena, he found that after several years of working in classrooms, "teachers developed an awareness of the political factors important to 'playing the game' and survival at work" (p. 189). As a result, teachers learned to strategically exercise power to influence students and to protect themselves from students or adults who intervened on behalf of students. Teachers identified several areas—classroom instruction, discipline, extracurricular activities, and personal factors—in which the exercise of power for influence and protection was important.

Classroom Instruction

To influence students instructionally, teachers learned over time that they had to develop a generally friendly or diplomatic orientation toward students. This diplomatic style was key for motivating students because most of the students placed little value on academic work and its connection to their future lives. This required teachers to be emotionally attuned to the individual needs of students and ready to make adjustments to them as their needs changed from one situation to another.

Teachers also found that they had to protect themselves instructionally regarding issues such as grading, homework, and discussions of controversial topics. In general teachers reported that in protecting themselves, "they were 'compelled' to compromise their educational standards" (Blase, 1991c, p. 192). For example, students (sometimes with the help of parents and administrators) would intimidate teachers into altering their grades. To protect themselves, "teachers sometimes changed grades for individual students and 'curved' grades for entire classes of students" (p. 193). To protect themselves from the conflicts generated by discussions of controversial topics, teachers chose not to bring up certain topics or used extreme care in how these topics were presented. These protective measures had negative consequences for the quality of teachers' classroom instruction. It limited the chances for students and teachers to grapple with important questions and topics.

Discipline

Teachers' use of discipline to influence students in particular ways was affected by several factors. If they knew that their principal would support them when they administered discipline, teachers reported being more honest and straightforward in trying to control students. Knowing that a student was attempting to manipulate them into administering discipline made teachers more cautious. Teachers generally perceived students as fragile. They also saw themselves as supportive of students. Both of these attitudes made teachers temper how, when, and if they doled out discipline to students. Teachers also knew that some administrators punished students too severely. This too made teachers soften their application of discipline.

Many teachers found themselves developing a protective orientation regarding the administration of discipline. They developed this orientation out of fear of parental and student reprisals and due to inconsistent administrative support. As a result, when teachers had to deal with inappropriate student behavior, they sometimes considered ignoring students' problems or, more frequently, they adopted more conservative discipline strategies than the ones initially contemplated. Additionally, teachers carefully followed school discipline policies to the letter and conscientiously documented incidents.

Extracurricular Activities

Many teachers told Blase that serving as a teacher-leader for student clubs, social events, and sports teams helped to increase their influence with students. These types of leadership opportunities offered teachers additional time to be with students, interacting outside the confines of an explicitly academic setting such as a classroom. This facilitated more meaningful interchanges between teachers and students and helped teachers to gain more recognition and respect from students. All of this aided teachers in being more politically influential with students.

However, increased involvement in extracurricular activities also made teachers more vulnerable to student criticism. Teachers found themselves having to develop protective strategies to manage the increased potential for conflict. Some of this was due to the possibilities of distorted information about the teacher being spread in the school. As one teacher explained:

> I had a situation when I was in charge of Key Club.... Some kids had left the club meeting ... picked up beer and liquor ... and went to the graveyard and sat around drinking and the cops came and took them all to jail.... Some parents said that the last I knew, my kid was on the way to a meeting that was supposed to be run by Mr. _____ ... I just don't know what they do at that Key Club ... I don't know if maybe Mr. _____ got them that beer. (Blase, 1991c, p. 198)

To protect themselves teachers sometimes chose not to get involved in future extracurricular activities or they would develop careful rules to cover themselves in case of problems with students.

Personal Factors

Teachers reported having more influence on students when they "conformed to conservative norms ... regarding personal demeanor (e.g., dress, hairstyle) and adherence to conventional values (e.g., social responsibility and respect for authority)" (p. 198). Consequently, teachers indicated that over the course of their careers they had become more conventional as individuals. As one teacher put it, "If you don't accept these expectations personally, your life will be miserable" (Blase, 1991c, p. 198).

Teachers also reported that over time, they had come to carefully censor personal or professional information they shared with students. Other closely guarded topics included personal thoughts on local political situations. This protective strategy grew from the possibility of students communicating distorted accounts of conversations. Teachers saw this as important because "the potential for people to misunderstand is great.... Information is spread and your problems are compounded.... It's all political because it's part of how you're perceived" (Blase, 1991c, p. 199).

We have discussed the political actions taken by teachers in the classroom arena. Students also engage in political patterns with teachers. For example, consider the narrative about Lou and Kelly. Although Kelly is not the governing force in the classroom, she, like other students, is not without power. She has the power to wield a key resource, her participation in class and her ability to potentially pull the students around her off task. By doing this, Kelly and her fellow students can waste time, one of Lou's most precious resources for helping the class as a whole. The teacher depends to some extent on students' ongoing cooperation and participation in the learning process. He also depends, as the research to follow explains in more detail, on the political strategies that students use in the classroom.

Research by Spaulding (1995) suggests that students exert political power in the classroom. They do this by intentionally using passive and aggressive resistance strategies with their teachers. Passive resistance strategies consist of student behaviors that are not particularly direct or confrontational, but nonetheless are effective in disrupting a teacher's work. Repetition, interruption, topic changes, ignoring, and partial compliance are different types of passive resistance that Spaulding found.

Repetition consists of asking the teacher to excessively repeat instructions or explanations. This strategy can be particularly effective if a number of students in the same period engage in this behavior. The amount of on-task time can be significantly reduced. Interruptions consist of breaking in on instruction or an activity already in progress. A consequence of this can be that the teacher becomes distracted and looses her train of thought, making it difficult to maintain the continuity of the instruction or activity.

Students can use two types of topic change strategies: responding to teacher questions with completely unrelated answers or asking teachers questions unrelated to the current academic focus. Again, as a result, teaching is delayed and the possibilities for becoming distracted are increased. Spaulding found that students used ignoring as a passive resistance strategy frequently when asked to quiet down or when focusing on something more interesting going on among peers. Partial compliance can be particular wearing on the teacher as the following quote from Spaulding's study suggests:

> During a math lesson, a group of boys begin talking and making quacking noises with their mouths. The quacking noises gradually get louder. [The teacher] looks sternly at the boys and tells them to "stop making that noise." Immediately, the boys stop making "that" noise (i.e., the quacking noise) but quickly convert to a new noise, a cheeping sound. The same pattern begins again. (p. 20)

Students are very clear as to why they use these passive resistance strategies. As one student told the researcher, "Some kids ask a lot of questions on purpose and Mrs. Cole has to keep repeating herself ... it keeps kids from having to do the things they don't want to do" (p. 22). Students use passive resistance more frequently than aggressive resistance because passive strategies are usually effective and less likely to result in serious consequences.

Spaulding found students only use aggressive resistance "when they experience an intense and almost unbearable dislike of an activity" (p. 33) such that they are not concerned with the disciplinary consequences of their actions. A perceived breach of fairness by the teacher can also be a trigger for the student. Aggressive resistance involves students engaging in very direct and overt behavior to prevent a teacher from doing something.

Protesting and the use of intermediaries are the two types of aggressive resistance. Protesting involves students using intense verbal objections and arguments. The students' hoped-for payoff is to have the teacher back down and capitulate to their wants or definition of the situation. Using intermediaries involves a student finding someone to intervene on their behalf. For example, Spaulding discussed two girls who greatly resented having their recess taken away when other members of the class were actually the ones misbehaving. Their teacher punished the whole class in hopes of using peer pressure to improve the true offenders. The girls spoke to their parents about the unfairness of this practice. The parents in turn spoke to the principal, who then spoke to the teacher. The teacher stopped using this form of discipline as a consequence.

Students generally deploy these resistance strategies to "delay, distract, modify, or prevent teacher initiated activities or instruction that they dislike" (Spaulding, 1995, p. 11). This dislike can be due to boredom and lack of interest or to avoid learning something the student has difficulty grasping. Again, students are very clear about their reasons and goals for using these strategies. "We tell [the teacher] because we don't like it, we hate it, we can't stand it ... we let her know how we feel and that we are going to feel that way until she changes it. She will change her mind" (p. 29).

THE FACULTY ARENA

Political patterns can also be found in the faculty arena. There are two general approaches for looking at political patterns between teachers. Ball (1987) tended to view the school as made up of different factions or groups; frequently these factions are based on divisions between formal entities such as departments in high schools or grade levels in middle and elementary schools. Groups may also be divided based on differing ideologies. In Ball's (1987) approach, ideologies consist of teachers' values and philosophic commitments regarding students, instruction, curriculum, or grading. Groups of educators will often form around a shared educational ideology. For example, Lou's district developed a shared ideology that a rigorous grading scale would motivate students to achieve academic excellence. Recently in the popular press much has been made over competing ideologies of reading: whole language versus phonics.

In the frantic, day-to-day effort of working with students, individual teachers may have little contact with their own department and/or grade-level colleagues, let alone entering into interdepartmental or intergrade-level conflicts over differing educational ideologies. However, a significant change in a school such as a new principal or a large-scale reform initiative can alter the surface calm between groups. As Ball (1987) wrote, "Change or the possibility of change brings to the surface those subterranean conflicts and differences which are otherwise glossed over or obscured in the daily routines of school life" (p. 28). Change can threaten the ideological interests tacitly held in common by a department or grade level so that teachers feel compelled to make more explicit their shared beliefs. This is illustrated by the next case.

Kruse (1995) studied the Evansville school district, which had recently hired a new superintendent. This superintendent had successfully spearheaded two junior high schools being restructured into middle schools in his former district. Within a short period of time, he proposed the same for Evansville. His plan called for changing the existing seventh- through ninth-grade junior high into a fifth- through eighth-grade middle school. The ninth grade would be moved up to the high school. According to the superintendent, this would relieve the population glut in the junior high. Demographically, the ninth-grade class was overcrowded. He also argued that a middle-school program would provide a better developmental transition for children as they moved from an elementary education and prepared for their future as high school students. A middle school would accomplish this by providing more student-centered learning, teacher teams working with smaller groups of kids, and the use of interdisciplinary units.

The superintendent's middle-school initiative was conducted in cooperation with the school board but without consulting any of the teachers involved. However, the ninth-grade teachers were happy to be, as they put it, promoted up to the high school. The fifth- and sixth-grade teachers likewise viewed the move up to the middle school as a new and exciting challenge. But the seventh- and eighth-grade teachers viewed working in the same building with elementary school teachers as a step down of sorts. They also had reservations about the middle-school educational ideology.

The seventh- and eighth-grade teachers entered the profession because of their strong interests in the content areas they taught. They viewed themselves as subject matter specialists whose job was to communicate important knowledge to students. Many of these teachers also placed an importance on excellence and high academic standards. They viewed sorting and classifying students, based on their mastery knowledge, as part of their responsibility as teachers. This educational ideology very much clashed with the new middle-school philosophy, a philosophy with which the fifth- and sixth-grade teachers felt very much at home.

The former elementary teachers regarded themselves as student-centered. They viewed teaching as helping to develop the whole child, not just their intellectual abilities. In their former positions, they taught a range of different subject areas so the transition to teaching interdisciplinary units was not off-putting. Neither was the prospect of teacher teaming; something many had experimented with informally in their former elementary school. Within a few months of the beginning of the middle school, the fifth- and sixth-grade teams had successfully made a transition into the middle-school structure and ideology.

The seventh- and eighth-grade teams struggled and to some extent resisted the middle-school structure and ideology. Their formal educational training and ideology had not prepared them to mix language arts, social studies, and science. They liked working with smaller groups of students, but resented having to coddle and spoon feed the students in the manner that the student-centered ideology suggested. Among themselves, the seventh- and eighth-grade teachers regarded many of the interdisciplinary units made by the lower grade teams as fluff and lacking in content. During schoolwide faculty meetings or in the teacher's lounge, interactions between the two factions started to decrease.

The split between the fifth- and sixth-grade teams and the seventh- and eighth-grade teams was exacerbated by the principal. Due to the successes of the fifth- and sixth-grade teams, they received more material and symbolic resources from the principal. He publicly lauded the units developed by the fifth- and sixth-grade teams during faculty meetings and in the school newspaper. He provided them with sub time to enable the creation of new units. He also sought advice and ideas from them for making the school better. Over time, the seventh- and eighth-grade teams began to withdraw and rarely spoke to the fifth- or sixth-grade teachers or the principal.

This case looks at politics in the faculty arena from the perspective of different factions clashing over competing educational ideologies. Blase (1987) offered another approach to politics in the faculty arena. He argued that teachers, over the course of their careers, develop a more general interpersonal political orientation regarding their interactions with fellow teachers. Teachers in his study described the genesis of this orientation:

> I thought that doing a good job in the classroom was all I needed to do.... I was very surprised after a couple of years to learn that I did not have the support of other teachers.... There are all these complex considerations ... (p. 293)

In response to these types of experiences teachers learned to become more political with their colleagues. As one teacher aptly noted, "You become more calculating ... plan your moves and learn to anticipate consequences" (p. 294).

There were two general types of interpersonal politics—positive and negative—that teachers described to Blase. Positive interpersonal politics seemed to be warranted by an overall sense that their colleagues' differing value stances and sensitivity to criticism made the potential for divisiveness to be ever imminent. To maintain a sense of mutuality and reciprocity, however fragile it might be, required ongoing positive interpersonal politics. This meant exchanges between teachers were generally diplomatic and worked to increase faculty cohesion.

Different types of strategies were thought to be important in the service of being diplomatic: control of self, friendliness, and support. Control of self meant that teachers learned over time that even when they felt otherwise, "biting your tongue ... and smiling" (Blase, 1987, pp. 299–300) was important in most interactions with other teachers. Open displays of aggressiveness or anger resulted in grave consequences for one's future standing and relationships. Teachers placed an important emphasis on being viewed as friendly. Friendliness could be communicated in a number of ways such as smiling or small talk. A range of different activities were indicative of support: sharing instructional materials; helping a fellow teacher by covering a class, taking over a lunch duty, or administering a make-up test; participating publicly in recognizing a colleague's accomplishments; offering advice to fellow teachers about students or other difficult situations; and providing therapeutic advise, gratitude, and empathy. Blase reported that each of these strategies helped build norms of reciprocity between teachers so they were more able to do their curricular and extracurricular work.

Due to the importance and stresses related to getting their work done, teachers depend on each other to a large extent. As a result, interpersonal politics that violated the general diplomatic orientation were seen as negative. Examples of this type of politics included confrontation, passive aggressiveness, and ingratiating behavior. These types of strategies resulted in "[l]ower levels of trust, support, friendliness, and morale, as well as increased conflict and alienation" (p. 303). Consequently, most teachers reported striving to use positive interpersonal politics with their colleagues.

Blase also found that the nature of the interpersonal politics—positive or negative—could very much be affected by department chairpersons. Even though department chairs had limited power to formally evaluate teachers, they did have control over important resources such as scheduling, room assignments, and creating the political climate in their departments. Not surprisingly, department chairs who handled the allocation of resources fairly and used positive interpersonal political strategies with their teachers increased these types of interactions among department colleagues. Department chairs who demonstrated favoritism in managing key resources and practiced negative interpersonal politics promoted the same types of interactions between faculty. However, even more than the department chair, as the next section explains, the principal plays an inordinately important role in fostering a particular type of politics in a school.

TEACHER–PRINCIPAL ARENA

In examining the politics between teachers and principals, it seems helpful to recognize a distinction scholars make between formal and informal channels of organization activity (Blase, 1991b; Malen, 1994). Formal channels of activity consist of situations intentionally and explicitly developed for discussing and deciding key policies and practices for a school. Faculty, site council, and committee meetings are examples of formal channels. Informal channels consist of the everyday exchanges between people that enable the work to get done in schools. Common informal channels are talking in the hallway between classes or brief interactions around the copy and coffee machines. The political patterns between teachers and principals need to viewed as taking place in both channels (Ball, 1987; Blase, 1991b; Malen, 1994).

Formal Channels

According to Malen (1994), the politics between teachers and principals found within formal channels centers on who has the power to make decisions that impact the classroom or the school as a whole. The content of these contested decisions often deals with issues such as the budget, personnel, curriculum, and instruction. Teachers tend to maintain their power over the classroom but they are also interested in influencing decisions that have schoolwide impact. Principals work to maintain control in those areas that their hierarchical authority in the organization formally establishes for them. This usually means maintaining control over schoolwide policy and issues such as budget and personnel decisions. However, depending on the school and the particular decision being discussed, teachers and principals will negotiate with each other over which party will influence a particular outcome.

In general, Malen found that, not unlike our discussion of Blase's work, teachers develop a generally polite and diplomatic orientation in dealing with principals in formal channels. This typically results in teachers being allowed to maintain their power in the classroom and principals retaining their power over schoolwide policies such as budget and personnel. This traditional pattern of power distribution in the schools seems to be caused by several factors. Principals tend to use a number of strategies to limit teacher participation and influence on important decisions. They do this by "controlling agenda content, meeting format, and information flow" (p. 155); by only involving teachers who already support their politics; and by overturning or ignoring decisions they disagree with.

Teachers, for their part, have been hesitant to question this traditional distribution of power. Some of this is a result of strong norms of positive interpersonal politics among teachers. But other research suggests that sometimes teachers have concerns that challenging the principal will result in "professional sanctions (e.g., being cast as a troublemaker, a malcontent) that may be applied by principals and peer alike" (p. 155). Such sanctions can affect the teacher's future standing in the school and the material and symbolic resources they are allocated by the principal.

Despite the maintenance of traditional power relationships between teachers and principals in formal channels, these avenues of communication and decision making continue to matter. The political climate established by the principal in faculty and committee meetings can play an important role in helping or hindering teachers' sense of efficacy and overall satisfaction with their work. Also, formal channels still provide legitimate opportunities for some participation in decision making and the airing of teacher concerns.

Informal Channels

According to Malen (1994), both teachers and principals experience a vulnerability in their work in the school and the wider community. This leads them to cultivate strategies to protect their spheres of influence and reputations and also to work toward maintaining a fragile sense of cohesion with their coworkers. Teachers adopt a range of strategies to be viewed as positive promoters of interdependence between themselves and principals. For example, they generally acquiesce to administrative expectations to protect their job security or key resources such as schedules, class load, and extra duties. They also hope not be tagged with reputations as trouble-makers. For similar reasons, teachers carefully conform to rules and policies regarding different facets of their work. They do this to communicate a willingness to cooperate or to protect themselves from particularly nonsup-portive or authoritarian principals. Diplomatic and nonaggressive strategies such as friendliness are frequently employed to keep the lines of communi-cation open and to increase influence.

Teachers also use some strategies, although less frequently, to undermine or question principals. Passive–aggressiveness through gossip and rumor are used to covertly discredit principals. Occasionally, teachers will directly confront principals. However, as this type of strategy is viewed critically by most administrators, it is rarely employed. Although many teachers view ingratiating behavior negatively, they still find some use for brown nosing, especially in situations with principals who are insecure or experiencing stresses from public relations work.

Principals frequently use an array of control strategies to contain teachers in their traditional domain of the classroom and maintain their own power on schoolwide issues. They can do this by avoiding conflict or making the appearance of soliciting teacher input and, also, by carefully handling opponents, engendering debtedness, or inducing loyalty. Additionally, prin-cipals may stifle talk or silence teachers by defining certain discussions as subversive, fragmenting faculty cohesion, and stigmatizing and isolating opponents. "They may also manipulate the information flow and 'manage the meanings' ascribed to actions" (Marlen, 1994, p. 158). The consequence of these principal strategies may be that teachers withdraw mentally and emotionally from their work and the school. However, principals can also use strategies with teachers to alter the balance of power between them. These types of strategies can increase and revitalize teachers' willingness to contribute to their classrooms and the school as a whole.

SCHOOL–PARENT ARENA

We have discussed each of the previous arenas as if they were distinct and separate from one another. And although a particular type of politics may frequently be centered in each arena, political patterns within one arena will not infrequently spill into one or several others. In short, the arenas interact with one another. This is particularly true regarding the school–parent arena. As you may have noticed from earlier discussions, parents can impact the student–teacher arena and the teacher–teacher arena. Therefore, in our discussion of the school–parent arena, we discuss some of the characteristic political patterns between the school and parents (Malen, 1994) and we present a case to demonstrate that the different arenas can influence one another (Corbett, 1991).

Teacher, principals, and parents interact politically in a number of formal channels of activity such as program specific advisory boards (for special education, Chapter I, or Title I programs) and school site councils (Malen, 1994). At issue between the parties in these formal situations is whether the professionals (teachers and principals) are offering adequate educational service and how much power parents will have to influence educational policies. In these meetings, teachers and principals typically view themselves as the experts regarding educational policy and parents tend to generally support this position. However, if an issue is of particular concern to parents, they will mobilize to influence school policy and practices. This makes teachers and principals vulnerable to parental criticisms and conflicts because they rely on maintaining the support of parents and the general community to smoothly conduct their daily work. This dependency generates a certain amount of tension for teachers and principals whenever they deal with parents and other community members.

The principal plays a key role in these formal channels (as well as in informal ones) in maintaining the power of the professionals and limiting the power of parents (Malen, 1994). The principal buffers teachers from parental influence through a range of strategies: by selecting the right parents to serve on advisory boards or councils; by educating parents to support the appropriate policies and take subordinate roles in relationship to professionals; and by using various resources to ensure that meeting agendas are controlled and move in directions useful to teachers and principals. Teachers also lend support in these meetings by typically aligning themselves with the principals. Also, as noted earlier, parents generally affirm the teachers and principal's authority to control the decision making in particular areas.

This picture changes to some extent when we shift our focus to informal channels of activity (Malen, 1994). The principal still plays a key role in guarding the boundary that separates the school from parents (or the rest of the community). The principal keeps parents from intruding into the school by dispensing important resources that cultivates and sustains parental support. He or she deflects and manages parental anxieties and conflicts through a variety of efforts. Most of the principal's strategies, in fact, work to ensure parents that the school is generally doing well and that parents have no cause for concern or need to intervene into school processes. However, principals may strike bargains or compromises with parents that influence a range of other political arenas within the school. Consider the case of the Westtown School (Corbett, 1991).

A group of Westtown school teachers and administrators jointly developed a new discipline system for the whole school. The hope was to create uniform standards for student behavior shared by students, teachers, and administrators. This would "separate academics from discipline ... by attaching specific consequences to particular students behaviors and thereby freeing teachers from having to make disciplinary judgments that could affect their instructional effectiveness" (Corbett, 1991, p. 80). It would also create a consistency in how students were treated in each classroom. Students would come to realize that in every class particular kinds of inappropriate student behaviors (e.g., fighting and disrespectfulness) would not be tolerated and, in fact, would result in particular kinds of sanctions. Different types of student infractions were assigned a certain point value. Teachers simply had to record the misbehaviors and report them to administrators, who would total the points and discipline the students depending on their total number of points.

The actual operation of the new disciplinary system did not reflect the ideal of consistency. Certain students were treated by administrators on a case-by-case approach and others were dealt with based on the uniform rules. Also, administrators did not suspend some students who accumulated the required number of points. Administrators found themselves disciplining students based on how parents might react. If administrators sensed that parents might respond negatively to the way their child was disciplined, they backed off to protect the school from a potential intervention by parent-influenced school board members or the superintendent. Administrators found that this case-by-case approach to discipline also helped to maintain parental support.

For teachers, administrators' inconsistent handling of student discipline eroded their authority in the classroom arena. In fact, the power seemed to shift from teachers to the parents and students. This empowered some students to act out in classrooms because they had less fear of potentially significant consequences. More importantly, the hoped-for increase in instructional time with students was jeopardized. This had a negative affect on the faculty arena. Teachers left Westtown or contemplated doing so. There were also reports of "increased mental and physical health problems, and increasing apathy" (Corbett, 1991, p. 87).

Clearly, as seen in the Westtown example, politics in and surrounding the school can affect the work of teachers. Recognizing this, some reformers have moved to change aspects of the traditional political patterns in schools.

POLITICAL SOCIAL PATTERNS AND REFORM

Many reformers since the late 1980s have called for restructuring schools through site-based management (Mohrman & Wohlstetter, 1994). One of the goals of this reform is to intentionally alter traditional political patterns. Site-based managed schools are governed by a council made up of teachers, administrators, and, sometimes, parents. The councils allow teachers and parents to play a more active role in shaping important schoolwide policies and practices. The power to make binding decisions about curriculum, budget, and personnel would ideally be shared with the person more typically in control of these areas, the principal.

The city of Chicago provides an example of how site-based management might alter the politics of schools to involve teachers and parents to a greater degree (Rollow & Bryk, 1994).

By an act of the Illinois legislature in 1988, the Chicago School Reform Act, the Chicago Public Schools' governance structure was transformed. (Political arenas at the state and federal level can significantly influence political patterns in schools as well; Ball & Bowe, 1991; Mazzoni, 1994.) Important powers, such as controlling the budget, were shifted from the Chicago Public School's central office and given to individual schools. Each school was governed by a local school council (LSC) made up of parents, community members, and teachers. The principal also served on the council, but on a 4-year performance contract. If the membership of the LSC felt that after 4 years a principal had not worked out, the current principal could be replaced. Additionally, teachers provided input into the governance of the school through the Professional Personnel Advisory Committee.

Researchers who tracked the implementation of this reform in Chicago found that school politics could be altered successfully to involve teachers more actively in key decision making (Rollow & Bryk, 1994). In some Chicago schools, teachers used their own initiative to develop expertise in particular educational programs and curricula. These teachers then sought to promote these new programs and curricula to their fellow teachers and the principal. If teachers successfully persuaded their colleagues and principal, the innovation would be implemented. If a principal vetoed their idea, teachers could potentially organize other members of the LSC to remove the principal at the conclusion of the 4-year contract. Teachers also became more involved in school governance through principals whose leadership style encouraged and supported collaboration. From this Chicago experience, we can also extract useful ideas for supporting teacher-initiated changes in other schools.

POLITICAL SOCIAL PATTERNS
AND TEACHER-INITIATED CHANGE

Many researchers have found that teachers become surprised when their reforms or school change efforts generate political responses in the form of conflict or opposition (Muncey & McQuillan, 1992). Therefore, a useful starting point for teacher-initiated change is an acceptance and tolerance of politics as an integral part of schools—conflict, power, and resources exist, and they matter. Before commencing a change effort, teachers may wish to draw on their organizational literacy to interpret the political social patterns in a school. The following questions might offer a useful beginning:

- Who are the particular individuals and groups that might have conflicts with the proposed change? Why would they oppose the change?
- What are the particular resources that might be at stake for these individuals and groups?
- What types of power and resources might these individuals or groups use to oppose or stall the change?
- Who controls the final power over whether the change is implemented?
- What is the process by which the final power might actually be used to implement the intended change?
- What resources and power does the change initiator have at her disposal?
- What is the ideology of proposed change and how does it compare with other ideological commitments in the school?
- Should informal, formal, or both channels of activity be used in the change process?
- In what arena or arenas should the change be advanced?

These questions are meant to offer a point of departure for interpreting the political social patterns in a school. The questions can help in the creation of a more effective and realistic plan for change. They draw on the concepts discussed in the chapter, but they are not meant to be exhaustive. Depending on the particular circumstances of a school, some will be more relevant than others. However, the discussions in this chapter, including the questions, should not be viewed as implying that any and all action in the name of politics should be approved of or used to assist in the change process. There is clearly political action that would be abhorrent to most teachers and administrators. The narrative that follows exemplifies how attention to political social patterns might be used to assist in teacher-initiated change.

Angela Perez, math department chair, was cautious when considering new educational reforms. She thought many reforms passed in and out of fashion like clothing fads and that they did so was reassuring. Most had little substance and few translated into something that meaningfully affected the learning of students. However, her attendance at several workshops and subsequent experimenting in her own classroom had changed her mind about one reform. Angela had grown increasingly confident that there was something genuine about the Funds of Knowledge approach for teaching math. It seemed to be particularly effective with the many disadvantaged Latino students who attended Garfield Senior High. It made a real difference in helping her students connect with mathematics and make sense of it.

The Funds of Knowledge approach argued that the everyday knowledge found in most students' homes was relevant to the subject-matter disciplines taught in schools. For example, in the daily family life of all students, math was regularly used: People bought things, paid bills, and brought home sources of money that needed to be allocated toward different ends. The Funds of Knowledge approach suggested that this everyday folk math could be built on as a bridge for students in moving toward the more abstract and unfamiliar math problems used in many classes and textbooks. Using the Funds of Knowledge from the home would allow students to begin with more familiar and meaningful problems. An added bonus was that it also frequently meant family members could help with their child's homework. Angela began to consider this reform an important change to implement in the math department's classes.

In moving forward with this reform, one of the problem spots would certainly be the sizable older contingent of faculty and their spokesperson-by-proxy Bill Winters. When Angela first brought up the Funds of Knowledge approach at a department meeting a few months ago a hush settled over the room. Finally, Bill broke the silence with, "I thought when you became chair you promised not to bother us with this kind of stuff." There were smiles and nods of approval from the older teachers sitting near Bill's end of the table. Bill and the others spoke frequently during "bull sessions" at lunch about the importance of upholding academic standards in the face of regular pressures to water down the curriculum. Many of the older faculty very much believed that the students' home culture was the problem rather than the solution, so the emphasis in Funds of Knowledge on the home did not sit well with them. Bill and the others very much had a principled stance that students needed to work hard to master math. If they did not, it was a matter of too little effort or a lack of ability.

After the initial failure at the department meeting, Angela talked to Bill several times after school over coffee. She knew from past experience that Bill was, despite his behavior at meetings sometimes, a dedicated math teacher. Angela explained her success in working with the Funds of Knowledge. She told him how several students they both had struggled with in the past were now succeeding. Bill seemed genuinely impressed, but did not think a few successes merited a change for the whole department.

With that avenue closed, Angela began chatting with the younger faculty in her department. Stories of her successes encouraged the younger staff to learn more about the Funds of Knowledge approach. Many of them became enthusiastic as they experienced improvements with their students. With a solid contingent of younger math faculty behind her, Angela approached her principal, Mort DeSilva, to get approval to develop a proposal to officially change the math department's general instructional approach. Mort was very excited by Angela's overview of the Funds of Knowledge approach. He regarded the high school's traditional instructional approach as having a limited appeal to a good portion of the student body. Mort was also someone who liked to be very visible and vocal in the wider district. He liked his building to be thought of in the district as successful and associated with progressive innovations. He gave Angela and the younger math faculty his blessing and scheduled a proposal presentation with the district's director of curriculum, Tovah Shapiro. Although the school board technically had control over a change in the curriculum, Tovah made most of the key decisions about what changed regarding the curriculum in the district.

When Bill heard that Angela had received Mort's backing, he knew the next step organizationally would be his old friend Tovah. He and Tovah had worked together for many years when she first started as a teacher. They both had children the same age and the two families had done things together during many summers until the children got older. Bill quickly gave Tovah a call and explained his concerns about Angela's Funds of Knowledge proposal. Tovah, like Bill, believed that traditional curriculum standards had slipped in the past years and that teachers needed to hold students more accountable for real math. Tovah assured Bill she would take his concerns into consideration when making a final decision.

Angela and the three teachers who accompanied her, made what Tovah thought was one of best proposal presentations she had seen in a long time. They had been clear and thorough. They had thoughtfully and carefully planned everything down to the last detail. Tovah told them how impressed she was and that she thought their proposal had merit. However, at this time she needed more substantial data to stand behind a full scale implementation in the math department. She encouraged Angela and her colleagues to consider applying again in a year or two after more student achievement data had been collected.

Angela and the other math teachers disappointedly met in the lunch room the next day and considered their options. After everybody grumbled for awhile, Angela indicated she still had one more idea for moving forward. With Mort's approval, Angela drew some money from her department's budget to arrange for a local expert on the Funds of Knowledge approach to do a workshop at Garfield. She invited all the department chairs and their faculty to attend. The workshop generated a fair amount of excitement. Many saw an opportunity to motivate students by connecting the standard curriculum to meaningful knowledge from students' homes and neighborhoods. The chairs of science, English, social studies, and many of their faculty approached Angela about the possibility of adopting the Funds of Knowledge approach and drawing on it to do some interdisciplinary work with the math department as well.

Angela was excited by the response, but also concerned that too much public discussion of changing several departments in the school might mobilize resistance from Bill and like-minded staff. Angela identified some of the key faculty from interested departments to meet privately at her home to make plans for another proposal. The meeting got a good turnout. The chairs of science, English, and social studies came, along with some hard-working and articulate teachers from all four departments. There were some disappointments and struggles in the meeting. Angela and her fellow math teachers had to give up some of the features of their earlier proposal to meet the needs of the other departments. After more debate and haggling back and forth a proposal agreeable to all was ready. Angela, along with the three other chairs, hammered out a few remaining details. Once again, Mort threw his full support behind the proposal. Additionally, Mort had an idea to create a stronger impression during the proposal presentation to Tovah.

With Angela's approval, Mort requested that the director of curriculum attend a proposal meeting at Garfield rather than the central district office. When Tovah arrived at the appointed time she was met by Mort, Angela, three other department chairs, and 36 teachers. Tovah found it difficult to turn down another solid proposal, especially one backed by an influential principal and a good sized contingent of Garfield's teachers. Following Tovah's approval, Angela initiated a series of inservice for the high school's staff and, subsequently, led several of Garfield's departments in piloting an interdisciplinary effort to implement Funds of Knowledge.

THE BENEFITS OF POLITICAL SOCIAL PATTERNS

There are several benefits to be gained from developing the literacy to read the political patterns found in organizations such as schools (Ball, 1987; Morgan, 1986). Putting politics out in the clear light of day may make it easier for school staff to accept and come to grips with the reality of organizational politics. Acknowledging political social patterns enables us to identify reportedly neutral bureaucratic features, such as goals, as the reflection of individual or group values rather than a nonpartisan effort to cultivate efficiency and consensus. Political patterns also enrich our understanding of the disintegrative strains and tensions in a school. Each of these is discussed in turn.

Morgan (1986) nicely captured a common practice regarding organizational politics and its potential consequences:

> One of the curious features of organizational life is the fact that though many people know that they are surrounded by organizational politics, they rarely come out and say so ... at times [this] makes it extremely difficulty to deal with this crucially important aspect of organizational reality. (p. 194)

As previously developed, power, conflict, and the allocation of resources play an ongoing role in schools and, for that matter, nearly all organizations. Accepting this facilitates a much more proactive stance regarding organizational membership in general and, especially, the initiation and management of any significant change process.

Those wishing to promote seemingly neutral bureaucratic social patterns such as goals may be employing politics to advance their own values and interests (Ball, 1987). The valued goal of one group such as administrators does not necessarily reflect the goals of teachers, parents, or students. Schools may be more accurately characterized as having goal diversity. Consequently, the apparent public consensus around a particular organizational goal in a school may be due to the power of an individual or group to impose its agenda in competition with other agendas. Acknowledging political social patterns helps us to recognize the potential for partisan motivations as the impulse behind any effort to promote bureaucratic control and efficiency or change and reform for the good of the whole school.

The political perspective adds to our understanding of the loose coupling often found in schools. It does this by highlighting the potential for disintegrative strains and tensions between different individuals and groups in the school. Attempts to unify the school around shared goals and educational ideologies may be fraught with conflict due to the diversity of values. As a result, political social patterns teach us to appreciate the provisional common goals that do emerge through conflict and negotiation. A provisional common good may be the best that can be hoped for in any human collective composed of a plurality of individuals and groups.

THE LIMITATIONS OF POLITICAL
SOCIAL PATTERNS

Although focusing on political patterns offers benefits, it also offers limita-tions as well (Morgan, 1986). Stressing the importance of politics, particu-larly its manipulative and conflictual elements, could result in negative consequences. Although the political perspective emphasizes plural sources of power in and around the school, in fact, as indicated earlier, some individuals and groups in the school—administrators for example—fre-quently have more power. Finally, some would argue that focusing on plural sources of power in and around the school obscures how inequalities present in the wider society based on class, race, and gender structure the distribu-tion of power within the school (Apple, 1982).

Organizations such as schools depend to a large degree on cooperation, openness, and trust among teachers, administrators, students, and parents (Blase, 1991b). Viewing schools within a framework that solely focuses on attempts to use power to acquire resources can lead organizational members to view all interactions as inherently strategic. This can potentially create a feeling of distrust that eats away at the necessary levels of confidence and mutuality that enable the shared sense of community necessary for the day-to-day work to get done. Additionally, adopting an interpretive stance that single-mindedly attends to conflicts between groups could increase the competitive spirit within a school. This might impede the necessary collaboration between different grade levels or departments and between teachers and administrators. Schools must be viewed as political entities that embody both conflictual elements and cooperative/consensual elements (Blase, 1991b). This emphasis is pursued further in the chapter on communal patterns.

As this chapter suggests, students, parents, teachers, and administrators all have the power to influence what happens in schools. Each group can employ a variety of strategies to influence the distribution of key material and symbolic resources. This insight has grown from a historically develop-ing acceptance of pluralism. What this growing acceptance of pluralism may inadvertently hide, however, is that among a plurality of individuals and groups, some frequently may have more power than others. For example, as implicitly noted previously, principals are typically more able to influence schoolwide policies and practices compared to teachers, students, and parents (Malen, 1994). This is not to suggest that principals have an absolute power, but they are generally able to control their schools, creating what some scholars term a *maintenance politics* (Rollow & Bryk, 1994).

Attending to the plural sources of power in schools can also conceal how inequalities present in the larger society structure the unequal distribution of power in schools. For example, according to one study, men hold 95.7% of the key leadership positions in government, business, media, and public service sectors of the United States (Tozer, Violas, & Senese, 1995), despite the fact that women make up 51% of the population. This inequality based on gender is reflected in schools as well. Women make up 71% of the teaching force, but only 34% of the principals (Shakeshaft, 1995). Similarly, only 7.3% of superintendents and 24% of assistant superintendents are female. This means that men typically hold the administrative positions in schools. As discussed previously, principals usually have more power to influence significant schoolwide issues compared to teachers, just as in the wider society men customarily have more power in schools than women. Patterns of inequality based on race and social class in the wider society are also reflected in schools (Apple, 1996). Focusing on plural sources of power can potentially hide the importance of these societal-based patterns of inequality and the role they play in school political patterns. These issues are discussed in more detail in chapters 5, 6, and 7.

SUMMARY

In this chapter, we presented the prominent role that political social patterns play in schools. The use of conflict and power to acquire important material and symbolic resources influences much of the daily activity in schools. Conflict and power are the natural consequences of any pluralistic human endeavor, particularly in situations of resource scarcity. Political social patterns in schools manifest themselves in different arenas: teachers and students, faculty, teachers and administrators, school staff and parents. Within these arenas, political action can take place within formal school channels and within informal channels. Different beliefs or ideologies about curriculum and instruction can play a role in mobilizing various factions of a school's staff. Acknowledging political social patterns more explicitly helps to promote a more proactive approach to school change and it highlights the potentially value-laded nature of any organizational practice. Focusing solely on political action within schools can erode the necessary amounts of cooperation and trust necessary for teachers, administrators, and students to work together each day. Acknowledging the importance of pluralism in schools may obscure that some individuals and groups consistently have more power than others.

PRACTICE CASE—POLITICS IN HOWARD COUNTY

Although many schools across the country have engaged in extensive reform in the last 15 years, our understanding of the role and influence of politics in this process is still developing (Ball, 1987; Blase, 1991a). One thing that does stand out in many investigations is that change has a significant effect on the distribution of resources and power and the ideological divisions within the school (Ball, 1987). Dealing with change effectively often entails understanding this and actively developing a power based through coalitions (Bolman & Deal, 1991). Coalitions involve individuals and different interest groups joining together to pool their power and resources toward a shared vision, frequently in exchange for future rewards. Developing a powerful coalition of people can help immeasurably in enabling the successful outcome of a change effort.

Located in rural Howard County, the Howard School District is a middle-sized school district with eight elementary schools (Grades K–6), two junior high schools (Grades 7–9) and one high school (Grades 10–12). Traditionally, Howard has had a strong sense of community and consistent parental support for its school system. Friday night Tiger football games are attended by students and their families, long-standing community boosters and graduates. The new 5,000 seat, astroturf football stadium is a source of pride for both the district and community. It is not unusual for families with elementary-aged children to attend sporting, drama, or music events at the high school as regular family outings. Children grow up with the sense that, "Mom and Dad had a great experience as a Tiger and so will I."

Howard has experienced rapid growth recently and the large, family-operated farms and showcase Victorian homes have been surrounded by new modern housing developments. Traditionally, it has been a stable district with little change, yet, recently, the new growth has caused some of the family atmosphere the town shared to vanish. Established residents lamented, "It used to be that you knew everyone on Main, their kids played with your kids, and you didn't have to worry about who might be trouble. Now you just can't be sure."

Sunset Hills Junior High School (SHJHS) is one of the two junior high schools in the district. The student population at SHJHS has been relatively stable since the school's opening in 1981, averaging around 900 students each year. Prompted by overcrowding of both the high school and junior high, and expanded development south of the main city, the decision to build SHJHS was painful for the community. Students had historically attended Howard Junior High, home of the Tiger Cubs, for Grades 7 and 8, before traveling the few symbolic blocks to the high school as ninth graders. The sense of long-standing community members was, "Howard Junior was a good experience for me. You got to know everyone in your class real well. By the time we graduated, everyone was friend for life."

For a brief period, the school board considered expanding the campus to include a second building, allowing students to remain at the same physical site, although the ninth graders would still be moved down to the junior high. The motion failed and SHJHS was constructed, on a site south of the center of town. Faculty, many of whom had attended Howard Junior High and High School, were among the reluctant voices. Many teachers had taught their entire teaching career in the same room and resisted the coming change.

The freshman faculty resented being demoted to the junior high, thus losing their ability to pick-up an occasional upper division class or coaching duty in their schedules. Furthermore, they were annoyed and offended by the added requirement of teaching little kids, seventh and eighth graders, in their academic course load. Many of the existing junior high staff were involuntarily transferred to the new building. They viewed their new assignment as being sent to Siberia.

Feeding directly from three different elementary schools, SHJHS opened its doors in the fall of 1981 to a reluctant teaching staff, a disappointed community, and a school board still hoping to convince everyone that it had made the right choice. In the words of one school board member:

We knew the new building was really was the best thing to do, educationally speaking. We are now able to offer more opportunity to students by having two teams, more electives and expanded academic offerings for seventh and eighth graders. But you know, I dread any decision related to building a second high school, this community just won't stand for it.

Sunset Hills Junior High school was, through the middle and late-1980s, a traditional junior high. The six-period day was structured around four academic offerings—language arts, mathematics, science, and social studies—and two electives chosen from art, foreign language, industrial arts, band, choir, physical education, home economics, study skills, and Junior ROTC. Faculty meetings were held twice monthly around an agenda planned and overseen by the principal, concerning issues related to the entire school. Scheduling, fund raising, student discipline, and district policy were among the most common themes. Discussions concerning curriculum were rarely held and when convened met by grade level and even more infrequently by academic subject area.

By 1987, the superintendent and director of curriculum and instruction, along with the building principals, were experiencing pressure to create a more nurturing experience for the seventh-grade students. Parental complaints concerning the abrupt transition to junior high for their children had consistently been an issue every fall for the school board and superintendent's office. From complaints about the inability of parents to determine the daily activities of their children and compounded by the perceived inaccessibility of faculty to address these concerns, to complaints about specific teachers being boring and unclear about expectations and workload, the complaint level had finally reached a critical mass. The district responded by transferring and hiring traditionally elementary-trained teachers to fill seventh-grade openings as they became available. The complaint level dropped somewhat and savvy parents learned to tailor their student's seventh-grade experience by requesting teachers known within the community as good teachers.

By 1987, the staff hired to fill these seventh-grade openings quickly found solace in each other and began to eat lunch together in one centrally located classroom. Occasionally, assisted by the instructional support teacher, conversation often focused on issues of curriculum—especially in the area of language arts—and students. The seventh-grade team felt better able to comment and provide assistance to each other across subject areas because, unlike their junior high colleagues, they had the primary responsibility for all subject areas when they had taught elementary school. Teachers began to jointly plan and share lesson ideas as well as group students for speakers, videos, and special events related to instruction. In some cases, teachers attended university and district-sponsored classes and inservice training related to areas of interest to the whole group. Morale was high and a sense of *esprit de corps* marked the unofficial seventh-grade team.

It was well known that a third junior high was on the drawing board. Since the school's opening in 1981, the district had grown by 1,800 new students. Three new elementary schools had been opened to accommodate the growth in population. A third junior high would need to be built. Given the modest success of the seventh-grade team and a growing national emphasis on children caught in the middle, the district administration had quietly begun to discuss the idea of opening middle schools. One method utilized by the administration to begin conversation around the notion of middle schools was to publicly call the third building the junior high/middle-school site. An April meeting of the seventh-grade team was called to discuss a pilot middle-school program to begin the following fall. Although the meeting was announced in the all-SHJHS bulletin, its occurrence seemingly went unnoticed. In attendance at the meeting were the superintendent, director of curriculum and instruction, 10 seventh-grade teachers, and the building principals of Sunset Hills and Howard Junior High. It was suggested that the instructional support teacher be added to the meeting but that idea was dropped by the building principal, who thought the instructional support teacher already had enough to accomplish.

Discussion was lively at the initial meeting. A majority of the seventh-grade teachers favored the idea of piloting a new program that would incorporate the elements called for by the community and the growing literature on middle-level schooling. Three SHJHS teachers volunteered to produce a proposal to be reviewed by the administration. Although the principal from SHJHS would be out of the country for most of May (he was chaperoning the high school band trip to China) it was decided the three would proceed with the proposal team reporting directly to the director of curriculum and instruction and the superintendent.

The three teachers all had taught with the Howard district for more than 7 years and jointly held expertise in language arts, geography, mathematics, science education. Dianne had taught elementary school for 7 years before joining the junior high school faculty as a language arts/reading teacher. She had also taught pre-algebra and seventh-grade honors biology. The second team member, Patti, had taught junior high school English and geography for her entire career. The third teacher, Anne, held expertise in special education and viewed the pilot as an effective means to begin an inclusion project.

The three split up research areas. Dianne took responsibility for doing the core research and developing a rationale for the project that would explore the essential elements necessary for a middle-school program. Patti decided to look into existing middle-school programs in the area and arrange for visitation, and Anne studied the mainstreaming literature. The three arranged to meet weekly for 1 month to develop the plan, rationale, and proposal. The final proposal would be ready for presentation at the May school board meeting. If approved, it would then be presented at the June SHJHS faculty meeting. The team eagerly went about planning the pilot program. For a while it was a hot topic at the lunch meetings, but predictably, conversation moved on to other subjects. Among themselves they met with little disagreement and were able to complete the proposal within the short time frame.

A professional and well thought-out plan was presented and approved by the school board in May. The plan included some requests for the following school year. Each of the three teachers was to receive an additional shared planning period for the year to develop integrated curriculum plans. They also received a travel and substitute budget so they could continue to visit and consult with other teachers involved in similar programs. Their assigned classrooms would be moved to the only portion of the school designed with moveable walls. This was to allow the teachers to meet and plan regularly, as well as to facilitate integrated, large-group instruction. Finally, the teachers were allotted an additional instructional budget of $1,500 for the purchase of new texts, trade books, materials, and classroom expenses. Each request was granted although the school board did require a detailed accounting of how the moneys would be spent and awarded veto power over all material requests to the director of curriculum and instruction.

Although the discussion never directly addressed any instructional plans for the new building, there was some private conversation between board members that the pilot program would provide an in-house study as to the feasibility of a middle school in Howard. A letter was drafted by the vice principal and sent home to sixth-grade students and parents announcing the new option available at SHJHS for approximately 60 students. The letter suggested to parents that students enrolled in the core learning program would receive a better educational experience than their traditionally educated peers.

Arrangements were made to present the plan at the June faculty meeting, held on the first Thursday of the month. It was decided that the presentation would use the same material that presented to the school board and time would be allotted for questions by the remainder of the faculty. The team entered the faculty meeting with high hopes that they would be as well supported by the staff as they had by district administration.

The vice principal began by announcing "an exciting new core learning program for the following school year." The three teachers rose and began presenting issues related to adoption of the new seventh-grade program. The presentation had barely begun when one eighth-grade faculty member interrupted and asked why they were only discovering this project when it already was a done deal. A second added that they knew about this only because their sixth grader had brought home a notice announcing the option. A third added, "If the district thinks they can build a middle school without input from the faculty they have another thing coming."

The vice principal unsuccessfully tried to bring the meeting back to the presentation by stating, "The school board has approved this project. The superintendent's office and Ben Stafford [the principal] and I are quite excited about this option for students."

At this time, the instructional support teacher rose and stated, "Decisions that are made behind the backs of staff can always be undecided. The school board wasn't allowed to hear the other side. I intend to appeal."

With that, she walked out, followed by many of her ninth-grade teaching colleagues. The meeting had lasted 5 minutes. Stuttering, the vice principal added, "Copies of the approved project proposal are available in my office, meeting adjourned."

Dianne, Patti, and Anne quickly headed back to a neutral classroom to discuss what might happen next. They were joined shortly by the other seventh-grade teachers, who expressed disbelief at the hostility exhibited at the meeting. It was decided that this would probably blow over and the staff would go back to ignoring the seventh-grade teachers, as they always had before. By noon the following day, the superintendent had called a special meeting of the school board, the project team, SHJHS administration, and three protesting faculty members. The meeting would be held the following Tuesday, at 3 p.m. in the board room.

Over the weekend the team met to discuss a strategy for the coming showdown. Feeling that they had already made their case, team members decided they would listen to the protests but not add anything to the discussion unless directly questioned. Anne summed up the group feeling by saying, "They've ignored us for years, managed to get out of teaching classes they didn't want and expected us to do the stuff they considered below them. They've treated us like second class citizens and now that we're being invited to the main dining room they don't like it." A general decision was made to be as classy as possible, and not to turn this into an open personal assault on anyone. If anyone wanted to discuss the attributes of the project, they were welcome to;

however the politics of the decision were not open for discussion and any comments about them would be answered by this brief statement, "Please speak with Ben Stafford about your concerns regarding that matter. We feel that we were as open about our plans as possible."

Monday and Tuesday, the tension was high at Sunset Hills. It was clear that weekend lobbying had occurred among the eighth- and ninth-grade staff and a few phone calls had been made to other seventh-grade faculty inquiring about the finer details of the project.

At 3 p.m., the board room was filled. The superintendent made a brief statement regarding the purpose of the meeting, "It has come to my attention that a portion of the faculty feel that they were left out of the decision-making process respecting next year's pilot program. We are here to listen to their complaint."

Janet, the teacher who led the walkout, began speaking:

> I've read the proposal and find no fault with the project as described here. My complaint was with the clandestine manner with which it was carried out. This project appears to be an underhanded way to get middle schools into the district without faculty input. Although the school board may find such schools appealing, I can tell you the majority of faculty at Sunset Hills do not.

Her comments were backed up by Stan. He taught a ninth-grade option program for at-risk students, a program that had been approved by the school board 2 years earlier by a narrow margin. The major issue in its approval had been the cost of one full-time faculty member for a reduced class load of 12 students. He argued:

> When at-risk was approved, I was made to jump through hoops for a full year. Everyone had to sign off before I could begin. Now these three can put though a new program in 6 weeks and everyone smiles. It may not look expensive on paper, but let me tell you, when it fails it will be very expensive to clean up the mess.

A silence filled the room. The director of curriculum spoke:

> I fail to see where your complaints are relevant. The core program will not affect your jobs, classes, or class size. It was not handled in a secretive manner. Those teachers affected were fully involved. As I see it this is a perfect example of administration and teachers working together to bring about positive change.

Bob Anderson, the school board president, summarized the school board's opinions by saying:

> As you may know, the school board met, over the weekend to discuss this issue. Our conversation boiled down to these ideas: One, the project in question appears to be a student-based project—that is to say the facts supporting the presentation come from work related to kids and what is best for them. Very little of what I do as school board president seems to relate directly to kids and I'm happy to support something that seems based in making schools better places for kids. Two parents in the community have been calling for something different for junior high kids for a long time. We all have received many

complaints about the unresponsive nature of junior high school teachers; in one project we can show those parents how we are responding to their concerns. Finally, we are ready to offer assurances that if or when the decision is made to decide what kind of school the new school will be, we will hold community and faculty forums to allow anyone who wants a say to have one."

Janet spoke again, "By then you'll have already started a program that will unfairly support one side of the argument."

Bob shot back, "We've supported the other side for years, and look what we have to show for it. Perhaps this is a way to make it a fair fight."

The superintendent interrupted, hoping to calm the discussion, "Any other comments?" Facing Dianne, Patti, and Anne, he asked, "Do you still want to do this?"

Anne answered for the group:

> Yes, we do. We feel like we informed everyone who was willing to listen. It is unfortunate that so few people heard what we and the other seventh grade teachers had been talking about concerning kids. We would like everyone to know that we consider this matter finished. Finally, we would like the opportunity to complete the staff presentation; we still feel it is important that the staff is aware of what we are doing. We no longer expect support but we feel that we are less likely to be questioned at every turn if they are informed.

The superintendent looked across the table to Ben Stafford, the Sunset Hills principal, and said, "Schedule the meeting. I believe we're done here."

EXERCISES

1. What was the problem the teachers were trying to address in this case? The principals? The school board and superintendent?

2. Using the case as your data bank, identify the features of politics that are present in the case. In what ways are material, social, or intellectual resources of concern in this case? How could a knowledge of the political help the members of this school district to have better addressed this change process?

3. Consider your school. In what ways are the features of politics present or absent at your workplace? In what ways are they characterized by the concepts in this chapter? Complete the following table, add rows as necessary:

Political Tension	Type of Conflict	Possible Political Remedy

4. In what ways can politics be seen as positive in a school or school system? In your experience, have there been situations in which a political climate helped to diffuse or clarify a potentially difficult situation?

READING YOUR OWN SCHOOL

Consider your own school. How are the ideas and concepts presented in this chapter present in your work setting? How might these ideas help you to make sense of your school and the events that occur there? List five examples of how you see these concepts in practice at your school; examples might include the actions of administration, staff, faculty, students, or parents, or specific issues or events such as a curriculum adoption or annual school celebration. Link each event to an idea or concept presented in this chapter. Do you think these actions or events facilitate student growth and learning, faculty and staff efficacy, and sense of well-being? Or do these actions or events create barriers to student growth and learning, faculty and staff efficacy, and sense of well-being? Finally, how could you use these ideas to initiate positive change within your school setting?

RECOMMENDED READINGS

Ball, S. J. (1987). *The micro-politics of the school: Towards a theory of school organization*. London: Metheun. Along with Joseph Blase, Ball played an important role in sensitizing educators to the importance of school politics. This is a very readable book that outlines an insightful theoretical perspective on the political patterns within schools. Each of the theoretical points is illustrated by richly detailed examples from case studies of schools.

Blase, J. (Ed.); (1991). *The politics of life in schools: Power, conflict, and cooperation.* Newbury Park, CA: Sage. Joseph Blase's scholarship has been instrumental in sensitizing educators to the importance of politics in school organizations. This edited collection has a useful introductory essay by Blase that overviews a number of the key concerns in the micropolitical perspective. Each of the contributors also offers illuminating case studies of school politics.

Bolman, L., & Deal, T. (1991). *Reframing organizations: Artistry, choice, and leadership.* San Francisco: Jossey-Bass. This book offers a very clear and readable introduction to politics in organizations. Additionally, it provides a introduction to other perspectives for studying organizations such as schools.

Malen, B. (1994). The micropolitics of education: Mapping the multiple dimensions of power relations in school politics, *Journal of Educational Policy, 33,* 147–167. This article provides an exceptionally thorough and well-organized overview of politics in schools.

4

Communal Social Patterns and Schools

◆ ◆ ◆

The chapter on political patterns suggested that conflict, power, and resources were central for reading the social life in schools. However, we also raised the problem of placing too much emphasis on these types of patterns. For example, excessive amounts of conflict can make it difficult to sustain a shared sense of belonging and trust among students, teachers, and administrators. This chapter speaks to this issue by highlighting the significance of communal patterns for school organizations. School organizations depend on the shared work and responsibility of all educators to successfully teach the next generation of children. Communal patterns enable teachers and administrators to achieve this goal. We downplay or dismiss them at our peril. As one author noted, a sense of "community is precious to people, although they often do not know how precious until it is lost" (Yankelovich, 1981, p. 227). Consequently, an understanding of communal patterns is an important form of organizational literacy for educators. Consider this case:

Miller-Main High School, located in a large urban district, has long been viewed as the worst school in the district. High on absences and low on test scores, an assignment to teach at Miller-Main was, until recently, a dreaded responsibility—reserved for either new teachers with no seniority or those teachers who had little time left on the clock until retirement. For new faculty, the goal was usually to do as little time in the building as possible and transfer somewhere else as quickly as possible. Yet, Miller-Main did not always carry such a disreputable reputation. Miller-Main was, at one time, the pride of the neighborhood. A school that attracted bright students from stable working-class families, the Miller-Main of the 1960s has been barely recognizable in recent years. The closing of local industry paired with failing school levies had taken its toll on both the neighborhood surrounding Miller-Main and the school itself.

Although the faculty at Miller-Main has been largely transient of late, there has always been a core faculty who never left the school. Having started teaching together in the late 1960s, these teachers have considered them-

83

selves friends, professional colleagues, and ongoing support. Known as The Seven, they stuck together, struggling to provide the best educational opportunities for students they could.

The fall's inservice was no different really than the other inservices they had attended over the years. A guest speaker came to discuss the new graduation standards and the programs that the state sponsored to help failing students. Although all the Miller-Main teachers attended, there was a sense among some faculty that it really didn't matter; the problems students brought with them to school could not be easily overcome. It was not that the teachers had not tried; they had. In the past years, the school had adopted a variety of goals and instructional foci to help in the effort to prepare students for graduation. However, no matter the effort, it always seemed to fall short.

During the lunch break The Seven joined together to talk. Although they agreed that the programs discussed in the inservice could provide help to their troubled students, they also agreed that they needed to provide a focus within the school day as well as better utilizing the external state-sponsored supports. The group decided to meet over lunch for the next few weeks to discuss such a plan and to develop ideas about in-school support programs for failing and at-risk students. However, as soon as the plan to meet was launched, problems surfaced. The principal pointed out that although he was supportive of their effort, they could hardly design any new instructional duties without the input of the remaining faculty. He also reminded them that the monthly faculty meeting was already to be used to develop a school diversity program and that the budget for extra meeting time had been slashed due to the most recent levy failure. He ended by pointing out the obvious, "You have a good idea, but no time to meet except lunch and even all of you don't share that same time period."

The Seven felt discouraged. They decided nonetheless that the idea of a school focus on the academic success of their students was important at this juncture. The issue of time, they believed, could be overcome. They decided to put out a memo asking the faculty if they would be willing to contribute one lunch a week to discuss issues of student graduation and academic success. The lunch, they explained, would be an ongoing working session open to any who wanted to attend and the rules would be simple. First lunch would begin the discussion, noting on a large sheet of butcher paper ideas, proposals, and needs of students. Second lunch would then continue the discussion, adding their ideas to the list and refining and questioning the ideas of first lunch. Third lunch would add on their comments and so on. The only rule would be that they must stick to the topic at hand—student academic success—and provide positive, helpful input. The message was clear—if you want to complain, do not come. The plan was also aided by the fact that although the lunches did not officially overlap, there were always teachers who wandered in early and a few who were able to stay later. Some had planning time and others classrooms close to the lunchroom. This way, someone would be available to provide a quick but necessary update of the previous lunch's progress. Finally, the butcher paper notes would be hung up and available for review for the following week.

Over the first weeks of school, the meetings were well attended, although many teachers seemed to come to check things out rather than participate. As the months progressed, more teachers attended regularly and more voiced their ideas. The lunches also became a site to share information between teachers about students who needed extra help in core subject areas—a social studies teacher could talk with an English teacher about writing skills or a math teacher could check in with the science teacher to discuss the development of measurement skills or equations in both subjects. By focusing and coordinating their actions, teachers began to feel that their efforts "mattered to more than just my students" and that, "if I had a problem it wasn't just my concern anymore." Other teachers found that "my students did better when we all gave them the same message."

The weekly conversations became a forum for discussion at Miller-Main. As teachers developed a shared sense of belonging to the lunch meetings and the conversations became more challenging of ideas, teachers became more able to really clarify what it meant to master particular material. The graduation standards began to take on a new importance. As one teacher said:

I used to hate those things. I thought they had nothing to do with my work, but as I began talking about them with other teachers I began to see how I could really not worry about them as long as I was providing good instruction. I found out that they could be guides for my curriculum not these iron-rods that I had to change everything to meet.

As the spring came and the annual process of transfers was begun, a real benefit of the lunches was seen. Teachers requesting transfers was down 65% from the previous year. Many cited the feelings of belonging and focus on the shared goals for students as an important reason for their staying at Miller-Main.

COMMUNITY IN SOCIAL, POLITICAL, AND HISTORICAL CONTEXTS

As the people who work in schools and other social organizations have become increasingly troubled by the constraints of bureaucratic forms of organizations, they have sought other, more personally fulfilling kinds of organizational forms. One currently popular form of restructuring the school organization focuses on the development of communities. Community resonates as a new metaphor for the school organization because of the word's association with connectedness, common interests, and a sense of caring that has been absent from discussions of the bureaucratic organization. School members, teachers, parents, and administrators often find the notions of community comforting in times of educational uncertainty and unrest. And scholars of schools are not alone in their interest in developing communities. Community has become a popular theme in contemporary political culture as well. Calls from the White House for increased national and public responsibility for health care, the elderly, the impoverished, and welfare reform all have a distinctly community-focused message. President Clinton appealed to a community ethic when he ended his 1994 State of the Union Address by stating:

> And so I say to you tonight, let us give our children a future. Let us take away their guns and give them books. Let us overcome their despair and replace it with hope. Let us by our example teach them to obey the law, respect our neighbors and cherish our values. Let us weave these sturdy threads into a new American community that can once more stand strong against the forces of despair and evil, because [then] everybody has a chance to walk into a better tomorrow. (U.S. Government Printing Office, 1994, p. 13)

Present in these words is a community-focused theme of a common value base providing a moral framework for shared, collective, ethical decision making. The president's words resonate with the notion that community can be formed by a people as diverse as those in the United States by establishing connections for people around basic shared purposes and dreams. For Clinton, the purposes and dreams are safety in the present and hope for the future.

Clinton's desire for community is part of a growing trend that reemerged in the 1970s after being relatively dormant for several decades (Carroll, 1982; Lears, 1983/1993; Yankelovich, 1982). In the bureaucracy chapter, we discussed how most Americans during the 19th century lived in small, rural communities. Many inhabitants of these communities grew up together and supported one another during common events such as harvest time, church, or school. Intimate bonds developed among people in these small-scale settings through their daily face-to-face life together and shared values (Weibe, 1967).

This communal pattern was altered considerably by the scale, complexity, and impersonality of life in urban areas and large work organizations during the 20th century (Karl, 1983). Ironically the increased productivity of modern agricultural equipment made farming as an occupation less able to support large segments of the population during the beginning of the century. Many moved to the cities to work in the large factories that offered good wages, through routine and often alienating assembly line work. By

1920, more than half the population of the United States lived in areas classified as cities (Noble, Carroll, & Horowitz, 1980).

Economic growth, efficiency, competitiveness, and technical know-how became the dominant values of this urban–industrial period. However, a few people raised concerns regarding the costs of these values and their embodiment in large-scale bureaucratic, commercial social patterns. One researcher summarized these by writing that

> in industrial society human relationships grow impersonal, commercialized. Giant institutions (big government, big business, the communications media) destroy ... the smaller, more human sized institutions of the society: the local church, the old neighborhoods, the small schools, the local shops and family relationships.... The ultimate consequence of this [is] the "destruction of community (Yankelovich, 1981, pp. 226–227).

The majority of U.S. citizens turned a deaf ear to these criticisms through the first half of the century. By the 1970s, however, many longed for more expressive and intimate connections than the ones provided by bureaucratic, industrial social patterns (Carroll, 1982; Lears, 1983/1993). They became more open to changing social patterns in organizations to support community. People also desired to make whole the fragmentation created by a number of events that rocked the consensus that formerly held the country together. The turmoil of the 1960s, the Vietnam War, Watergate, the impeachment of Richard Nixon, the OPEC oil crisis, and the hostage crisis in Iran divided Americans and shook their faith in the power and legitimacy of the country and its institutions. Renewing the bonds of community began to seem very appealing to many, even those in schools.

To focus on the development of community is, at its essence, an attempt to move beyond the focus on individual rights within contemporary liberal philosophy. Suggested instead is a union around a politics of common good (Sandel, 1988) rather than the politics of rights (Dworkin, 1977, 1989). By shifting the focus to the common good of a society or organization, one must shift from a focus on individual ideals and practice to a jointly held set of ideas and practice. This challenges the traditional social organization of the school. It challenges teachers to move beyond their concerns for their kids and to develop a more articulated long-term view including all students in the school. It challenges teachers to move out of isolated, individual classrooms to begin sharing lessons and planning and instructional ideas, as well as holding all members of the school community to a shared standard of pedagogical excellence.

For schools to become communities in the true sense of the term, the social organization of schools must then be arranged around commonly held beliefs and the action necessary to support the practice of those beliefs. One way of looking at reformed social organization is to consider the notion of communtarianism. *Communtarianism*, as a viable system for social organization, is based in two arguments. One is anthropological, the communitarians arguing that the only way to understand individuals' behavior is in their social, cultural, and historical contexts. The argument follows that the only way to realize or perceive individuals is within the context of their communal relationships (Gusfield, 1975; MacIntyre, 1981; Sandel, 1988). The second argument is normative in nature. Communitarians assert that the moral consequences of contemporary liberal philosophy are undesirable and unsatisfactory for society today (Bellah et al., 1985, 1991; Etzioni, 1991, 1993).

THE IMPORTANCE OF SOCIAL, HISTORICAL, AND CULTURAL CONTEXTS

The anthropological argument in support of community suggests that an individual's aims and values, developed within the community, inherently constitute who the person is. In any consideration of an individual's behavior the aims and values of the person must be understood in relationship to the community. This stands in sharp contrast to the individualistic notion that one's behavior stands outside the community's values. Although individualists think in terms of the self as having priority, the communitarian position holds that this distinction is artificial and, in practice, impossible.

MacIntyre (1981), a philosopher of communtarianism, argued that one understands one's life only by looking at life actions in a story, a narrative. Furthermore, the narrative of one's life couples and connects with the narratives of others' lives. Thus, an understanding of oneself can only be attained in that of the community—a community that sets the background, form, and shape of the narrative story. The methods of discovery concerning individuals are necessarily rooted in the methods of discovery of the cultural context—the community—that the individual inhabits.

For teachers, this argument suggests that understanding the context of the school environment, the surrounding neighborhood, and the lives of their students is important in developing schools that can address the concerns of the student population. This argument also suggests a more personal focus. The notion of narrative assumes that each of us has a story to tell in relation to why we entered teaching, what we hoped to bring to children, and how we ourselves approach learning and knowledge. If the notion of school as community is to include these narratives, we then must learn to tell them to each other, and perhaps more importantly, learn to listen to others' tellings as well.

NORMATIVE CONTEXTS OF COMMUNITY

Beyond the narrative argument concerning community is another argument that suggests that the standards of societal behavior must change. The normative argument suggests that, as a society, we have too long held that whatever is good for a given individual is the paramount concern rather than holding the well-being of the community foremost. The normative argument for the development of community suggests an obligation of the individual to the community and a responsibility to the common good of others in the society. The community described here is a desired level of relationships in which members of the greater society act in ways designed to benefit others as well as the self. The communal ties are seen as morally good and supportive of the community, responsive to those who comprise the community (Bellah et al., 1985; Etzioni, 1991).

The responsive community appeals to the values that members already possess (the value of education) and appeals to the internalization of values that are not currently in their command (equal opportunity for education). The community is, in one sense, always in the processes of affirming new values as the needs of its members change, shift, and evolve. Thus, the construction of community becomes a responsibility of the membership as it self-corrects, reflects, and scrutinizes its growth.

These two arguments suggest that movement to a communal notion of society, as opposed to the current focus on the individual, will benefit society and schools by creating strong, durable ties among its members. Community ties are those that unite, inform, and connect the membership. This is in sharp contrast to the enduring and persistent focus of the U.S. legal system on an individual politic of rights that has been posited to be a contributing factor in the increasing feelings of alienation, isolation, exclusion, and polarization experienced by the U.S. population (Bellah et al., 1985; Dworkin, 1989; Etzioni, 1991, 1993; Minow, 1990). Teachers are no strangers to these feelings as they work to advance change and reform within the walls of our public schools.

ASSOCIATIVE TIES

Educators, be they teachers, administrators, para-professionals, parents, or coaches, have long worked side by side in schools linked together by ties of association. Educators associate with the other people who work and learn in schools through their day-to-day social contacts with each other. However, associative ties do not bind people together in significant or substantial ways. Associative ties join people loosely, rather than providing a firm, meaning-filled connection.

Associates do not enjoy full status in our lives. Instead, they are held separate, apart, and isolated from the meaningful relationships of our lives. Associative relationships lack the strong degree of intimacy, trust, and commitment that other, more personal relationships hold for us. Associates share in part only the status, reward, and esteem enjoyed by full members of an organization (e.g., consider the status of the associate in a law firm or that of an associate professor). Conversely, they are freed from responsibilities borne by full members. In turn, the organization does not gain a full commitment from members of associate status (for an interesting discussion of elementary and middle school teachers' commitment to their work, see Kushman, 1992).

Schools have long been considered bureaucratic organizations and places of association for teachers (Rowan, 1991; Sergiovanni, 1994). As bureaucratic organizations, schools have sought the approval of the public. In seeking approval, they have attempted to gain legitimacy by appearing rational in their decision-making and organizational processes. Such behavior has resulted in the creation of departments, curriculum plans, instructional delivery services, and mission statements. As places of association, public school organizations have proven to be isolating, alienating places that lack motivating external reward structures (Apple, 1985; Darling-Hammond, 1984; Grant, 1983; Grimmett & Crehan, 1992; Lortie, 1975; Louis & Smith, 1992; Warren, 1989).

To escape these feelings of isolation and alienation, Sergiovanni (1994) suggested a need to change the metaphor for the school from that of an organization to that of a community. The metaphoric shift he suggested will provide schools the opportunity to "do things differently, to develop new kinds of relationships, to create new ties, [and] to make new commitments" (p. 153). Thus, teachers and administrators would design their work in ways that focus on the creation of a new vision of schooling centered around new roles, relationships, and responsibilities for the members of the school community. However, such a vision does not bind its members to total agreement but instead to a commitment to communicate about the important aspects of the construction of the school goals and vision (Carter, 1985).

A commitment to communicate gives members of the community a method for conversing and a set of shared, substantive topics to communicate about. Much like the example in the beginning of this chapter, a commitment to communicate sets forth a way for teachers to identify concerns related to the models of learning and teaching employed within the school. These concerns may be individually or jointly held. In turn, concerns may also relate solely to an individual student or faculty member or they may pertain to other members of the community, much like the concerns of Miller-Main teachers about their students scoring well on the graduation standards exams. Thus, commonly held concerns serve to center the community by providing a sense of communal responsibility for their eventual resolution (Arnett, 1986).

MODELS OF COMMUNITY

School leadership, whether in the form of a traditionally placed principal or a newer site-based management model, provides an important catalyst in this change. Inasmuch as the leadership of the school sets the tone for the larger school culture, the emergent school community takes its lead from the leadership model the school employs (Murphy & Louis, 1994). It is important that the school leadership be aware of the differing patterns and forms of community relationships that can develop. As schools work to become communities of learning, two models of community are useful to consider: democratic community and voluntary community.

Democratic Community

Setting forth some assumptions and notions about leadership for democratic community and its converse, autocratic rule, would be useful at this juncture. Simply stated, democratic communities are marked by a fair and equal process that assures the fair and equal treatment of members of the community (Bryk, Lee, & Holland, 1993; Bull, Fruehling, & Chattergy, 1992; Kymlicka, 1991). A democracy is more than a form of government; it is primarily a mode of shared living through communicated experience. The process of communication of ideas, ideals, shared concerns, and interests forms the foundation of democratic practice. Democracy in schools takes on many forms. In many schools site-based management, building leadership teams, and shared governance structures are taking hold. These forms of democratic governance provide places where teachers can share their ideas and concerns as well as participate in the day-to-day running of the school.

In contrast, the autocratic community is marked by a lack of a concern for the process by which decision making occurs and the subsequent treatment of individuals for whom those decisions have import (Crowley, 1987; Gutman, 1987; Kymlicka, 1991; Mann, 1986). The autocratic leader holds all the cards; his or her power is unlimited and domineering. The leader decides, perhaps with the help of a few trusted confidants, the policy and practice for others of the community. School climate and culture are marked by set notions, unquestioned policies, and a sense of the status quo as all there is or could be.

Access to influence, school goals, which topics are open for discussion, who gets what information and when, decision-making models, and group cohesion are all influenced by the style of leadership employed within the school. The style of leadership, be it democratic, autocratic, or somewhere in between, influences the probability that communal ties, rather than associative ties, will emerge.

The democratic group permits dissent among members. The intent of the group is to increase the amount of participation for all members of the organization rather than that of a few chosen individuals. Tradition is not blindly preserved; rather it is challenged, discussed, and utilized as a means to clarify those common basic underlying principles on which the community rests.

In schools, democratic practice evidences itself when teachers work together to create learning environments best suited to the students served within their classes. When teachers are encouraged to schedule classes flexibly across grade levels or subject areas, the democratic processes of schooling are underscored as teachers work through the decision-making process necessary to create strong interdisciplinary teaching units. Democracy in classrooms is furthered when teachers ask students to focus on cooperative learning as they work to sort out and grasp the meaning of a difficult idea. As Stiles and Doresy stated in their 1950 classic, *Democratic Teaching in Secondary Schools*, "Democratic teaching aims at helping the learner to plan, execute, and evaluate learning experiences that are functionally related to purposes that are consciously accepted by the learner" (cited in O'Conner, 1993, p. 11). Their work rests on that of John Dewey, who pointed to the importance of method and its relation to subject matter when considering democracy and education. Dewey (1915/1944) stated:

> Methods have [been] authoritatively recommended to teachers, instead of being an expression of their own intelligent observations. Under such circumstances, they have a mechanical uniformity, assumed to be alike for all minds. Where flexible personal experiences are promoted by providing an environment which calls out directed occupations in work and play, the methods ascertained will vary with individuals—for it is certain that each individual has something characteristic in his way of getting at things. (p. 168)

Thus, democratic education is rooted in a reflective communicative process related to the methods a teacher employs, the content a teacher presents, and the process by which the learning occurs. Democratic conceptions of school practice can be located in all areas of the school as they encompass the historic triad of school practice—instructional methods, subject matter, and administrative governance.

Voluntary Community

The notion of voluntary community helps us to view schools as places in which teachers and students choose to participate. We all participate in many voluntary communities in our lives outside of school. Religious and sports organizations, quilting and book groups, or political and community gatherings all are examples of voluntary communities. We can, and do, choose to join and leave these groups regularly. However, it is not common to consider schools as places of voluntary associations. A look at the Catholic system provides us some help in viewing schools as places where people might come together in voluntary ways. In their work on Catholic schools, Bryk, Lee, and Holland (1993) set forth three important features of a voluntary community: structures for daily life, school autonomy, and increased identification of students and teachers with the school. Structures supportive of voluntary associations include both instructional and curricular functions. Catholic schools are marked by strong organizational forms concerning schedules and content of courses, disciplinary codes of conduct, and academic standards. Schools that embody voluntary communities possess a relatively high degree of autonomy in managing their affairs. This autonomy is tempered by a tradition of local input into decision-making practices and judgments. Thus, the school operates not as separate unit but as an independent decision-making body in a distinct, rational tradition of practice. Third, the voluntary association of both students and teachers with the school marks individual membership. Norms of membership are enforced not by coercion and constraint but rather by an individual's choice to be part of this community and thus to consider it "my school" in ways that public schools may not enjoy.

COMMUNICATION FORMS FOR BUILDING COMMUNITY

Communication is a term we use readily on a daily basis. Yet few of us consider what it means to communicate. We successfully talk to and with others about a multitude of topics—some charged and tension-filled and others familiar and comfortable. The words we use and the tone in which we state them enhance the communicative action. A raised eyebrow, a warm smile, or an expansive hand gesture all add meaning to the spoken word. The forum in which we choose to share our words also colors the meaning and influence our words hold for others. Finally, who speaks influences the communication as well. Communication, then, is some combination of words, tone, gestures, and forums of speech and speaker. It is a complicated notion.

We cannot here take on all those topics. Instead, we focus on three forms spoken communication can take: the monologue, information-centered dialogue, and dialogic communication (Arnett, 1986; Brown & Keller, 1973).

Monologue

Monologue is a self-centered conversation. By centering the conversation on oneself, a speaker focuses attention on his or her ideas, values, and beliefs. Openness to new thoughts, attitudes, opinions, or values are not only not considered, they are not invited. The stance of the speaker is one of defense rather than candor and straightforwardness. By adopting a defensive posture, the speaker limits the amount of interaction that may occur between the two participants. A monologue allows parallel conversations to take place. Two speakers work to make their points, in their argument, without a sense of what the other has to offer. The others position may not be honored, as the self is placed above the community and the consequence is often rather unproductive conversation (Arnett, 1986; Friedman, 1992).

For teachers, engaging in monologue has two negative consequences. First, community is not cultivated by monologic conversation (Arnett, 1986). Quite the opposite occurs as monologue isolates rather than joins. Imagine a teacher who asks for the help of another in working through a difficult discipline problem with a student. The first teacher, a somewhat new staff member, is frustrated; she has tried everything in her bag of tricks with no apparent improvement in the student's actions. On hearing the first teacher's dilemma, the second, a seasoned veteran of the staff, interrupts and launches into a long account of "How I do it." The first listens, takes a few notes, and mentions that yes, she has tried some of these ideas already, and elaborates on her use of them. The second reflects a moment and responds by saying these techniques always work for her and she really does not have any other ideas. The conversation proves frustrating for both teachers as the younger leaves with the problem unsolved and the veteran teacher feels she has not provided needed help to a younger colleague.

The second negative consequence of monologue for teachers is that it does not promote a sense of trust among colleagues (Arnett, 1986). Teachers who engage primarily in monologue rarely offer their colleagues a sense of who they are as people, and although respect for their knowledge may be fostered, trust is not. Trust relies on the interaction between two people who both value each other's thinking and know that their ideas and words will not be used to harm them at a later time. Monologue does not allow trust to grow, as true listening does not take place. Rather, people are listened to long enough for the second speaker to mount an argument against the first speaker's ideas. Understanding is not fostered and frustration results. In our example, it is easy to see how trust between these two teachers was not furthered (Arnett, 1986; Ayres, 1984; Darnell & Bruckriede, 1976).

Information-Centered Dialogue

Information-centered dialogue is conversation focused on the transmittal of information (Arnett, 1986). Technical conversations about content, instructional technique, and pedagogy are all forms of information-centered dialogue. Inasmuch as technical dialogue focuses on the objective understanding of information, technical dialogue, in and of itself, does not help to create community. Technical dialogue is information-centered; it does not concern itself with other people as people, it concerns itself with transmission of facts and data. What technical dialogue offers the community is the opportunity to expand the cognitive and skill base of its members.

It provides the community with a common vocabulary and set of understandings around a particular issue to begin a sustained, reflective conversation about that material (Fischer, 1978). Quality inservice is a good example of technical dialogue. When teachers share experiences in school or district inservice that result in changed classroom practice technical dialogue has proven useful and successful.

Technical dialogue is important in creating shared understandings of techniques and content-related information. Shared information, however, is not sufficient to create ties that bind community members to each other. For information to become knowledge shared by all members of the school organization, it must first have a shared social construction (Kruse & Louis, 1997; Leithwood, Dart, Jantzi, & Steinbach, 1992; Leithwood, Jantzi, & Steinbach, 1993; Louis, 1994). Such shared understandings come from a dialogue that does more than impart information. The dialogue that fosters shared understandings places the relationships of community members equal to that of the transmittal of the information—it is dialogic in nature.

Dialogic Communication

Dialogic communication allows teachers the opportunity to take information gained in technical conversation and use it to create shared knowledge (Brown & Keller, 1973; Johnstone, 1981; Mittroff, 1981). Once knowledge is shared, teachers can then utilize it in ways that enhance community. Makay and Brown (1972) identified characteristics considered essential to dialogic communication posture. Among them are:

1. Human involvement from a felt need to communicate.
2. An atmosphere of openness, freedom, and responsibility.
3. Dealing with real issues and ideas relevant to the communicator.
4. Appreciation of individual differences and uniqueness.
5. Acceptance of disagreement and conflict with the desire to resolve them.
6. Effective feedback.
7. Mutually held respect and trust.
8. A willingness to admit error and allow persuasion.

Emphasized are both the importance of the relationship and the necessity of conflict, persuasion, and disagreement in a dialogical perspective. The mix of conflict and caring is the earmark of a dialogic conversation. Although this appears paradoxical, it is in this place of conflict and caring that teachers can begin to clarify what are the important features of their

community. The collective spirit can then be forged, creating an environment where teachers can begin to identify the principles that guide their
decisions and practice.

School-based efforts to conclude conflict resolution strategies in the
curriculum come closest to providing us a model for dialogic conversation
in schools. In these models, students and teachers are taught to actively
listen to one another. Students are taught to listen and mirror the concerns
of other students, to wait without interrupting to voice their side of the story,
and to work to resolve the conflict in ways acceptable to both parties. The
focus in conflict resolution is to delegate problem-solving authority to both
parties, offering each the opportunity to gain new insights into what it means
to be a member of the larger community of the school.

By creating a dialogic community, democracy is furthered. Dissent is
voiced, listened to, and honored. The objector is not shunned from the
relationships formed by other members. Instead, challenges are offered for
the community and these serve as opportunities for the members to reaffirm
and clarify the common principles and values that guide the decision-making process (Bryk, Lee, & Holland, 1993; Crowley, 1987; Gutman, 1987;
Kymlicka, 1991; Mann, 1986).

COMMUNAL SOCIAL PATTERNS AND REFORM

Teachers and administrators have long been engaged in a search for ways to
develop community within their schools. Although there are many good
examples from which to choose—the development of house structures or
schools-within-schools in large high schools, the creation of families of
learning at many elementary schools, increased volunteer efforts among
members of the business community to bridge the gap between school and
work environments—perhaps the best known and most successful is the
organizational structure of the middle school. The middle-school movement was founded on the belief that small, stable communities of learning,
a core of cooperative academic programs, and teachers who are expert in
early adolescence are necessary prerequisites to improving the academic and
social success of 10- to 15-year-old students (Carnegie Council, 1989, p.
10). Calling the adolescent years, "crucial in determining the future success
or failure of millions of American youth," the council set forth an agenda
determined to make the transformation of middle-grade schools a reality.
The transformation has occurred in schools all across the nation. In fact,

few other large-scale reform projects have had the impact of the middle-school movement (Kruse & Louis, 1997). And few middle-school teachers would suggest the transformation has been anything but positive for their teaching. One benefit to teachers was the addition of teaching teams. Teachers have discovered that assignment to teams has increased their sense of community with the school.

In general, teaching teams consist of teachers from varying disciplines who are organized into core groups to share the instruction of a given community of learners. Teachers who are part of such teams often speak of them glowingly. In the words of an eighth-grade math teacher, "I love my team; teaching is so much better and more interesting since we started the teams." She credited the team with "keeping me more on task, helping me to look at students as whole individuals who take more than just [my class]." Another middle-school teacher said:

> Teaming helps me to know what is going on in other teacher's classes. I can plan lessons to work with what other teachers are doing and help kids understand the concepts better. I love planning a unit that uses some social studies and some English.

It was the interdisciplinary nature of teaming that attracted the Carnegie Council (1989) to the idea. They called for the development of teacher teams to provide:

> an environment conducive to learning by reducing the stress of anonymity and isolation on students. Common planning by teachers of different subjects enables students to sense consistent expectations for them and to strive to meet clearly understood standards of achievement. Teaming creates the kind of learning environment that encourages students to grapple with ideas that may span several disciplines, and to create situations to problems that reflect understanding, not memorization. (pp. 38–40)

Although the Carnegie Council's initial focus was on the educative possibilities teams offered students, the benefits to teachers were not lost. The council noted that, "Interdisciplinary teams also provide a much-needed support group for teachers, eliminating the isolation teachers can experience in departmentalized settings. Morale among teachers often increases significantly with team teaching" (p. 40).

Thus, the council stressed two critical aspects of the teaming arrangement. The first was to "foster continuity of relations and to create the learning climate students need to delve deeply into complex ideas" (p. 40).

The second was to create small teams ensuring that teachers can know the students on the team well.

Teaming has provided teachers many of the benefits that our discussion of community offers. First, it has placed small groups of teachers in daily contact with each other. Teacher teams are usually marked by a shared planning period in which teachers discuss important instructional and curricular issues. Some teams have structured agendas in which they address specific issues on specific days—special education on Monday when the specialist is available to meet, long-term planning on Tuesday, and so forth. Other teams have a less structured approach, favoring an open agenda where members feel free to add issues to a growing list, signing up on the posted butcher paper as time and interest allow. Either way, the daily meeting allows teachers to begin the conversation necessary to develop shared values, visions, and plans. Such conversation results in increased community and the development of teacher dignity and efficacy.

Teaming also provides teachers with profound personal rewards. Perhaps the most frequently mentioned reward for teachers in teams is the support system they experience. Support comes in many forms and manifests itself in different ways. Many teams emotionally support each other through both their school lives and their home lives. Teachers who team come to know each other on a level unusual for coworkers. For example, in a recent study, a teacher credited the team with helping her through the long and painful process of her father's extended illness and death, and another veteran teacher noted that her team provided moral support that carried her through a low point in her professional career (Kruse & Louis, 1997).

Intellectual assistance is at the core of the practice of many teams. Teams provide a place for teachers to try out new ideas, share exciting workshop insights, and talk about issues germane to their practice. Such reflective dialogue fosters truly innovative teaching efforts.

Closely linked to intellectual assistance and emotional support is the notion of personal encouragement (Louis, Marks, & Kruse, 1997). As teachers stretch their cognitive and skill bases in public ways, they report that team members provide positive reinforcement for their sharing and risk taking. In teams where teacher talk focuses on instruction, teachers report that they feel more likely to confess their failures with trusted members. The trust and subsequent conversation result in further risk taking and an increased sense of efficacy and personal dignity.

Finally, the development of middle-school teams provides teachers greater access to the decision-making systems within the school governance structure. In typical faculty meetings at nonteamed schools, a designated individual (usually the principal) presents an issue for discussion, vocal members of the faculty present their opinions, and then the full faculty votes. Most teachers feel left out, underrepresented, and silenced. In schools with interdisciplinary teams, teachers are often given topics for all-school decision making before the scheduled faculty or governance board meeting. Teachers then provide input from the team level into a schoolwide decision. The benefits to teachers in such a system are twofold. First, they have more time to think and discuss issues before they come to a final decision. Second, the team approach allows more informal participation in the decision-making process, as greater access to data and supporting information is also usually available. Given an extended timetable for decision making, teams can actively seek out information to better guide their process.

Because the middle-school movement was founded on the notion that all members of the school community must become responsible for the learning and well-being of students, the reform lends itself well to supporting the development of schoolwide community. Teachers are able to both increase their sense of affiliation with each other and the school while focusing on the development of student learning and growth.

COMMUNAL SOCIAL PATTERNS
AND TEACHER-INITIATED CHANGE

Washington Elementary School is a school that has been considered an excellent elementary school over the years. Centrally located in a suburban community, the school has enjoyed strong parental support, a stable population of students and teachers, and continued financial backing of the community. The district proudly and correctly claimed that a levy had never failed. In fact, most passed with strong support and little effort.

Teachers who work at Washington delight in the supportive environment. One benefit they appreciate is the ability to regularly attend local, state, and national conferences. They look forward to these opportunities to learn the latest ideas about instruction and curriculum and bring ideas back to their own school. It is expected that following attendance at a conference, teachers are to hold several short meetings to share the newly gained ideas with other members on the faculty. Although teachers enjoy these informal get-togethers, it is generally believed that they are more social than educational.

Yet the principal at Washington had wanted more from these meetings. She believed that her teachers needed to view these opportunities as meaningful ways to gain expertise as well as new skills and knowledge. Turning to her site council, she requested help in developing a new process for sharing and developing the ideas teachers brought back with them from conferences and inservice.

The site council outlined a proposal to bring to the faculty. Included in the proposal was a review of the purpose of inservice to support the faculty's goal of educational excellence. Furthermore, the proposal included the ideas of the faculty as brainstormed at a faculty meeting. At the faculty meeting, the staff had agreed that creating a system in which they were more accountable for the material they had learned at conferences and inservices could provide an opportunity to develop their professional skills. They also agreed that if a system was provided for the required sharing, they would be more likely to make the opportunity count for their own learning as well as the learning of others. In short, a loosely structured system could provide the necessary arrangements to make the occasion to gather as a faculty devoted to the education of children matter in the educational sense of the school.

In the end, the system designed by the site council was simple. Faculty would continue to attend the workshops, conferences, and inservices as they always had in the past. What would differ would be on return. Teachers would be responsible for using the material in their classes, curriculum planning, or instructional pedagogy over a period of a month or so to test drive the ideas. At this juncture they could then decide to go one of two ways, to progress forward in the sharing process or to determine that the material did not fit their philosophy or program. If the latter occurred, the site council teachers would then discuss whether or not other teachers should go if the opportunity presented itself again. A few workshops have been considered off limits for future attendance.

If they chose to continue in the process of sharing, they then needed to have a trusted colleague visit their classroom when the teacher was practicing the new innovation or curriculum method. This activity was designed so that teachers would have a second critical view of the new practice as well as to give them a reflective partner with whom to discuss their new learning. After several observations the teacher was to have developed a clarity or facility with the new method. They were also to have had ample time to have the innovation work well, badly, and somewhere in between. This allowed teachers to speak more knowledgeably with their colleagues when the final part of the sharing process occurred—the staff inservice. When the teacher had had enough time to learn and think about the new idea and they felt ready, an inservice was scheduled. The inservice was to be an in-depth sharing of the new idea. Often lessons were demonstrated, either live or on video, teaching tips were distributed, always with invitations to come see the new innovation demonstrated in the classroom. Teachers credited the new process with "better understanding of our new ideas and a clearer understanding of what other teachers are doing in their classes."

Many elements of community building are present in this story. Leadership is supportive of learning and change. An open communication network exists to support teachers' improvement efforts as well as a continued focus on student learning and academic achievement. All members of the school community share a responsibility for student growth. From the shared sense of responsibility, a willingness to risk and improve has grown among the staff. As the process of discussion and open dialogue focused on the creation of shared understandings of the new ideas grows, the staff remains resolute in their efforts to create a school remarkable for the caring and concern they show students.

THE BENEFITS OF COMMUNAL SOCIAL PATTERNS

Creating school communities holds several potential advantages for schools. Among the positive outcomes that writers on professionalism and community have asserted are the growth of increased responsibility for instructional expertise, increased personal commitment to work, and the replacement of bureaucratic, rule-based controls over teacher behavior with values that promote self-regulation, resulting in a climate of innovation and effectiveness. The outcomes of increased professional community can be categorized under three broad headings: (a) an increased sense of efficacy relating to work that results in increased motivation to teach well in the classroom; (b) an increased sense of satisfaction with the personal dignity of work; and (c) greater collective responsibility for student learning (Louis & Kruse, 1995).

Teachers' sense of affiliation with each other, with the school, and their sense of mutual support and individual responsibility for the effectiveness of instruction is increased by collaborative work with peers (Louis, 1992). As affiliation with peers increases, so does a teacher's sense of belonging to and being part of the school organization. As the sense of belonging increases, so do opportunities to improve classroom practice as teachers may become more open and sharing of their instructional skills and classroom abilities. Building school community can reinforce a collective sense of efficacy as well as that of the individual members. Teachers can work to get through their own day—or they can perform daily tasks with the intention of contributing to the organization's objectives (Louis & Kruse, 1995). As teachers' actions become more aligned with those of the organization, community increases, providing teachers a continued sense of well-being and belonging to the organization.

One issue that frequently arises in talking about teachers' work is the discouragement that many of them feel when they believe that their best efforts are neither respected nor valued by peers, supervisors, or the public. However, when it is combined with other strategies for improving teachers' work, community appears to contribute to teachers' sense of responsibility for student learning (Lee & Smith, 1993) and also their sense of efficacy (Louis, Marks & Kruse, 1997). As teachers develop a sense of communal support and personal reward for their efforts related to the development of overall school community their sense of dignity related to their own work increases. As teachers begin to communally work toward the development of shared strategies, instructional skills and new conceptual understandings about teaching and learning teachers develop a greater sense of ownership of and responsibility for quality in student learning resulting in respect for their work both in the public and private arena (Louis, Marks, & Kruse, 1996).

Just as there is a link between efficacy and dignity, there is also a link between dignity found through meaningful participation in schoolwide decisions about teaching and learning and there is individual accountability. Teachers' engagement with the school community can stimulate more concerted efforts to resolve the dilemmas and problems associated with student development, and, in turn, reinforce a shared sense of purpose such as in Miller-Main, the school example that began this chapter. Collective responsibility also suggests a shift in the way in which schools think about controlling teacher behavior. Rules, regulations, and division of labor have traditionally been the means to control life in schools and these are usually developed and applied by an individual district or state. Collective responsibility, on the other hand, reinforces policies that promote decentralization and debureaucratization of schools. Successfully transformed or restructured schools substitute professional norms, values, and beliefs for these traditional external control structures. Thus, teachers can then become personally and professional responsible for their work-related behaviors.

However, it is important to remember that community is difficult to foster in schools. In part, this is due to their bureaucratic nature. Bureaucracies have not traditionally focused their efforts on the interpersonal relationships present within the organization. Instead, the bureaucratic organization remains focused on roles, hierarchies of power, and charts of responsibilities for those in particular positions.

In addition to the often rigid, bureaucratic structure of schools, other limitations have been placed on the development of personal professional relationships as well. For nearly two decades, schools have experienced greater and greater limits on both the financial and intellectual resources available to them. The arts, many humanities classes, and other important programs have felt the pinch as referenda failed and student rosters declined. Teachers have had professional opportunities reduced as competition for scarce resources has grown at the building and district level. The competitive struggle for resources has become a commonplace within the walls of our schools. However, competitive struggle is not the only possible outcome of the changing environment that schools face. The development of a strong schoolwide community is both a desirable and possible outcome as well.

Therefore, three implications for the creation of schoolwide community are offered. They include a commitment among members based in need, an embracing of variety of complementary interests, and individual success as necessarily linked to communal success.

For the schoolwide community to be initially created and long-lasting, it must offer readily observed and indisputable benefits to all school members. The relationships that are forged must be ones in which the members choose to participate due to a shared perception that membership within the schoolwide community is preferable to other, more individual options. Research data on middle-school teacher teaming support the conclusion that, when supported with strong leadership, time to meet and plan, and trust and respect from relevant colleagues for their communal efforts, individuals will participate with greater collaboration and deprivatization of their practice (Kruse & Louis, 1997; for a discussion of teaming as an example of school community, see the next section of this chapter). The commitment of teachers in teams to each other and to the goals and mission of the team is based in a strongly felt individual need for the communal team relationship. The supportive benefits teachers derive from teaming are at least as great as, and in most cases greater than, the benefits teachers derive from individual practice. Thus, teachers engage in team work for the concrete benefits it offers them as individuals as well as the benefits the teamed structure provides to students and their peers.

Within a system where extended relationships among staff are considered beneficial, focused reflection on practice may occur more frequently. Reflection in the communal organization may then become a way of thinking about future needs rather than only a way of resolving current problematic situations. Reflection may then become an important part of the school culture as conversation about things that matter to the participants becomes commonplace.

However, if broad, inclusive conversations are to become part of the standard fare of the school, the community must embrace a variety of complementary interests. This is necessary for two reasons. First, topics must capture the collective imagination and, to do so, must provide avenues for broad participation. Second, the interests must be complementary so that the faculty do not lose their focus on the shared goals and mission of the school organization. Rather than following the model of random and uncoordinated adoption of innovation, schools must embrace a clearly articulated and understood focus and utilize that focus to channel staff development and shared teaching efforts. Within the school, personal identity is then honored and fostered concurrently with the creation and refinement of a focused, shared, and ongoing improvement effort. The school then serves to provide a context within which personal identity is formed and where awareness about ones' teaching and professional learning follows the currents of communal conversation and contributes to them. By the creation of a variety of complementary interests—cooperative learning, higher order thinking skills, writing across the curriculum—staff may then focus their involvement in ways that contribute to their personal growth as well as to a schoolwide improvement effort. Professional community is fostered as staff work toward shared goals in ways that increase personal as well as communal intentions.

The creation of schoolwide community emphasizes both the importance of a supportive relationship between teachers and the necessity of conflict between teachers as the practical affiliations between members grow. Although this appears puzzling, it is necessary if teachers are to hone out the important features of their shared vision for students. Conflict, if managed responsibly, can help forge a collective spirit in which teachers can begin to identify the assumptions and principles that guide their decisions and practice.

As individuals succeed, the communal group succeeds. Individual success is necessarily linked to communal success. When individuals learn new ways of practice and thinking, they can contribute to the group process in ways that are supportive of the shared goals of the school organization. By creating a system in which the growth of one teacher benefits all teachers and students through extended focus on improved practice and student learning, teachers can learn to utilize their reflective skills for the benefit of communal goals.

Community creates a center by which teachers can begin the process of defining and refining their educational mission and goals. Although there is likely no one center that can capture the attention of every member of the school community, teachers can simultaneously consider a variety of closely linked complementary interests allowing individual members to participate in a diverse ways. The goal of schoolwide community becomes the creation of individual reflective habit leading to an ongoing, focused, reflective conversation. The benefits to the teacher within the system of the school—and to the students the school serves—are many. If teachers can keep alive a reflective conversation that permits the telling of new narratives and visions of a better school, future generations of teachers may inherit a system of schooling in which all members can benefit from the efforts of a truly professional community.

THE LIMITATIONS OF COMMUNAL SOCIAL PATTERNS

However engaging community is as an answer to the growing frustrations of members of bureaucratic organizations, it too has its detractors. An obvious, but necessary, critique concerns that of the size of the school. In large schools it is simply more difficult to gather the members for meetings, to encourage participation of all members, and to provide opportunity for the involvement of large numbers of teachers in the daily workings and decisions of the school (Lamdin, 1995; Lee & Smith, 1995; Meier, 1995). Recently, a doctoral student of ours received a new position in a large, prestigious high school. After several weeks of being on the job, she was lunching in the faculty room. Trying to learn the names of all the faculty had become a goal of hers, believing that she would do better as an administrator if she knew all the faculty of the school. She leaned across the table to discretely ask the name of a faculty member at the end of the lunch table. After checking with one teacher who did not know, she turned to another and yet another who did not know who this teacher was. It was only after asking six people that she was able to determine the teacher's name. However, most surprising for her was to discover that this teacher had taught in the building for more than 5 years! Clearly, lack of even personal identification among faculty compounds the difficulty in developing community.

Hargreaves' (1994, p. 23) work also develops a theme that critiques community as an organizational form. His work suggests that although the benefits of community and teacher communal work are widespread, they may be overrated in their ability to promote lasting school reform. In particular, he suggested that well-meaning efforts fall short when school leaders are "less than fully serious about their commitment" to develop community. He called the results of such efforts "contrived collegiality." That is to say that on the outside, the school looks communal. Teams are in place, meeting times arranged, inservice and other external resources are available yet no real change occurs. Teachers may even go through the motions of the changed programs, meetings may occur that are more social than educational in focus, teachers may observe each other teaching in an effort to communally focus on improved instructional ability, yet they shy away from critique and reflection on practice. They are instead contrived. Bargains may be struck—"I'll say you're a good teacher if you say I am also." Hargreaves suggested contrived behaviors may be the result of inflexibility on the part of administration to include faculty in the initial planning of programs resulting in political action to undermine mandates to be communal. His critique reminds us that community is difficult to achieve and cannot be implemented by bureaucratic methods.

High schools also have additional issues that create problems for the possibility of community as an organizational form in schools. In particular, the work of Little (1990) makes a compelling argument that, for most high school teachers, who are located in large schools fragmented by discipline, schedules, and student tracking, factors other than community may have a bigger impact on school performance and student achievement. She noted that four aspects of high school teaching—students, instructional assignment, departments, and subject matter—can erode a teacher's sense of community with other members of the school.

In each case, the status of the teacher and their sense of belonging to the larger community is what is at stake here. For teachers who may find themselves teaching either students or classes seen as less desirable and therefore lower status, it is less likely they would choose to remain involved with the larger school community. In the case of large high schools, teachers of vocational and noncollege-bound courses often experience their classes as a dumping ground for difficult students and believe themselves to be enjoying fewer of the academic resources the school has to offer (for a discussion of similar concerns at the middle-school level, see Kruse & Louis, 1997). Teachers who perceive they are second-class citizens to those who teach the college-bound students are less likely to support the efforts of the larger school community because they do not feel a part of those goals.

In summary, Little's work suggests the attitudes of teachers within a school toward students, formal departmental structures and design, and the demands and opportunity to interact with challenging and interesting students on a regular basis, appear to form the primary identification for high school teachers. As these identifications serve to separate teachers from the larger school environment, community is unlikely to develop.

SUMMARY

Over the last decade, the work of teachers has been one of the most salient themes in the school reform literature. The literature has addressed a distinct focus on the need to establish schools as communal places of caring and concern for children (Bryk & Driscoll, 1988; Bryk, Lee, & Holland, 1993; Bull, Fruehling, & Chattergy, 1992; Sergiovanni, 1994; Strike, 1993; Tom, 1984). Thus, schools were faced with a key dilemma concerning how to create lasting and increased community within schools.

Research conducted in the late 1980s and early 1990s focused on identifying the important resources necessary for teachers and school administrators to radically change the schools in which they worked (Corcoran et al., 1988; Firestone & Bader, 1992; Firestone & Rosenblum, 1988; Fullan, 1991; Levine, 1989; Louis, 1992; Mann, 1986; Metz, 1988; Newmann & Rutter, 1987). Portrayal of the necessary structural and social resources became a shared goal of researchers interested in school reform.

Such portrayals included descriptions of work conditions. The variables researchers focused on included increased respect from relevant sources within the educational community (Firestone & Rosenblum, 1988; Louis, 1992); participation in school governance structures (Johnson, 1990; Kanter, 1983; Mann, 1986; Meyer & Rowan, 1983); collaborative work structures (Little, 1990; Louis, 1992; Louis & Smith, 1992); opportunities for professional growth (Caldwell & Spinks, 1992; Levine, 1989; Lieberman & Miller, 1992); adequate resources of time, space, and institutional control (Louis, 1992; Miller, 1985; Newmann, 1991; Raywid, 1993); and a continued sense of congruence between personally held beliefs and those of the organization (Bryk & Driscoll, 1988; Metz, 1988). These variables were suggested to be foundational in the effort to improve the quality of teacher work life and in the endeavor to transform schools from fragmented bureaucratic organizations into communities of caring and concern for both the students they serve and the teachers who work within their walls (Bryk & Driscoll, 1988; Smith, 1994). Restructuring initiatives such as cooperative and small group learning, teacher teaming, site-based management, or magnet schools are consistent with this theme. Within these structures, it is suggested that the opportunity exists for teachers to create strong communal ties by engaging in joint discussion and reflective problem resolving of the daily struggles of the classroom. The following case portrays the struggle of one small school district to develop into a community-based school organization.

PRACTICE CASE—REFORM
AT OAK LEAF MIDDLE SCHOOL

Oak Leaf Middle School lies tucked away in small, southwestern rural community. The town has a population of 5,000 people, the middle school a population of 440 students instructed by a faculty of 26. This case study tells the school's success story—one that includes a transition from a traditional junior high school to an innovative middle school as well as from a school in which isolated teachers taught fragmented lessons to one in which teaming, integration, and cooperation are the norm. The story of Oak Leaf Middle School draws from 4 years of data—the planning year, the first year of operation under Dan Jackson, the second year under Marta Seward, and the third year under Jim Meyers. Interestingly, the story also spans two very different financial periods for the district—the first 3 years were ones of plenty, the fourth one of destitution following the failure of a major referendum.

The Creation of Oak Leaf Middle School

Many of the current success stories in education have been celebratory stories of charismatic leaders. However, this is a story of shared rather than individual leadership, one in which the school board, administration, teaching faculty, and community worked together to create a model middle school.

Oak Leaf Middle School, its structure, programs, successes, and struggles are thought of as belonging to a team rather than to an individual. Many faces, ideas, and personalities are present in the narrative. No one person can be pointed to as the creator of Oak Leaf Middle. In this reality lies the strength of the school and its program. Ownership, whether it be of the curriculum, instructional program, or school philosophy, is more than a buzz word. It is practice. Those educators who worked to create the structure now teach within it. More importantly, they believe in it.

Interestingly, Dan, the principal who began the change effort and worked through the initial planning is now district superintendent. Faculty ownership in the school's programs and practices smoothed the way for a new principal, Marta, to enter in the fall of 1992. In part, Marta was selected for the job because of her ability to harmonize with the existing philosophy and practice.

However, the transition occurred with little tension among faculty because they knew that they—not the principal—were the possessors of the skills and knowledge that made their teams and classrooms function. Ongoing rather than first-generation ownership had been established.

Housed in an aging building and cramped for space, Oak Leaf Junior High was like most rural junior high schools around the country. Good teachers taught good lessons to students who were attentive, interested, and involved with their learning. Yet the school board, bolstered by the recent publication of *Turning Points* by the Carnegie Council (1989), felt that the educational opportunity offered to students in Grades 5 through 8 could be improved. Specifically, they were interested in providing a balanced curriculum, utilizing varied instructional strategies, offering a full exploratory program of electives, maintaining continuous student progress toward academic goals paired with high expectations for all students, and placing students of the same grade and their teachers in close physical proximity for planning and learning purposes. These priorities would remain inviolable.

All staff were invited to participate in the research effort concerning the new middle school. Word went out that positions on the faculty were open to all—commitment to the new school would involve a commitment to a new form of teaching and learning. In the end, many elementary and high school teachers applied for and were transferred to newly created middle school positions. Faculty were chosen based on their commitment to the principles by which the new middle school was to operate. Thus, teachers who signed on clearly understood and embraced the assumptions that governed the school with which they were about to become involved.

The process of educating the staff and faculty was only half of the effort. In order to build the new school structure, the community needed to be educated. As with any bond issue, the community wanted assurance that their tax dollars were well spent and the proposed changes necessary. Parental concerns varied and were often in conflict. Whereas the parents of sixth graders wanted assurance that their students would be treated with caring, compassion, and concern, the parents of seventh-grade students expressed anxieties related to high school competition and readiness. The steering committee established for the creation of the new middle school responded by offering a comprehensive rationale, based on the guiding principles and adopted philosophy.

The final agreement affirmed the communities' appeal that the middle school be a positive environment for all students. Fifth graders would remain in a self-contained classroom, whereas sixth, seventh, and eighth graders would departmentalize. All teachers would teach reading, in addition to a subject area specialization, assuring small classes and individualized instruction in such an important content area. Throughout the school, students would see fewer teachers each day, allowing for increased student attention and ac-countability. Learning at all levels would be integrated and interdisciplinary. Thus, a focus on the American Revolution in social studies would be paired with the reading of *My Brother Sam is Dead*, set in that time, as well as with activities designed to focus students on the contextual and problematic issues related to the revolution rather than the recitation of fragmented superficial facts. Higher order thinking skills would be central to all teaching and efforts would be made to extend learning beyond the classroom. Faculty would receive 1 hour daily to cooperatively plan and monitor instructional activities and homework. A report card system was designed to incorporate both letter grades and extensive teacher comments to maintain effective and ongoing parent contact.

Once the bond had passed and district personal were assured of both the middle-school concept and the new building, the steering committee began developing the staff for their new endeavor. Believing that discerning, enlightened teachers would make quality decisions about education, curriculum, instruction, and strategy, Dan led a committee that decided to bring university courses on site to teachers. Consistent communication with the school board throughout the planning process translated into a willingness to pay for both for the classes and the corresponding salary increases the additional credits would provide the teaching staff. Negotiation with the university ensured that course content would connect philosophically with the newly formed Oak Leaf Middle School. Both the board and the administration spoke volumes with their actions; teachers felt support for their efforts unlike any they had felt in years. Conservative instructional approaches utilized in earlier years were abandoned in favor of new, innovative, integrated curriculum and pedagogies.

Furthermore, the newly formed teaching teams were given quality time to begin their work together. Three years later, teachers fondly point to the summer institute as the place the team became cemented and learned to trust and respect each other. Teachers assert that the summer courses were the difference between success and failure. By simultaneously working on both new curriculum and new techniques with which to teach students, teachers felt that they approached the new school year better equipped to address the needs of students. The institute also provided time for the teams to begin to know each other and develop professional relationships that later would turn into strong friendships.

Following the summer institute, the teaching teams felt ready to begin the school year. Much of the curriculum for the year had been planned and a process existed for completing the remaining curriculum modules. More importantly, the daily schedule contained an hour for team planning and an hour for individual planning, so teachers understood that time existed during the regular school day to complete ongoing work.

Team planning time was inviolable. Members would gather daily in shared office space with coffee, calendars, and curriculum and use the hour to discuss difficulties with lessons, successes with students, or the next interdisciplinary unit. Tasks were often divided between the team members. One member would arrange films, speakers, or gather science and math materials; another would draft an assessment rubric for discussion at the next meeting. The time was viewed as cherished and used accordingly. Both content and instructional strategies are discussed with equal regularity—the process of concurrently planning what to teach and how to teach it had become commonplace. Teachers actively reflected on lessons and activities from the previous days and weeks, searching for cues as to what this particular group of kids responded well to, where their interests lay, and which teaching techniques were best to get the message across. Classrooms norms evolved in which students were deeply and continuously engaged in pursuing substantive learning. On-task learning behaviors became commonplace and lessons were often modified to extend or remediate previous learning.

Nevertheless, solid planning and extensive preparation could not completely prepare teachers for the radical changes that Oak Leaf Middle School teachers had chosen to undertake. Some teachers found the transition a straightforward and simple innovation. They enjoyed the unconstrained atmosphere and found the opportunity to explore new curriculum and pedagogy stimulating. Others struggled under the responsibility of teaching reading, finding it difficult to address disparate content areas. The formidable goals the staff had set forth seemed insurmountable to some teachers. At this point in time, it would have been easy and expected for the principal to step in and order people to get on board. Instead, he chose to trust the team plan, allowing the teams to mediate their own struggles.

Teachers were encouraged to talk through concerns with their team before taking them to a full staff meeting or to the administration. Through the process of working through conflicts as they arose, the teams built confidence, interdependence, and trust. Dan, the principal, would drop by classrooms, not to evaluate teachers, but to keep abreast on what occurred in classes. This policy provided him with ready topics for informal conferences with students, parents, or teachers interested in discussing the progress at the middle school. Additionally, he could offer ideas from the experience of observing instruction and put teachers with similar interests in contact. The individual development of a teacher's potential became the shared goal as everyone learned new skills together. Increasingly, the staff felt comfortable with the new structure.

Strong parental communication structures were viewed throughout the planning process as an important practice for Oak Leaf Middle School. Report cards were a combination of grades and comments, with emphasis placed on the comment section. Additionally, teachers provided written midquarter reports for both students and parents. Although operative, the process was cumbersome. Willing parent volunteers spent 3 full days each trimester collating the teacher-written progress reports and stuffing envelopes in preparation for mailing. Teachers were beginning to feel that the process was both increasingly unmanageable and perhaps antithetical to the goal of increased communication, as the stuffing process meant that comments were often due weeks before they were to go home.

Finally, it was the volunteers who questioned the system. Suggesting that a new streamlined process be adopted, the parents of Oak Leaf took on the report card process as their project. Marta, now principal, viewed this as not only appropriate but as a concrete example of community ownership in Oak Leaf's policies and procedures. The parents quickly decided that students could handle the courier roles. Envelopes need not be shuffled and stuffed; students could be responsible to collect their grades and comments. The mailing process would be bypassed, allowing students to share their school progress in an open manner with their parent(s). Thus, the student's role in and responsibility for their progress was increased; further, the message was conveyed that they were trusted to honestly, willingly, and straightforwardly discuss their school progress with their parents. During spring quarter a trial balloon was launched. The system ran smoothly, saving both time and energy.

Oak Leaf Under Fire, the Third Year

Oak Leaf Middle School was thriving in the fall of 1992. Teachers had become comfortable with teaching in a teamed format and the teams were beginning to reach out and consider stronger, more powerful ways to link curricula. Concurrently, the district was also attempting to raise a substantial amount of money in a levy referendum. Residents of the farming community surrounding Oak Leaf had experienced a series of lean years and were reluctant to raise their taxes. Although the district fought a strong battle, the levy failed. Suddenly, efforts to create strong teaching and learning environments for students fell a distant second to efforts designed to help alleviate the budget crisis the school district was facing.

Because the middle school was considered Dan's baby, rumors held that the middle school would be less deeply cut than the high school, elementary, or community education programs. In fact, Dan and the school board held true to campaign promises that all schools would face equal cuts based on 30% of their budget. Faculty would be laid off in all buildings and voluntary early retirement would be viewed favorably.

One possible solution to the financial problems of the district was to dissolve the middle school and return to a junior high school format. This would save money in two ways. First, staffing of the middle school is expensive. Flexibility in scheduling is lost as teachers remain locked into team assignments and unavailable to teach in other grade levels. Second, teaching assignments could be shared between high school and middle school faculty if the middle-school teachers were freed from the team focus.

The middle-school faculty and governance council banded together to launch a campaign to preserve the middle-school philosophy of the building. Although the teachers felt that this was a shared, communal understanding, discussion proved otherwise. A majority of teachers defined the middle-school philosophy as including maintenance of the focus on reading instruction; retaining jointly shared, team planning time; and continuing the school policy of single-grade assignments for teachers. For the community and school board members, the notion of what comprised a middle school was far less focused. Many members felt that as long as the structure of the building, pods of students by grade, were maintained, Oak Leaf had a middle school. For others, parents most notably, maintenance of the middle school meant preservation of the team focus so that their students would have the fewest number of contacts with different adults per day.

The conversation and its disturbing findings quickly filtered out to the full faculty. A meeting was called to discuss the feelings of the staff. Following much conversation, it was decided that reading and team planning were the important defining factors for the faculty. Although many teachers believed that the maintenance of single grade-level assignments for teachers was preferable, in reality the budget probably could not sustain such an expensive practice. More troubling was the discovery by the faculty that many teachers felt a stronger bond with their team than with the school itself. As one teacher stated:

> We'd put all our energy into the team focus, and the pods only work against seeing other faculty. It's possible to get to school, enter your pod, and not come out until you go home. We'd lost our shared focus.

Marta decided that in the following year, the faculty must begin working toward a greater shared understanding. A committee was formed to brainstorm ways to address the problem. Solutions were creative. Leading the list was the suggestion that the school sponsor a series of round table discussions with invited educational leaders on issues of interest to the full faculty. This would prove fairly inexpensive because no credit would be offered but a dialogue could be sustained. Other solutions included faculty meetings focused on issues such as assessment and instruction, and the use of preschool meetings in ways designed to enhance schoolwide community.

However, first there were the pressing problems of staffing and budget cuts. Like most other schools, teachers to be let go came from the bottom of the seniority list. Thus, cuts in the staff rooster did not fall evenly across the schools. Many teachers, due to certification requirements or licensure restrictions, held their positions while more senior members (in years) were scheduled to be laid off. Involuntary transfers, a practice never used in this small district before, were necessary for some teachers to hold a position. As Dan stated, "I could offer these people jobs, but sometimes it was way out of their usual placement, so the choice for some staff is a position they would rather not take or no job." The tension around who would stay and who would go was palpable.

A positive outcome of the district budget cuts was the creation of a shared, faculty wide planning period from 8 to 9 each morning. District and schoolwide committees meet during this time to discuss issues of importance to the school community. Although many of the committees appear to be traditional department or grade-level affairs, three committees hold great promise for the school. These include a research committee for faculty interested in reading widely in the educational literature and bringing into the school new ideas for pedagogy and practice, an interdisciplinary committee designed to focus on integrating the curriculum across subject matter and traditional grade-level boundaries, and a committee designed to focus on community–school relations and student apprenticeships.

These new committees are said to be, "some of the most interesting and thought-provoking professional activities [teachers] have ever attended." As one teacher stated:

> I feel alive here, we are talking about real change, and since everyone started at ground zero, no one can be a prima donna. No one has more experience than any other of us in doing this [districtwide curriculum planning] so all our sharing is on equal turf. I try new things and others are eager to hear about them. I'm talking to people I haven't talked to about school stuff in years.

A Future for Oak Leaf

Under Jim's principalship, Oak Leaf Middle School was able to weather a difficult year following the budget cuts and transfers. His previous status as the school technology teacher proved useful in strengthening cross-team ties. Because Jim had experience working with all the teams, he was able to develop the needed conversation between teams. He, better than an administrator hired from outside the organization, was able to locate places of communality between teachers and help to identify their shared interests.

In conclusion, Oak Leaf Middle School was able to create a community by looking both backward and forward. A teacher glancing backward could draw on an organizational history rooted in positive memories of support, professionalism, and success. A teacher looking forward is provided a clear vision supported by adequate, focused, and available information and the opportunity to reflect, discuss, and study the information presented to them.

EXERCISES

1.   Using the case as your data bank, identify the features of community as an organizational form that are present in the case. List these. How do these features positively or negatively affect the professional or scholarly interactions between the members of the case? How do these features affect social interactions between the members of the case?

2.   Consider your school. In what ways are the features of community present or absent at your workplace? In what areas of your school could these ideas be incorporated to create an increased focus on student learning

and progress? Identify the barriers and facilitators to creating community in your school setting.

3.   As discussed in the critique section, schoolwide community can be difficult to obtain, especially in large or departmentalized schools. What are some ways to mitigate against these barriers or are they simply one of the enduring dilemmas of schooling?

4.   Team teaching has been suggested to create strong community among the members of the individual teams, yet, paradoxically to create distance between teachers in the larger school community. This argument seems particularly salient when applied to teachers who are not assigned to teams, such as teachers of elective subjects. They often claim to be left out of important school decisions and events. How can a school create strong teaching teams and still maintain a strong level of community among the full faculty?

READING YOUR OWN SCHOOL

Consider your own school. How are the ideas and concepts presented in this chapter present in your work setting? How might these ideas help you to make sense of your school and the events that occur there? List five examples of how you see these concepts in practice at your school; examples might include the actions of administration, staff, faculty, students, or parents, or specific issues or events such as a curriculum adoption or annual school celebration. Link each event to an idea or concept presented in this chapter. Do you think these actions or events facilitate student growth and learning, faculty and staff efficacy, and sense of well-being? Or do these actions or events create barriers to student growth and learning, faculty and staff efficacy, and sense of well-being? Finally, how could you use these ideas to initiate positive change in your school setting?

RECOMMENDED READINGS

Arnett, R. C. (1986). *Communication and community*. Carbondale: Southern Illinois University Press. Arnett illustrates the narrow ridge definition of interpersonal communication with rich examples. His vignettes demonstrate effective and ineffective approaches to human community; an effective approach, he makes clear, incorporates not only openness to other's points of view but also a willingness to be persuaded.

Bellah, R. N., Madsen, R., Sullivan, W. M., Swidler, A., & Tipton, S. M. (1985). *Habits of the heart: Individualism and commitment in American life.* New York: Harper & Row. Based on a 5-year research study of various U.S. communities, the authors explore the traditions Americans use to make sense of themselves and their society, arriving at one of today's major moral dilemmas: the conflict between individualism and our need for community.

Etzioni, A. (1993). *The spirit of community: Rights, responsibilities and the communitarian agenda.* New York: Crown. Arguing that Americans need to move from me to we, Etzioni calls for a reawakening of our attentions to the issues of shared values and the creation of institutions that support and sustain those values. In proposing a new balance between the me and the we, this book offers new insights into emerging social attitudes and our responsibility toward members of our community.

Louis, K. S., Kruse, S. D., & Associates (1995). *Professionalism and community: Perspectives on reforming urban schools.* Thousand Oaks, CA: Corwin. Louis and Kruse examine the question: "Why do some school communities succeed and others fail?" Using longitudinal case study accounts, they explore the progress of five urban schools working toward the development of professional community. Focusing on the structural, social, and human conditions of schooling, the authors describe how to form a professional community and offer evaluative criteria for assessing the variety of elements that constitute professional community.

5

Patterns of Inequality: Earlier Critical Approaches to Schooling

♦♦♦

People frequently view schools as benevolent organizations, transmitters of knowledge and skills that ensure the development of individuals and the survival of society. Schools are also regarded as meritocratic institutions. Students receive rewards such as test scores and grades based on individual talent and hard work. Ascribed characteristics such as social class, race, and gender are not to play any legitimate role in the allocation of rewards in schools. Based on high levels of talent and work, schools hold out the promise of a good college and, in the not-to-distant future, upper mobility.

As noted in chapter 1, some research indicates there are limits to the accuracy of this view. Patterns of social inequality exist. Compared to Anglo-Americans, African-American and Latino children have much lower rates of high school completion (Ballantine, 1997). Despite the public rhetoric about schools and social mobility in the United States, parent occupational status continues to be fairly predictive of a child's occupational future; schooling does not always contribute to upward mobility (Hurn, 1993). Female students receive significantly less interaction and supportive feedback from teachers than male students (Bennett deMarrais & Le-Compte, 1995). These patterns of inequality based on class, race, and gender are reflected in the wider society as well. For example, at every level of educational attainment (doctorate, master's, baccalaureate, and high school) Whites in the workplace earn considerably more than African Americans and Latinos; males earn from 30% to 50% more than females (*The New York Times*, 1993). A disproportionate percentage of African Americans and Latinos experience poverty compared to Whites; a higher percentage of females live in poverty compared to males (Tozer, Violas, & Senese, 1995).

Critical approaches to schooling attempt to explain why these patterns of inequality exist and what role schools play in sustaining or alleviating them (Apple, 1982; Giroux, 1981; McLaren, 1997). It is important to stress the plural form of approaches because there are a wide range of scholars working in the critical tradition and who hold different views on the nature of schooling and inequality. Additionally, critical scholarship began during the 1970s and 1980s and has evolved considerably since then. It has changed in response to identified weaknesses and the growth of new theoretical and empirical work. However, making sense of the most recent work, in some ways, requires understanding the earlier critical scholarship. The recent work shares many concerns with the earlier scholarship, and the later work has built on some of the original assumptions and understandings developed in the 1970s. As a result, we present some of the key ideas from earlier critical work in this chapter and more recent critical scholarship in the next chapter. The hope is that by starting with the older work, the more recent scholarship will be more accessible. Also, because our discussion of critical approaches stretches over two chapters, our presentation of the benefits and limitations of critical scholarship and the practice case is found in the next chapter, rather than this one. This chapter introduces a focus on economic and cultural reproduction. Each of these older approaches offers an important starting point for developing the organizational literacy to read patterns of inequality in schools. Consider the narrative here.

Jamal Franklin stood in the hallway outside his classroom and for the hundredth time in the last 2 years shook his head angrily as groups of expensively clad students streamed past him heading toward the advanced placement (AP) English classes that met down the hallway. Meanwhile, proud but poorly dressed students strolled into Jamal's room and John Prather's across the hall. Jamal and John taught regular English classes for sophomores. Many of the students from the poorer neighborhoods near Albert Meadow High School ended up being tracked for one reason or another into the regular English classes like Jamal and John's rather than the AP or honors sections down the hall.

Jamal knew from his own reading that tracking working-class students into lower level courses meant many of the them would not receive the knowledge and skills that were critical for a strong performance on college placement tests and for the possibility of attending a good college. More and more, a good college education was a minimum entrance requirement to compete for good-paying jobs. Based on this understanding, Jamal and a group of supportive faculty and parents had mobilized 3 years ago to get rid of tracking in Meadow High. The hope was that without tracking, Meadow High would offer the same high quality curriculum to every student. That way all students would have the knowledge and skills to go on to college after high school if they chose.

The school board had initially been willing to consider the plan, but a number of the wealthy parents whose children attended the honors and AP classes created a public furor. They argued that their children would be held back by all the slower kids. Teachers would regularly have to be working with the slower children to catch them up to the brighter students. Flooding all the slower kids into these classes would dilute the quality of their own children's education. Their children had worked hard to succeed in the AP and honors classes. Getting rid of tracking in effect would discriminate unfairly against the brighter kids. These arguments carried the day and the school board quickly distanced themselves from Jamal's coalition of teachers and parents. Jamal still carried hard feelings about this when he stared down the hall toward the AP classes and thought about John teaching regular English at Meadow High.

John was a sincere, hard-working, first-year teacher from the suburbs who was very inexperienced, especially with poor inner-city youth. Jamal frequently heard the unmistakable sounds of a classroom on the brink of boiling over the threshold of the door. Unfortunately, it was common practice in Meadow and other high schools to put young, inexperienced teachers like John with those students who in many ways were most in need of the most experienced and skilled staff. Senior faculty at Meadow, as in many high schools, opted to forgo the challenges of teaching all but the best students in the AP and honors classes. It was one more way Meadow's poor kids were disadvantaged unfairly.

As a 20-year veteran, Jamal had willingly given up his own AP assignments to devote himself to regular English courses. He really enjoyed the challenge of working with his students. It gave him the opportunity to make sure his curriculum at least helped them toward a college future even if they often fought him occasionally along the way. Many of them were quite bright but also very rowdy. Jamal knew some teachers actually regarded this boisterousness as an indicator of disinterest in academics or, worse, as a demonstration of low intelligence. Some teachers worked to get these kids transferred out of honors and AP classes and into regular classes. Jamal, however, refused to give up. He liked them and believed in them. He always envisioned the possibility that they could and would make it. This kept him coming back each day renewed with hope.

This story illustrates some of the key concerns of the older critical approaches to schooling: the relation between the economy and schools, the tendency to hierarchically rank different social groups in schools similar to the wider society, schools as potentially reproducing or transforming this social ranking system, the power of the wealthy to dominate schools, and the hope of teachers and students to alter inequitable patterns. As noted in chapter 1, common explanations for what happens in school classrooms and corridors often point to the individual rather than social patterns in the wider U.S. society. Critical approaches to schooling in general insist that to understand what goes on between students, teachers, and administrators, we need to think relationally (Apple, 1979). School organizations must not be seen as separate from the economic, political, and cultural webs of the larger society:

> [A]s far as possible, we need to place the knowledge that we teach, the social relations that dominate classrooms, the school as a mechanism of cultural and economic preservation and distribution, and finally, ourselves as people who work in these institutions, back into the context in which they all reside. All of these things are subject to an interpretation of their respective places in a complex, stratified, and unequal society. (Apple, 1979, p. 3)

RETHINKING POWER AND ITS RELATIONSHIP
TO SCHOOLS

Thinking relationally is particularly important for reconsidering the concept of power. In the chapter on political social patterns, we suggested that different groups in society employed power to further their values and interests. The image conjured up was of multiple groups, of generally equal strength, skirmishing on a level playing field to meet their needs and interests. Also, power was employed by a neutral authority to umpire the struggle for resources for the good of all groups. The umpiring ensured that resources were distributed fairly and that no group consistently dominated.

Critical scholars suggest that the characterization by pluralism that all the groups have about the same chance and status in the struggle is false. Historically and currently, certain groups have consistently held more power in relationship to other groups in the United States; these dominant groups have not umpired the struggle for resources in a neutral and fair manner so that most groups benefit equally. Rather, power has been used by dominant groups to maintain their own control and advantage in America (Carroll & Noble, 1989; Takaki, 1993).

For example, in the chapter on politics, we sketched a history of the United States in the 19th and part of the 20th centuries in which there was an emphasis on social harmony and a distrust of conflict and factions. Critical scholars would point out that this focus on unity was promoted by the dominant group in the United States, wealthy White Anglo-Saxon

Protestant males; and this belief was used to exclude less powerful groups from full participation in the country's political, social, and economic institutions (Carroll & Noble, 1989). The poor, Catholics, Jews, women, African Americans, Native Americans, Asian Americans, and Latinos were not afforded equality of opportunity in the 19th century (Spring, 1996; Takaki, 1993).

Nineteenth-century public schools also participated in fostering inequitable social patterns (Kaestle, 1983; Spring, 1997; Tyack & Hansot, 1982). White Anglo-Saxon Protestant culture dominated the curriculum and educational practices of public schools. A range of social groups was excluded from full participation in public schooling. Even into contemporary times, the United States and its public school system continues to exhibit patterns of social inequality (Allison, 1995). Critical approaches have played a key role in bringing the use of power to foster inequitable patterns to the attention of a wider public (McLaren, 1997). Older critical approaches first attempted to do this by focusing on the importance of reproduction.

POWER, REPRODUCTION, AND SCHOOLS

Scholars who focused on reproduction found patterns of inequality to be duplicated generation after generation (Bowles & Gintis, 1976). Individuals who grew up in lower class homes would frequently end up later in life in lower class occupations much like their parents. Similarly, because women and minorities have frequently been stratified in the lower rungs of the workforce, with a high level of probability they also found themselves later in life in low-paying jobs, not unlike their parents. How does this happen and what role do schools play in this reproduction process?

Reproductionists particularly emphasize the means by which various social institutions such as schools function to replicate the advantages of the powerful (Giroux, 1981). This perspective is not advanced simply for the sake of critique. The hope is to identify how dominant groups unjustly structure inequality in society and schools and then work toward a more just society. As critical scholar Apple (1979) noted:

> for a society to be just it must ... contribute most to the advantage of the least advantaged. That is, its structural relations must be such as to equalize not merely access to but actual control of cultural, social, and especially economic institutions. (p. 12)

One step in moving toward a more just society involves the identification of how dominant groups structure inequality in society and schools through economic reproduction (Bowles & Gintis, 1976).

ECONOMIC REPRODUCTION

For economic reproductionists such as Bowles and Gintis (1976), the key to understanding inequality is a recognition that capitalism is the country's dominant form of patterning relationships between people. Capitalism was mentioned in the chapter on bureaucracy and in that chapter we emphasized the calculability of profits. Bowles and Gintis (1976) drew on the work of Karl Marx and Friedrich Engels to understand capitalism. For Marx and Engels, capitalism was a particular mode of production: the organization of human social patterns and resources to produce the food, shelter, and goods necessary to meet important societal needs (Schmitt, 1997). Historically, there have been a range of alternative modes of production: communal, slavery, and feudal to name a few. Each involves different types of social relationships, different technical means for producing goods and services, different forms of ownership, different distribution of power, and a different allocation of goods and services. For example, during the medieval period, craft artisans such as shoemakers were controlled by a relationship with a craft guild that set the general rules for local shoemakers. However, each artisan was independent and owned the resources necessary for shoemaking such as tools and raw materials like leather. Shoemakers sold their shoes to consumers but the money provided just enough to support the artisan and his family.

Capitalists and Workers

Capitalism as a mode of production structures human relationships so that there are generally two classes of people: capitalists and workers. Each class differs with regard to their position and power in the general processes by which food, clothing, and shelter are produced and distributed. Capitalism as a mode of production supports the private ownership of property. In a corporation-dominated capitalist economy being competitive typically requires owning vast amounts of property that enable the production of goods and services on a very large scale. This essentially means having the monetary resources necessary to produce things in large factories. Hence, corporate capitalism tends to favor those who step into a supposedly fair and equal marketplace with very large amounts of money, for example, capitalists.

By virtue of their wealth, capitalists own and control most of the re-sources—tools, factories, machines—needed to produce goods and services for sale in the marketplace. Consequently, the relationship between the two classes is exploitive. Due to their relative lack of wealth, "[w]orkers ... do not own the products of their labor, nor do they own or control the tools, buildings, and facilities of the productive process" (Bowles & Gintis, 1976, p. 67). The concentration of money, power, and control in the hands of capitalists "means the majority [the workers] must exchange their only productive property (their capacity to labor) for a wage or salary, thereby agreeing to give formal jurisdiction over their economic activities to owners and managers" (p. 55).

Capitalists work to maintain their control and power over workers to ensure their ongoing accumulation of profit. Profit is the driving force in capitalism (Nelson, 1995). Profits are the surplus value that extends beyond the cost of paying workers and other expenses for producing a particular good or service. Workers are excluded by capitalists from sharing in profits despite the fact that workers' labor enables capitalists to accrue profits. "Capitalists [also] make profit by eliciting a high level of output" from workers and by keeping workers' wages low (p. 54). In other words, capital-ists are motivated to pay workers as little as possible to ensure the profitabil-ity of their companies.

Capitalists are able to maintain this inequitable relationship through the legal right to hire and fire workers. This legal right is buttressed by the existence of a large pool of unemployed workers available to replace any worker critical of capitalists' undemocratic power in the workplace or unwillingness to share profits. Hence, consistently high levels of unemploy-ment, 4% to 6%, year in and year out, work to help capitalists maintain their dominance and exploitation of workers. A large pool of unemployed workers also helps to generally ensure stability in the workplace and the continued generation of profit for capitalists. Because if workers were to collectively work to reorganize this system into a more equitable distribution of power and rewards, the government would step in to support the power of capitalists. Historically, the government has accomplished this through the passage of various antilabor laws and the use of armed forces (Zinn, 1990).

The Rise of Managers as a Class

An important way capitalists maintain their power is through organizing the work process (Bowles & Gintis, 1976). Before the 19th century, capitalists rarely intervened into the way the working class performed its labor. They loaned money or provided raw materials to individual workers who often toiled in their own homes. When workers produced their finished product, capitalists collected and brought the products to the marketplace to sell. During this early history, the execution of work tasks was under the personal discretion of the individual worker. With the rise of entrepreneurial capitalism in the first part of the 19th century in the United States, capitalists began to directly supervise workers or delegate that responsibility to white-collar managers or foremen.

In many regards this represents the genesis of a new class of employee, a managerial class that worked to directly regulate workers for the benefit of capitalists and their businesses. Henceforth, management would directly supervise workers to control their pace and the length of the work day. Or, they would generate the company policies that structured the behavior of workers. This form of direct hierarchical domination meant less independent workers but more control of the work process and, consequently, more profits for capitalists. This hierarchical set of relationships provided an important foundation for the subsequent bureaucratic organization of work between capitalists and workers, particularly in the large corporations that developed at the turn of the 20th century. Hence, the large bureaucratic work organizations in 20th-century United States enable capitalists' domination of the workplace.

The Technocratic–Meritocratic Ideology

Ideology is a critical resource for stabilizing capitalists' bureaucratic, hierarchical power over workers. In the chapter on political patterns, we discussed ideology as a set of beliefs about what students and teachers should do in schools. In this chapter, *ideology* is used in a different sense. Again, in line with the work of Marx and Engels, the concept of ideology argues that "[t]he ideas that are dominant in any given historical period appear self-evident because they the fit snugly with the dominant economic institutions" (Schmitt, 1997, p. 73). In other words, ideologies serve to legitimate a particular mode of production like capitalism as the best possible one for a society like the United States (Bowles & Gintis, 1976). Legitimacy refers to the process of creating and maintaining the support for a particular distribution and use of power. Because capitalism, as sketched earlier in this chapter, distributes considerably more power to capitalists and managers than workers, an ideology is required to make this distribution of power seem just and natural. For Bowles and Gintis (1976), the ideology that serves to legitimate capitalism in the United States is the technocratic–meritocratic ideology.

The technocratic–meritocratic ideology suggests that the hierarchical, bureaucratic structures of work organizations "arise from [their] natural superiority as a device to coordinate collective activity and nurture expertise" (p. 105). In short, the technocratic part of the ideology argues that organizations work more efficiently when an individual is assigned to a particular job and has the opportunity to develop expertise in that job. This same individual along with others who perform the same job will work more efficiently as individuals and as a coordinated group when supervised by someone above them who specializes in the supervisory job. In turn, the supervisor will work more efficiently with his subordinates when appropriately supervised by his boss. This hierarchical chain continues upward to the management and ownership of the organization.

The meritocratic part of the ideology argues that individuals should be assigned to the different hierarchical positions in an organization based on merit, the cognitive skills developed through an individual's level of educational accomplishment, and their "natural" intelligence; "natural" intelligence is believed to influence an individual's ability to acquire education and cognitive skills. Individuals of greater intelligence will be able to acquire more education and, therefore, have more cognitive skills. Individuals with a low IQ will acquire less education and, as a result, will possess fewer cognitive skills.

Each position in the organization requires a particular level of education/cognitive skill. As one moves up the hierarchical ladder in an organization, the jobs require higher and higher levels of education/cognitive skill. To encourage individuals to aspire toward the highest position possible, each movement up the organizational ladder is rewarded with a higher wage or salary. As previously noted, individuals differ with regard to their merit, their intellectual competence and ability to reach higher levels of education. The hierarchically ordered organization inevitably ends up placing those individuals who are best suited educationally/cognitively for each position. Bowles and Gintis described some of the bureaucratic social patterns discussed earlier in the book; however, they had a slightly different take on bureaucracy.

Bowles and Gintis (1976) drew on a body of research to argue that, contrary to what the technocratic–meritocratic ideology suggests, individuals are not rewarded with more money by virtue of their attaining higher levels of education. Rather, an individual's socioeconomic status influences the monetary return they receive from additional education. For example, research indicates that, "Whites of high social class backgrounds enjoy economic returns to education that are 66% higher than those for either whites of low social class background or blacks" (p. 99). Individuals classified as managers earned substantially higher economic returns from more education than did those individuals classified as workers. Additionally, individuals classified as workers, be they White, African American, or female, similarly earned small amounts of economic return from seeking more schooling.

The Technocratic–Meritocratic Ideology and Public Schools

The technocratic–meritocratic ideology not only obscures inequalities in the workplace, it also hides how the public school system actually works. Bowles and Gintis (1976) asserted that, in part, public schools legitimate existing economic inequality in America. They do this by encouraging society to believe that economic success is tied solely to the mastery of the technical and cognitive skills that schools dispense. Individuals are sorted and provided with differing levels of technical and cognitive skills in schools based on meritocratic principles. For Bowles and Gintis, this image of public schools is false: "Beneath the facade of meritocracy lies the reality of an educational system geared toward the reproduction of economic relations only partially explicable in terms of technical requirements and efficiency standards" (p. 103).

They based this claim on studies that indicate that "the intellectual abilities developed or certified in school make little causal contribution to getting ahead economically" (p. 110). The research indicates that even a supposed inherited intellectual ability like high IQ contributes little to economic success. Rather, the findings indicate that the social class background of an individual makes the most significant contribution to future economic success. Individuals who come from high social class backgrounds have a greater chance of economic success than individuals who come from lower social class backgrounds. Again, this is contrary to what the technocratic–meritocratic ideology suggests.

When the facade is taken away, what do schools actually do? For Bowles and Gintis, public schools perform a number of functions in society, but a particularly important one is to socialize children into the capitalist economic system. This is accomplished via a correspondence between the kinds of social relationships structured in schools and those in the capitalist workplace:

> Specifically, the social relationships of education—the relationships between administrators and teachers, teachers and students, students and students, and students and their work—replicate the hierarchical division of labor. Hierarchical relations are reflected in the vertical authority lines from administrators to teachers and to students. (p. 131).

Schools and the Hidden Curriculum

These hierarchical relationships become what some have called the hidden curriculum of public schools. Schools teach a formal curriculum—English, science, math, social studies, and so forth—but they also teach the appropriateness of relating to authority in particular ways. Generally, the hidden curriculum of hierarchical relationships teaches students to develop personality traits in keeping with submission to authority. These personality traits will be rewarded in the capitalist workplace and help maintain the current hierarchical structure of capitalist power and worker obedience.

Additionally, the hidden curriculum rewards the development of personality traits specific to the social class origin of students. These personality traits serve students in their projected class-based positions in the workforce. For example, Bowles and Gintis indicated that individuals destined for the lower level worker roles in the capitalist economy need to be taught to be careful rule followers. Individuals slotted for top executive positions need to think independently and act creatively to meet the demands of the changing marketplace. In other words, the hidden curriculum provides different types of schooling based on students' social class origin and, consequently, their probable class-based work futures.

Finally, according to Bowles and Gintis, schools perform a function that complements the hidden curriculum. Schools socialize students to accept the technocratic–meritocratic ideology. In the course of being taught the hidden curriculum specific to their class background—rule following or independence—students come to understand their hierarchical relationship with their teachers and administrators as the natural way to organize the work of large groups of people. They also come to understand their placement in the academic ladder—college preparatory, general, and vocational—in relationship to their fellow students as actually based on merit. The technocratic–meritocratic ideology comes to be their sole way of understanding how they ended up as bad, average, or good students and, eventually, worker, manager, or capitalist. The end result is that the economic reproduction of a class-based society comes to be seen as necessarily just and inevitable.

Research in Schools and the Hidden Curriculum

An important study by Anyon (1980/1995) supported Bowles and Gintis' thesis regarding the hidden curriculum in public schools. Anyon studied the fifth-grade classrooms in schools from working class, middle class, and very affluent neighborhoods. She found that the school experience of the students "differed qualitatively by social class" (p. 177). Although all the students received instruction in similar subject areas, the hidden curriculum provided them with very different lessons regarding their relationship to work and authority.

In the working-class schools, students were directed to follow a set of steps in a fairly rote fashion. Little explanation was given of the concepts behind the steps or why the particular steps being followed were important. Evaluation of student work also concentrated on whether the correct steps were followed. This relationship to work was evident in math and language arts instruction. For example, a teacher took the students through a step-by-step process of constructing a 1-inch grid. However, the teacher never informed the students why they were in fact making something called a 1-inch grid and that they were doing it to study the concept of scale. During this lesson a student interjected that she had a faster way to develop the 1-inch grid and the teacher responded by saying, "No, you don't; you don't even know what I'm making yet. Do it this way or it's wrong" (Anyon, 1980/1995, p. 166).

Similarly, language arts instruction in the working-class schools focused on the mechanics of punctuation. Little emphasis was put on creative writing or the use of language as an expressive tool. As one teacher noted regarding the language arts curriculum, "Simple punctuation is all they'll ever use" (Anyon, 1980/1995, p. 166). Writing assignments that were given to students frequently required answering questions on a ditto sheet. Even an assignment that asked students to write an autobiography actually involved answering questions such as, "Where were you born?" or "What is your favorite animal?" on a ditto labeled "All About Me."

Teachers asserted their authority through giving orders to students and not explaining why particular decisions were made. Students also had no input into decisions about the use of classroom time and space. A premium was put in working class schools on controlling the movement of students by saying things such as, "Why are you out of your seat?" (Anyon, 1980/1995, p. 167). A general stance was communicated in the classroom that authority figures such as teachers were to be obeyed and not questioned. Students in these working-class schools were clearly being given an education through the hidden curriculum more congruent with a work situation that required following directions and submitting to authority.

By comparison, the more affluent schools offered a very different hidden curriculum. For example, in one affluent school, math and language arts instruction by teachers communicated that work was creative and for the purpose of developing the individual. Teachers encouraged students to express their thoughts and ideas and work at applying them to different situations. Teachers evaluated students based on the originality and quality of their written stories, essays, murals, or graphs. In math, students learned about deriving averages by having students collect data about the average number of possessions among the fifth grade students. Students had to take home sheets on which the number of televisions, cars, games, and rooms were listed for each home. Students used the data from the sheets and calculators supplied by the teacher to arrive at averages. Some students decided on their own to extend this project by comparing the averages of the fifth grade to the fourth grade.

Language arts instruction emphasized the importance of creative writing and the development of individual expressiveness. Students wrote stories for the first graders in the school after they had interviewed them about what kinds of stories they liked. They also wrote editorials about issues confronting the local school board and wrote radio plays, some of which students performed for the whole school. When teaching the use of punctuation such as commas, emphasis was put on use being dependent on the expressive context. For example the teacher told students, "Where you put commas depends on how you say the sentence; it depends on the situation and what you want to say" (Anyon, 1980/1995, p. 172).

Students learned that authority in the classroom needed to be negotiated with the teacher on an ongoing basis. Teachers rarely gave direct orders to students. Instead, teachers encouraged students to consider the consequences of their actions and to then choose accordingly. There were few explicit rules governing the movement of students in the classroom. If students wished to leave the classroom for the bathroom or the library, they signed their names on the board and walked out. The school as a whole allowed all students to decide on their own to go to the library to get books.

Students could make decisions and influence what work was to be done as well as whether they were ready to go on to another topic area. Again, supportive of Bowles and Gintis' (1976) thesis, the hidden curriculum in the more affluent school prepared their students for work roles very different from those of the students in the working-class schools.

CULTURAL REPRODUCTION

Until this point in the book, the focus has been on the importance of social patterns in U.S. society and its schools. However, we have also been implicitly discussing the importance of different beliefs, values, knowledge, ideas, and symbols. Many scholars refer to these collectively as *culture*. And, along with social patterns, culture plays an important role in the United States and its schools in creating and sustaining inequality (Apple, 1979; Giroux, 1981; McLaren, 1997). Just as in economic relations, where some groups—capitalists and managers—dominate other groups—such as workers—some cultures dominate, whereas others are subordinate. The dominant culture " ... affirm[s] the central values, interests, and concerns of the social class in control of material and symbolic wealth in society. Groups who live out social relations in subordination to the dominant culture are part of the subordinate culture" (McLaren, 1997, p. 176).

Cultural reproduction generally asserts that there are a number of ways that the knowledge, beliefs, and values distributed by public schooling creates and maintains inequitable patterns based on social class. Students from poor backgrounds are not given the curricular knowledge that will enable them to be socially mobile and/or to question their subordinate status in society. This is accomplished by disproportionately sorting working-class students into the lower academic tracks of public schools (Oakes, 1985); these tracks are less likely to lead to college and eventually to better job opportunities in the future. The opening narrative in this chapter provides an illustration of this type of cultural reproduction. Another way is the school curriculum's relationship to hegemony and ideology.

Hegemony and the Curriculum

The exercise of cultural power is typically not accomplished by force, coercion, or even by a small group of powerful individuals conspiring to place particular types of knowledge in textbooks and teachers' heads. Rather, the control and power of dominant groups is established through hegemony

(Apple, 1979; Giroux, 1981; McLaren, 1997). *Hegemony* refers to intellectual leaders, either in support of or in dominant political and economic groups, actively working in different social spheres to argue for particular types of culture as inclusive and universal. By establishing particular types of culture as inclusive and universal, intellectuals seek to organize and frame reality in such a way that alternative and oppositional beliefs seem unnatural or without any merit. If not successfully challenged, over time this selective presentation of culture comes to be seen as the taken-for-granted view that structures our everyday notion of common sense.

Cultural control by dominant groups is typically established, not through force, but by a set of interrelated steps. First, dominant groups transmit culture in such a way that they draw a tight boundary around what is considered reality and what is not. Cultural ideas that support dominant groups are included. Cultural ideas that threaten this power are excluded. Second, by not challenging this exclusionary process, subordinate groups essentially offer, over time, their implicit consent to this selective cultural presentation. Third, eventually the dominant cultural ideas are generally internalized by subordinate groups and everyone else in society; this leads to the dominant culture being accepted as a type of common sense, both emotionally and intellectually. Ultimately, this enables the cultural beliefs that dominant groups use to sustain and legitimatize their power and control to seem natural and inevitable.

Because all children must legally be schooled in a modern society like the United States, schools are a major social institution for preserving and distributing culture to the next generation of citizens (Apple, 1979; Giroux, 1981). This makes schools, particularly the curriculum, a key site for the intellectual leaders supportive of and in dominant groups to cultivate hegemonic consent. Because of this, cultural reproductionists argue for viewing the curriculum as a selective tradition (Apple, 1979; Williams, 1975); the curriculum typically covers only a small portion of the ideas, concepts, and beliefs from the enormous range of what could be included. Yet this very selective presentation of knowledge in the curriculum is passed off as the tradition. In short, the curriculum can be part of the hegemony of dominant groups. The selection process of what gets included or excluded from the curriculum is based on the maintenance of dominant social group power and control in society. For example, up until the 1960s and 1970s, U.S. history textbooks in schools excluded a focus on women, the poor, and people of color (Fitzgerald, 1979). U.S. school children would have never known from reading these textbooks that women, the poor, and people of color ever took part in the history of our country.

Curriculum as Ideology

As just discussed, hegemony works in the curriculum by framing reality, by excluding certain subjects or views that challenge the power of dominant groups. Hegemony does this exclusionary work in the curriculum in conjunction with ideology. Ideology, as we noted earlier in the chapter, is the actual content of the beliefs and values that justify a particular distribution of power and privilege in society. Apple (1979) asserted that examples of hegemony and ideology occur in both the overt formal curriculum and the hidden curriculum a number of ways.

One way has to do with the relative status of different portions of the formal curriculum and their accessibility. Technical knowledge such as science and math, as compared to the humanities and arts, is the high-status knowledge that schools attempt to maximize. The maximization of math and science in the public school system works in much the way that unemployment and profit do in the capitalist economy of the United States. For corporations to sustain high levels of profits, 4% to 6% of the labor force must typically remain unemployed at any given time. If corporations had to find jobs for all these unemployed people, it would cut into their profit margin. It would also probably require significant changes in the way jobs and other resources are allocated by corporations. This would potentially be disruptive, requiring reorganization, costs, and time that would probably cut into their profits. Therefore, the current corporate economy naturally generates certain levels of unemployment because it is based on the maximization of profit rather than the equitable distribution of jobs and different resources.

According to Apple (1979), the distribution of curricular knowledge to the various student groups in the public schools seems to work in a similar manner. Capitalist corporate economies need schools to produce students with high levels of technical knowledge such as math and science to enable the continued efficient operation and expansion of the economy. Just as corporations do not worry about employing everyone to sustain their level of profitability, schools also do not have to worry about the distribution of high-status technical knowledge to everyone in the populace. As long as there are enough students with high-status technical knowledge to help maintain and increase the profits of corporate economies, "certain low levels of achievement on the part of 'minority' group students, children of the poor and so on, can be tolerated" (p. 37). Just like the corporate economy, where the maximization of profits sustains a certain level of acceptable unemployment, "so do cultural institutions [like schools] 'naturally' generate levels of poor achievement" (p. 37). Over time, we come to accept that high-status knowledge will not be distributed to schools serving poor and minority students. This practice becomes a kind of hegemonic common sense that makes this inequality seem natural.

There is another way, Apple (1979) believed, that technical knowledge plays a role in sustaining hegemony and promoting a particular ideology. With technical knowledge as the high-status knowledge in the curriculum, it becomes the standard of legitimate knowledge for solving societal problems. Technical ways of knowing place a premium on developing neutral, efficient means for accomplishing society's goals. The essential moral and political questions about the appropriateness of various goals for a democratic society become delegitimatized by an a-critical and technical focus on means rather than ends. By legitimatizing technical knowledge in this manner, students come to believe that schools and the curriculum embody a calm and unquestioned societal consensus on technology as the key to solving America's problems. This, too, communicates a kind of common sense from which the exercise of power in the curriculum, school, and society is silently pushed to the sidelines and out of the sight of students. It also emphasizes the importance of people who have technical knowledge as the ones capable of solving social problems. Many individuals with large amounts of technical knowledge are employed by corporations. The power of corporations is, again, reinforced.

Ideological hegemony is further supported, for Apple, by the silence in the curriculum on the general importance of conflict for society. As noted in the chapter on political social patterns, an older emphasis in the United States on harmony and homogeneity has frequently delegitimated conflict as a positive social force in the country. This nonconflictual bias often infuses the science and social studies materials in the curriculum. However, this does not happen through negative portrayals of conflict, but by the "nearly total absence of instances showing the importance of intellectual and normative conflict in subject areas" (p. 87). In other words, this is accomplished through hegemony, excluding conflict from the reality of U.S. life presented in the curriculum. The actual ideology that is promoted in the curriculum appears to be an inordinate emphasis on consensus and order. As a result, students are not offered an opportunity in the curriculum to view human beings as actively engaged in conflict for the purpose of creating a better society.

Conflict can, in fact, serve to revitalize and improve society. It can bring to people's awareness problems that need to be addressed and it can lead to the creation of new and more just laws. An especially important function of conflict in the curriculum could be providing students with a:

> more viable and potent political and intellectual perspective from which to perceive their relation to existing economic and political institutions. At the least, such a perspective gives them a better understanding of the tacit ideological assumptions that act to structure their activity. (Apple, 1979, p. 99)

By contrast, a consensus orientation in the curriculum can influence students to unreflectively take up a politically quiescent position that sees no need to challenge the current system of class-based power arrangements.

Cultural Capital

Scholars looking at how culture plays a role in reproducing class-based stratification from generation to generation also stress the importance of cultural capital (Giroux, 1983). The concept of cultural capital was developed by French sociologist Bourdieu (1986/1997). *Cultural capital* is the educational background, speech patterns, manner of dress, cognitive skills, and exposure to different forms of media—television, radio, music, movies, museums, books, theater and the arts—that parents pass on to their children. The children of upper class homes acquire very different types of cultural capital from their parents than the children of lower class parents. Upper class children receive relatively more experience with books, intellectual activities, and the arts than their lower class counterparts. As a result, upper class children come to public schools with a cultural capital very much valued by teachers and administrators. Schools further reward and reinforce this cultural capital, facilitating the upper class students' academic success and future job opportunities. Students from lower class backgrounds, by contrast, come to school with a type of cultural capital that is often devalued by teachers and administrators. Consequently, lower class students have trouble succeeding in schools and, consequently, do not achieve the academic accomplishments that will enable them to go on to high-paying jobs. However, due to a focus on individualism, schools will sometimes overlook the contribution that the cultural capital of a particular social class offers children. Upper class children with high levels of academic and intellectual cultural capital may be regarded as loaded with individual talent and intellectual ability by educators, whereas children with the cultural capital acquired from lower class homes may not be regarded as academically able.

Earlier critical scholars believed that educators should not give up in the face of economic and cultural reproduction. There are things that educators can do. The next example demonstrates how teachers drawing on the insights of the reproductionists might combat and oppose inequitable economic and cultural patterns.

ECONOMIC AND CULTURAL REPRODUCTION AND TEACHER-INITIATED CHANGE

To find an example of teacher-initiated change related to economic and cultural reproduction, it is necessary to draw on methods that a few teachers used in the 1970s. The approaches discussed here are not typically found in schools in the late 1990s. This narrative is meant as an example of how the insights from economic and cultural reproductions might be employed in the classroom to initiate change.

> Sheila Sullivan and Samantha Grabowski both taught U.S. history to pre-dominantly working-class students at Spencer High School. Each teacher herself had grown up in a working-class home and strongly identified with the everyday problems and concerns of the students at Spencer. Sheila's parents, uncles and aunts, and even her cousins were long-time members and staunch supporters of the local teachers' union. Samantha's dad had been the president of the local pipe fitters' union. From this family background, both had developed a thoughtful skepticism toward capitalism as an economic system and management of all kinds in the public and private sectors. Personal experience told them that business owners and management frequently did not act in the best interest of workers. Their study of U.S. history in college also suggested that this had been a regular theme over the course of the past two centuries in the country. Consequently, they saw teaching at Spencer High as a means to inform students about the use of power in the United States and its impact on the lives of working-class Americans. Sheila and Samantha felt strongly that through their teaching they could play an important role in empowering their working-class students to struggle against the problems of economic and cultural reproduction in their own lives However, each approached this task in a different way.
>
> Sheila approached this task through the content that she taught. She drew on the work of U.S. historians who used Marx-based theories to interpret the past. These historians placed a large emphasis on the role of capitalism in the

United States and its influence on the politics of different periods. Another important part of the narrative was how capitalists effectively exploited the working class in different ways over time. These historians also described the ideologies that publicly legitimated the power of capitalists. To enrich this approach to U.S. history, Sheila also brought into her classroom different examples of high school U.S. history textbooks. She helped the students to analyze how these textbooks actually played a role in either legitimating capitalist domination in America or highlighted the problems and negative consequences of capitalism. Students learned to analyze these and other U.S. history textbooks in terms of how they obscured issues about social class or made them more salient.

Once students began to understand some of the basics of a class-based approach to U.S. history, Sheila made a transition. She began to tell the history of public schooling in the United States and how schools had played a role in legitimating the economic and cultural reproduction needed to sustain capitalist domination. Public schools did this sometimes by teaching children from wealthy backgrounds how to become the next cohort of leaders in the country and children from poor families to accept their current economic status in life. This was accomplished through the hidden curriculum and through sorting some into formal curriculum tracks that led to college and some into formal curriculum tracks that led to little economic opportunity.

Samantha approached empowering her working-class students in a very different manner. She did it through changing the traditional social relationships in the classroom. Samantha hoped to alter the boredom and oppression common to classrooms organized in what she saw as the same manner as factories and other businesses. For her, many classrooms with the teacher standing in front lecturing and students passively submitting to teacher authority simply duplicated and legitimated the hierarchical authority in the capitalist workplace. This resulted in students rarely developing a sense of autonomy at school or experiencing more egalitarian relationships. In fact, as a result of traditional schooling, most students incorporated into their social identities a sense of being dominated and oppressed as natural. Samantha's class was designed to counter the ways schools often reproduced capitalist economic relationships in the traditional classroom.

At the beginning of the semester, Samantha allowed students to negotiate what topics would be covered in the class as a whole. The class voted on the order in which the topics would be covered. To eliminate an emphasis on competition and grades, a direct importation of capitalism as far as Samantha was concerned, she assured everyone they would receive grades of A. Students were also encouraged to individually select, in consultation with Samantha, historical topics that were personally meaningful to them. A significant portion of class time focused on discussing student thoughts and feelings about the topics from past and current U.S. history. Much of the U.S. history Samantha did cover dwelled on individuals who had broken from traditional social practices or opposed capitalist domination to make a positive change in their lives and for other Americans. Consequently, students were especially to consider how U.S. history influenced them as individuals; additional writing focused on the students' own personal histories and the futures they would like to create for themselves and others. In all these ways, Samantha sought to cultivate each student's sense of autonomy and personal power.

SUMMARY

In this chapter, we focused on the organizational literacy provided by some of the earlier critical approaches—economic and cultural reproduction—for understanding inequitable social patterns in schools. Economic reproduction emphasized the way that the hierarchical, social relationships in schools correspond to the hierarchical, social relationships in the capitalist economy where capitalists and managers exploit and control workers. This is the hidden curriculum taught in schools. Through this hidden curriculum, schools cultivate in students from lower class backgrounds the personality traits—for example, rule following and submission to authority—that will prepare them for jobs at the lower end of the economy. By contrast, the hidden curriculum found in the schools of wealthy neighborhoods teach students to negotiate with authority and to take individual initiative. This prepares students from wealthy backgrounds for jobs at the upper end of the economy. Schools help to reproduce a stratification based on social class. Additionally, schools teach students to understand this reproduction process through the meritocratic–technocratic ideology. This ideology hides the actual social class bias of the capitalist economy and its schools.

Cultural reproduction focuses our attention on how the knowledge distributed by public schools creates and sustains inequitable patterns based on social class. Students from poor backgrounds are not given the curricular knowledge that will enable them to be socially mobile. This is frequently accomplished by disproportionately sorting students from lower class backgrounds into the lower academic tracks of public schools. Another way is through hegemony and ideology in the curriculum. The school curriculum excludes ideas, views, and beliefs that might threaten the control and power of dominant groups in America. An example of this is the absence of any focus on conflict within the curriculum. Instead the curriculum includes an emphasis on technical knowledge because it supports the productivity of corporate capitalism. The curriculum also places a strong emphasis on consensus and order. Finally, teachers and administrators valorize the cultural capital that students from wealthy background bring to schools, which helps these students achieve academic success and eventual economic success. Schools devalue the cultural capital possessed by students' lower class backgrounds, making it difficult for students to negotiate between the culture of schooling and the culture of their homes and neighborhoods. In general, cultural reproduction teaches lower class students not to question their subordinate status in the United States. Problems with both economic and cultural reproduction are discussed in the next chapter on more recent critical scholarship.

RECOMMENDED READINGS

Anyon, J. (1995/1980, pp. 162–178). Social class and the hidden curriculum. In E. Stevens & G. Woods (Eds.), *Justice, ideology, and education.* New York: McGraw-Hill. Anyon provides a very closely observed study of the hidden curriculum in several schools. The writing is also well organized and easy to follow. A nice starting point for those new to critical scholarship.

Apple, M. (1979). *Ideology and curriculum.* Boston: Routledge & Kegan Paul. This book is also a classic. It was one of the first books in the United States to systematically explore the role of ideology in the school curriculum from the perspective of cultural reproduction. Apple's subsequent work has retained an important focus on social justice while contributing to our understanding of how patterns of contradiction, resistance, social movements, gender, and race play a role in public schools.

Bowles, S., & Gintis, H. (1976). *Schooling in capitalist America: Educational reform and the contradictions of economic life.* New York: Basic Books. This book is a classic. It describes, in fairly readable prose, how schools play a role in economic reproduction.

Giroux, H. (1983). *Theory and resistance in education: A pedagogy for the opposition.* Hadley, MA: Bergin & Garvey. Giroux has played a key role in the development of critical scholarship in the field of education. Although this book articulates ideas that move beyond those present in reproductionist works, it provides a very accessible summary of the past trends in economic and cultural reproductionist work. It also offers a very convincing critique of this scholarship.

6

Patterns of Inequality:
More Recent Critical
Approaches to Schooling

◆ ◆ ◆

The economic and cultural reproduction approaches highlighted important connections between the capitalist economy and schools (Giroux, 1981). Focusing on the power of dominant groups to sustain inequitable social patterns in schools through hierarchical social relations and the curriculum also provided important new insights for educators. Additionally, this scholarship made the research community more aware of students from working-class backgrounds. However, as critical scholars spent more time in schools and as the U.S. society entered the 1970s and 1980s, a number of problems with reproduction approaches became apparent (Apple, 1982; Giroux, 1983). Reproduction approaches seemed unable to account for the behavior of working-class students and parents as illustrated by the following narrative.

> Michele Webster stood in her third period language arts class at Redfield Middle School and came to a brief stop in the middle of an activity. She strolled over quietly to two of her students and leaned over to whisper to them. "Jim and Augie, please stop paging through that car magazine. You're supposed to be focusing on Shakespeare right now." Jim looked at Augie and rolled his eyes. Augie laughed. "Thank you, Jim. Thank you Augie. Will both of you kindly chat with me right after class?"
>
> "We got another class to get to," said Jim with mock concern for being tardy to his next class. Some of the other boys sitting around Jim started to chuckle along with Augie. The bell rang and the students gathered their things and started their trek toward the next class.
>
> Jim and Augie walked up to their teacher after class. She looked at them for a moment. They were not bad kids. They just did not see any use for Shakespeare or much of anything related to the writing and reading required for her class. Michele had spoken to many students like Jim and Augie before. She tried to explain to them that the knowledge and skill developed from her class could open up new ways of thinking about the world. Literature and

140

writing offered a window into so many different perspectives that were otherwise unavailable to them. Literature and writing could help them to reflect more critically and thoughtfully on so many aspects of life. Reading was fun. Their lives would be richer from all that reading could offer.

Like the many other working-class kids she worked with, Jim and Augie were not buying this speech either. They actively resisted the knowledge and skills she offered in class. One student, Tony, had clearly felt sorry for her when she tried to persuade everyone about the importance of poetry: "Mrs. W., you'd probably like my mom and sister. They read all the time." It was typical that many of her male students viewed reading poetry and literature as something that women did. Her male students gladly talked about sports, cars, and all-star wrestling with her, but the academic knowledge in her class was obviously of little interest. And, in truth, her female students did not respond much differently. They too resisted engaging with the language arts curriculum. They too found other topics far more interesting; topics such as boys, clothing, and music.

At one point in her career, when her talk about the intrinsic joys of reading failed, she shifted to a more practical argument. Her language arts class, she told students, would provide a foundation for more advanced work with literature in high school. Additional literature classes in high school would be important for getting into a good college. Getting into a good college was critical for getting a good job. She related how she and her husband went to college and were able to get good jobs as teachers. "How much do you make Mrs. W.?" one of them had very gently asked her. "My dad and uncles make plenty down at Gelason Steel. I don't need a college education to get a good job." That had stopped her for a while.

After reflecting on this exchange for quite some time, Michele realized that this same issue was reflected in the wider Olson City working-class community. For many of her students' parents, their lives were tied to local factory jobs that did seem to pay reasonably well. The parents were certainly fierce supporters of their local schools and stood behind Michele's authority as a teacher 100%, as they did most of the teachers in the district. However, the last levy put forward by the district had been defeated by a block of voters primarily made up of working-class constituencies in Olson City and the very wealthy owners and executives of the city's few remaining manufacturing enterprises. Exit polls indicated that the working-class neighborhoods did not see the need for increased taxes to improve the schools. Increased taxes would just take money away from their families. From this levy experience, Michele came to believe there was a basic contradiction between these parents' expressed interest in the importance of schools and their actual behavior. The parents did not seem to be completely supportive of upward mobility through an increased attention to academics. This contradiction was expressed by their sons and daughters in her class.

Based on this experience, Michele came up with a new approach for her language arts class. She tried to link the importance of language arts with the students' future roles as democratic citizens. Michele lectured in class about the importance of an educated citizenry in the United States and that critical reading skills were needed for people to be effective and empowered in dealing with sources of information such as newspapers and magazines. It would also help in selecting appropriate candidates and voting for particular policies. Democracy, she frequently told her class, is a society ruled by its people rather than by a select and elite few. This meant all must learn to participate in the active governance of the community. Having told her students this for so long, it came as something of a shock when one of her female students asked her in an annoyed voice, "Mrs. W. if this democracy stuff is so important for making good people, why don't we have more of it in this class? You make most of the decisions in here, not us." A number of the other students nodded in assent. A few verbalized "Yeahs" surfaced in affirmation of the questioner as well.

Michele was stunned. She had thought that her students and their parents were the ones living a contradiction. Not her. Her students had detected a basic contradiction in how she taught. She stressed the importance of democracy in her content, but her relationship with the students promoted a traditional stance toward authority and social hierarchy. She did not provide students in her class with an opportunity to engage in their own governance. She would have to reflect some more on the contradiction between her content and her teaching practices. It also made her curious about other contradictions that might be present at the Redfield Middle School.

CHALLENGES TO REPRODUCTIONIST APPROACHES

More recent critical scholarship raised several concerns about the reproductionist approaches discussed in the preceding chapter (Apple, 1982; Giroux, 1983). Newer critical scholarship argued that these approaches robbed working-class individuals, let along educators, of any hope of successfully struggling against the power of capitalism. As one noted scholar wrote, "Too often it is assumed that capitalism implies thoroughly effective domination of the subordinate class" (Willis, 1977, p. 175). Similarly, reproductionist accounts of school life tended to depict working-class students as unwittingly forced into their class-based life positions by dominant groups through ideology, hegemony, or hierarchical social relationships. Working-class students were rarely depicted as actively opposing reproduction. A number of critical scholars began to argue that, in fact, students from the working-class and other subordinate groups asserted themselves in school (Giroux, 1983). They, like all human agents, have the capacity to resist, to struggle against the fate structured for them by dominant groups. The work of Willis (1977) became an important example of the significant role that resistance actually played in the lives of working-class students.

Resistance

Willis (1977) followed 12 working-class boys who were friends as they progressed through their final year of high school and into the first 6 months of their work at a factory. Contrary to the reproductionist model, Willis found that these boys did not remain passive and compliant while teachers and administrators attempted to teach the knowledge, skills, and work habits required for success in a capitalist economic system. Rather, the boys developed a counter-school culture in which they actively opposed teachers and other school authorities. They accomplished this by playing jokes on teachers, being truant, roaming the halls during class time, and generally attempting to get out of schoolwork.

In addition, the 12 boys actively disapproved of students who accepted and conformed to the traditional educational ideology that schools offer important skills, knowledge, and attitudes helpful for future occupational mobility. In fact, students who listened to teachers and did their schoolwork were picked on and made the butt of the boys' jokes. A good deal of the boys' critique of academically engaged students grew from their negative view of mental labor. The boys looked down on mental work because it was unlike the physical labor performed by their fathers, older male siblings, and neighbors in the various factories in town. Physical labor was associated with strength and masculinity. Mental labor such as schoolwork was regarded as feminine and was performed by those who were thought to lack the ability for physical labor.

In fact, the boys' behavior in school in many ways mirrored the shop floor culture of the factories, as did their respective relationships to authority. Male shop floor culture put an important emphasis on physical labor over mental labor as a source of pride and identity. Also, the intellectual work of factory managers was looked down on. The boys' talk and actions focused on the power of their physical abilities and the low esteem in which they regarded academics. Father, brothers, and male neighbors working in the factories viewed management as forcing them conform to rules and procedures. Similarly, the boys viewed teachers and administrators as forcing them to conform to the rules and content of school. Male relatives resisted management's exercise of control over them. Likewise, the boys resisted teachers and administrators.

Resistance enabled the boys and the factory workers to carve out a sense of freedom and dignity in the face of having their daily lives controlled by those hierarchically above them in the bureaucratic structures of capitalism. Additionally, the boys' rejection in school of the individual achievement

and competition ideology of capitalism represented their almost uncon-
scious recognition of the unequal reality awaiting the working class as they
step into the economy. Conformity to this ideology may help particular individuals but not the working class as whole. The boys have plenty of evidence
in their neighborhoods of economic reproduction based on social class.

However, in consciously rejecting the mental work of school, the boys
played a significant role in reproducing their parents' working-class status.
In all probability, only mental labor such as school work would enable them
to move up and away from factory work. Hence the boys' resistance to
school, while providing them with some control in the short run, significantly structured their life chances in the long run. This suggested significant problems with reproductionist accounts. Reproductionists stressed the
power of the capitalist economy and its schools to keep working-class individuals in their lower social status generation after generation. Willis (1977)
demonstrated an interplay between capitalism and its culture, as taught in
the schools and the culture of the working class. The culture of the working
class helped the boys to struggle actively against being completely incorporated into capitalism. However, the culture of the working class also operated in conjunction with the economy and schools to sustain and reproduce
a future with less economic opportunity for the boys.

Contradiction

Another important critique of the reproductionist approaches challenged
the assumption that schools completely embodied capitalist social relations
and culture (Apple, 1982; Giroux, 1981). As noted in the preceding chapter, reproductionist approaches viewed the relationships between administrators, teachers, and students as corresponding to the unequal, hierarchical
relationship between capitalists/managers and workers in the capitalist
economy. Also at issue in reproductionist approaches was that the culture
transmitted in schools mostly reflected the interests of dominant groups.
Newer critical perspectives argued that this view was incorrect and overly
pessimistic. More accurately, schools reflected contradictory forces in the
wider society, a struggle between the imperatives of capitalism and the imperatives of creating a more just society. Work by Carnoy and Levin
(1985/1993) attempted to incorporate the concept of contradiction into
our understanding of schools and patterns of inequality.

Carnoy and Levin (1985/1993) agreed that the expansion of the capitalist
economy was an important force structuring public schools; however, so was

America's democratic political system. As they pointed out, "on the one hand, schools reproduce unequal, hierarchical relations of the capitalist workplace; on the other, schooling represents the primary force in the United States for expanding economic opportunity for subordinate groups and the extension of democratic rights" (p. 5). For Carnoy and Levin, these opposing structural forces impinge directly or indirectly on public education and result in schools having to deal with three types of contradictions: contradictions in resource allocation, contradictions intrinsic to the educational process, and contradictions from the reproductive process.

Contradictions in resource allocation deal with the fact that public education is a part of the country's governmental structure (federal and state). Many critical scholars refer to both levels of government as the State. The State in a democratic capitalist society faces opposing demands for the use of its resources. Capitalists desire resources from the State to increase their profitability. Different subordinate groups such as minorities, the poor, the disabled, and people from bilingual and immigrant backgrounds desire the State's resources to help their children acquire more opportunity through schooling. These contradictory demands pose problems for the State because more funding for public education may reduce the resources available for capitalists. This may take the form of greater State tax burdens placed on businesses, taxes that support increased benefits to subordinate groups. Targeting State money for public education and subordinate groups can also result in less State money being available to directly benefit businesses.

There are also conflicts between capitalists and workers over State spending on education. Sometimes capitalists wish to increase educational funding with the hopes of securing a better trained workforce. Sometimes increased taxes to support education are resisted by workers because it cuts into moneys available for their families. In the last decade, U.S. businesses have struggled to compete in the international marketplace and in the process have laid off workers and moved overseas for cheaper labor. This climate of stiff international competition and rising unemployment have made capitalists and workers politically resistant to State spending on education during the 1980s especially.

Contradictions intrinsic to the educational process refer to the fact that schools work to teach students the necessary cognitive and vocational skills to perform well in the capitalist economy. Schools socialize students to accept capitalism as essentially beneficial. And schools teach students to accept as legitimate and fair that individuals from differing race, class, and gender backgrounds are sorted into appropriate occupational slots. "However, at the same time the schools are charged with producing citizens who know and care about democratic rights and equal opportunity" (Carnoy & Levin, 1985/1993, p. 8). Schools spend time teaching things that contradict the goals of preparing workers for the capitalist workplace. For example, schools are required to prepare students to participate in a democratic society. This frequently means that students, compared to workers, have more opportunities for expressing their opinions freely, gaining support through various legal rights, and influencing the path they take regarding courses, teachers, and schedules. Additionally, students learn about the importance of legal justice through government and history classes. Finally, to some degree, students can affect school decision making.

In comparison to the workplace, schools also place more emphasis on social equality. From the 1950s onward, public education has stressed the importance of providing equality in the form of funding, educational processes, and educational results for groups that have historically been disadvantaged in U.S. society. Important social movements and court cases focusing on issues of race, gender, and class equality have given schools an egalitarian thrust that is frequently quite contrary to the traditional role of worker preparation. Similarly, schools have historically held out the chance of upward mobility for many groups. Particularly in the last decades, with the number of small businesses declining in response to the growth of large corporations, advanced schooling remains one of the few paths still available for social mobility. Contradictions arise, however, when far more well-educated individuals are generated by schools than the economy can actually absorb.

The kind of education students receive in schools contradicts the dictates of the workplace. Students are exposed in school to a range of cultural subjects—art, music, drama, physical education—that have nothing to do with work preparation. Some of these subjects may in fact engender values and beliefs in students that are contrary to the materialistic aims of capitalism. Finally, another contradiction posed by the internal dynamics of schools is that, generally, businesses cannot directly control what goes on in schools on a day-to-day basis. Capitalists can certainly attempt to influence the curriculum and different teaching practices but teachers by virtue of tenure and their professional associations and unions can also exert influence on capitalists through political processes.

Another general type of contradiction for schools comes from the reproductive processes itself. At the same time that schools import the unequal, hierarchical relationships of the workplace, they also introduce social conflicts based on class, race, and gender that are generated by these hierarchical relationships. Just as capitalists' attempts to control and dominate the labor force has the contradictory effect of increasing worker alienation, similar dynamics in schools can foster student alienation, teacher alienation, and class-based resistance. For example, although students do have more freedom than workers, much of the structure and content of schoolwork is outside their control just as it is for workers. Students, typically, do not have a choice about whether they go to school. They are compelled by law to do so. Students perform in school for the sake of attaining external rewards such as grades and promotions. As a result, obtaining the appropriate credential sometimes becomes more important than learning for the sake of learning. Because of this, students frequently take shortcuts that result in them having less knowledge than a grade or educational credential may actually indicate. During this process, students frequently become alienated by the schools' attempt to impose the hierarchical social relations of capitalist production. This significantly reduces the efficacy of schooling in preparing an educated workforce.

Capitalist hierarchical relationships at schools can also be alienating for teachers. Unlike other professionals, teachers do not have nearly the amount of autonomy and control that doctors and lawyers do. Their activities are structured and controlled by laws and administrators with little to no input from teachers themselves. Although teachers have organized into association and unions, this frequently puts them in the position of bargaining or striking for wages and benefits against the community of families that they serve. "Since parents pay teachers through taxes, it is against parents' interests [just as it is for capitalists] to have higher teachers' salaries or cuts in teacher services" (Carnoy & Levin, 1985/1993, p. 14).

Teachers working to improve their salaries and benefits through collective bargaining and, if necessary, through strikes can facilitate students and families coming to believe that teachers are greedy and not working in the best interest of the community. Administrators and local businesses have built on a growing anti-union bias in the last decade to create a pubic image of teachers as a typical union just looking for more money. This type of conflict can serve to cast teachers in a similar position as other alienated female workers in business. As the teaching force is 72% female, the gender-based inequality of the capitalist workplace can be reproduced.

By and large, schools teach a version of middle-class culture (Sleeter & Grant, 1993). Students who come from the lower class experience a discontinuity when bringing their neighborhood and family cultures into school (Heath, 1983). Schools subtly and overtly signal to children from lower class backgrounds that they will not do well unless they assimilate to middle-class norms, values, beliefs, and practices; otherwise reduced expectations are held out for lower class children in schools. In response, some working-class children will oppose the class-based agenda of the school and actively work to be seen by their peers as not caring about school. Many will just drop out. This is how a class-based stratification process is reproduced.

Race

Another key criticism of traditional economic and cultural reproduction approaches was that they tended to view class as the most important dynamic for explaining inequality in society (Apple, 1982). Racism and sexism in traditional reproduction accounts were considered of secondary importance compared to the key dynamic of class conflict. Newer critical approaches argued that race and gender dynamics have significant conse-quences for inequality that must be attended to in and of themselves (Weis, 1988). For example, Ogbu (1988) argued for the importance of under-standing the role of race regarding social inequality and schools.

Ogbu devoted more than two decades to investigating the inequitable social patterns in schools and society. He conducted his studies through interviewing and long-term observations of schools, families, and neighbor-hoods. From this work, Ogbu found that inequality cannot be understood solely in terms of social class because the United States also has a racial stratification system. For example, the racial stratification system influences African Americans from different social classes in very similar ways. Afri-can-American children "on the average, do less well in schools than white children from similar social class or socioeconomic backgrounds" (p. 169). This is evident from studies of SAT scores and other academic records. This same pattern is evident for Latinos as well. However, Ogbu made clear this does not mean that membership in a racial group determines academic performance. Rather, "[g]aps in school performance appear and persist only when racial groups are stratified in a caste-like form" (p. 169). Traditionally, a caste system places people from a particular group at birth to a specific rung on the social ladder. Over the life span, generally, this ranking cannot be changed. Ogbu argued that the U.S. racial caste system influences African-American children in schools settings.

Another crucial point to understand about African Americans and racial stratification is that Blacks are a nonimmigrant group. Unlike White Americans, Blacks did not immigrate to this country of their own accord, seeking political and economic opportunity. They were brought to the United States against their will and forced to play a subordinate role in the institution of slavery. Following slavery, African Americans, compared to Whites, were denied access to a range of political, economic, and educational resources that would have enabled them to climb up the social ladder in the manner of White immigrants. When African Americans were finally given access to education they were frequently provided with a curriculum tailored to preparing them for subordinate or menial positions in the economy.

Based on this historical experience, African Americans have developed several collective solutions to their treatment as a caste-like social group. One, they evolved an oppositional cultural frame of reference:

> That is, minorities like Blacks often develop an identity system or sense of peoplehood which they perceive and experience not merely as different but more particularly as in opposition to the social identity system of their dominators or, in the case of Blacks, "White oppressors." (p. 176)

Two, Blacks evolved folk theories that were informally shared amongst family and community members. These folk theories argued that, due to a variety of barriers (political, economic, legal, and educational), African Americans could not succeed in the United States through the typical channels. Blacks created a range of alternative survival strategies to get around these barriers and move up the social ladder. Third, African Americans developed perceptions that the many barriers and forms of discrimination were enduring and built right into the very fabric of many institutions in the United States. This led to a general, collective distrust of White Americans and the institutions they controlled.

Each of these collective solutions has consequences for African-American children in schools. One consequence is that the folk theories of making it tend to regard academic pursuits as an unlikely avenue for advancement. This has been reinforced historically and through watching family and neighbors struggle unsuccessfully to get ahead through the public schools. As a result, some Black families and neighborhoods do not develop a strong academic tradition or orientation. Also, many of the alternative survival strategies put an emphasis on skill and knowledge that is at odds with the skills and knowledge required by formal schooling. Ogbu also believed that the alternative survival strategies may divert Black children from a sustained focus on academics.

A second consequence is that a general distrust of White institutions has carried over into a distrust of schools and their White-dominated staffs.

Vocal public conflicts between African Americans and the White staff of neighborhood schools reflects this distrust. Ogbu indicated this distrust may also be transmitted to Black children. This probably makes them less likely to accept, internalize, and follow school rules related to behavior that focuses on academic performance.

There is a third consequence. The oppositional cultural frame of reference has led African Americans and other involuntary minorities to believe that school learning involves mastering the culture of dominant Whites. Black children may view this as a subtractive process. In learning the knowledge and skills of White culture, their perception is that they must progressively give up the attitudes and beliefs that are a part of their Black culture. Hence, successful academic performance is equated with acting White and "abandoning Black people and Black causes, and joining the enemy, namely, White people" (p. 177).

Being concerned with acting White can lead to troubling outcomes for Black students. By defining many of the behaviors and attitudes necessary for succeeding in school as White, African-American and other involuntary minority children reject those things that will enable them in the long run to break away from the racial stratification system. Another consequence of acting White is that Black peers who retain their oppositional frame of reference may openly criticize and taunt them. Students run the risk of losing their sense of support from Black friends and colleagues. They become isolated and struggle to articulate a new identity for themselves, one that allows them to cope with their discomfort around the rejection of their Black peers and their continuing discomfort around Whites. Many Black students faced with these consequences opt for retaining their oppositional identity and not succeeding academically thereby maintaining the inequitable patterns of the racial stratification system.

Gender

In addition to acknowledging the importance of race, more recent critical scholarship has placed a growing emphasis on the significance of gender. Valli (1983) did an early study of female working-class students in a high school cooperative education program that nicely illustrates some of the important issues in this developing area. One of Valli's starting points for the study was that early family life, peer groups, schools, and the mass media often socialize females to assume an identity constituted by a limited range of roles: wife, mother, and sex object. Accepting these limited roles reproduces a traditional sexual division of labor in which taking care of family and home and being sexually attractive for men becomes a women's primary foundation for her identity. Labor performed outside the home in the workplace becomes a man's primary foundation for identity. This frequently leads to a weak workplace identity for women and their subordination at work and at home. A traditional feminine identity makes women less likely to acquire the education needed for a high paying job or to take something other than a low-level supportive role in the workplace. It also makes them more likely to be dependent on a male provider at home.

Valli (1983) found that a high school cooperative education program actually reinforced these inequitable patterns for female working-class students. The program required these female working-class students to attend classes during the morning to learn various business skills and concepts. In the afternoon, students left school to apply their new knowledge in an actual job setting. Valli's observations and interviews indicated that students were taught a traditional feminine work identity in their morning classes and in their afternoon work experience. Both school and work placed a significant emphasis on students' sexual appearance and behavior. Both settings also required that students model their behavior according to the traditional feminine roles of mother and wife.

For example, during morning classes, students received messages about the importance of their physical attractiveness for securing a job and getting promoted. In one instance, a speaker addressed the students about their appearance and its importance for the interviewing process. The speaker told students they should, "[d]ress like you already have the job, like you would to find a boyfriend. That's a good parallel. You have to attract someone" (p. 220). Similarly, the students' primary teacher coached them on how to speak and answer questions in an interview situation. As a potential model for them to follow, she encouraged them to do this "just like the finalists in the Miss America contest" (p. 220). Appearance was also heavily stressed in evaluations conducted by the primary teacher. In one evaluation the teacher noted that, "She's a pretty girl. She could do a lot with herself and I don't think she's doing it. She could capitalize on that. She was wearing some very sexy shoes the other day" (p. 221).

Students received similar messages at their work sites in the afternoon. For instance, every student but one was placed on a job by the end of the first 2 weeks of the program. The unplaced student was more overweight than the others and also frequently garbed in older, less expensive clothing. It took 2 months for this student to secure an evening position that featured no public contact. This situation was inequitable because the employers' perceptions of this student's self-presentation stood in contrast to several facts Valli discovered. The student had more business experience, a higher class rank (third), a higher score on a standardized math test (90th percentile), and faster, more accurate typing skills than the other students in the class. Valli found that his was not an isolated example. The primary teacher informed the class one day that an employer had called her to complain that the students she was sending for job placements were not pretty enough.

The female students were also sent messages about assuming a traditional identity in the workplace; this happened through the active encouragement students received to assume roles that females traditionally perform at home—wife and mother. Again, this took place both in school and work settings. A speaker brought into the morning classes made clear references to the female worker as a mother figure. She told students about her second career as an office worker. "My first family was all raised and scattered around the country. I thought my parenting days were over. Then, 6 years ago, I began a second family. And in 6 years I had 42 offspring" (p. 226). Similarly, students heard their primary teacher thank that speaker by saying that the cooperative education students "gained so much from being in your office. You became the mother at work that I was in school" (p. 227). The primary teacher reinforced this message in other ways as well.

The different work settings also socialized students to assume the role of wives and mothers. Students had jobs that required them to pick up after and support the presumably more important work of men. In one instance, a student was asked by her boss to fetch coffee for the men at a meeting and to smile while she did this. This division of labor was so taken for granted by students that Valli discovered that students were surprised when this was pointed out. As one student noted, "All of the big bosses are men. I've never noticed that before, but that's the way it is. And all the secretaries are females ... and all the key punch operators are ladies. I've never thought of that before" (p. 225). The differences in roles were also communicated by how males and females were addressed in the offices. Male employees were addressed as "Mr. so-and-so". Female employees were referred to by their first names. Businesses also made distinctions between males and females based on the kinds of work areas distributed to employees. Men were given private or closed-off work spaces on the tops floors of buildings, and women shared large, open areas on the lower floors. Each of these distinctions played a role in communicating superiority and subordinate status that students took note of. One student commented, "I don't know if there are any ladies up there—at the very top." (p. 226).

All the female students in Valli's study did not completely accept and internalize the messages that fostered a traditional feminine identity. Some students resisted what was communicated and some negotiated by appropriating pieces that made sense to them and rejecting pieces they disagreed with. However, in general Villi found that the culture of femininity students drew on and developed during the cooperative education experience resulted in defining wage labor as a secondary or peripheral identity, and affirmed the ideology of male supremacy in the workplace. In doing this students "inadvertently confirmed their own subordination, preparing themselves 'for both unskilled, low-paid work and unpaid domestic service'" (p. 232). Traditional patterns of gender-based inequality were maintained.

MOVING BEYOND REPRODUCTION
AND RESISTANCE

Although a focus on resistance and contradiction considerably enriched critical scholarship, there were still problems with this work. Wexler (1987) provided an important critique of reproduction and resistance approaches to schooling and inequality. He argued that these approaches were not really attentive to historical change. Both reproduction and resistance posited static, eternal social patterns—class conflict between owners/managers and workers or individual workers carving out autonomy for themselves through resistance—that organized industrialized societies like the United States and their school systems. During times of societal stability reproduction and resistance approaches were probably appropriate analytic tools. However, societies such as the United States since the 1970s had undergone considerable change. In particular, three important changes remained unexamined by reproduction and resistance approaches: the power and influence of social movements, the change from industrial society to postindustrial society, and the growing importance of mass cultural forms such as television, movies, and advertising. The first two are discussed directly; the third is presented later in the chapter.

One of Wexler's key concerns was to emphasize the importance of social movements in the construction and changing nature of society. As one scholar put it, "society is best understood as a dynamic set of social movements—as the material accomplishment of conflicting groups struggling for control ... " (Weis, 1990, pp. 9–10). Consequently, schools as an important part of society are shaped by social movements as well. For example, the civil rights movement from the 1950s to the 1970s worked to develop a shared identity among African Americans that enabled them to struggle against the social, political, educational, and economic discrimination that they collectively faced as a people (Omi & Winant, 1994). This new social movement successfully organized large numbers of people who changed many areas of U.S. life including the public schools. Desegregation, multicultural education, and increased federal funding for disadvantaged school systems are just some of the accomplishments of this social movement. The successes of the civil rights movement also helped mobilize other social movements—the women's movement, the antiwar movement, gay liberation—that also significantly altered inequitable social patterns in the United States and its schools.

More recently in the last 20 years, a social movement called the New American Right has become ascendant in the public sphere (Apple, 1993). An alliance of economic, political, cultural, and religious conservatives, this new social movement has successfully contested many of the changes created by the civil rights and women's movements in the 1960 and 1970s. For example, the New Right has successfully transformed the meaning of equity in public discussions in the United States (Apple, 1993). From World War II into the 1960s, the civil rights and other liberation-oriented social movements helped the concept of equity to be linked publicly to a recognition of the oppression of different groups in the country's past. As a result, prominent public officials explicitly acknowledged that African Americans, Latinos, Asian Americans, Native Americans, the poor, and women had been disadvantaged compared to middle and upper class Anglo-American males. These views often translated into federal and state programs such as affirmative action, welfare, and increased educational funding designed to redress past wrongs and create a more level playing field.

During and since the 1970s, the country has experienced a serious economic crisis, the most significant since the Great Depression of the 1930s, as we leave behind the old industrial forms of producing goods and services (Apple, 1993). In this transitional period, minorities, women, and the poor became the scapegoats for people's economic insecurity and frustration as businesses cut thousands of good paying jobs (Apple, 1993; Rifkin, 1995). The public began to view the government as unfavorably advantaging minorities, women, and the poor through particular federal and state programs. Additionally, government funding, targeted to help disadvantaged groups and generated in part through taxes on corporations, came to be seen as a burden to U.S. businesses trying to compete in a more competitive international market.

The New Right successfully played on the anxieties and resentments during this period of economic and social turmoil. This new social movement argued that the government had overstepped its bounds and actually practiced reverse discrimination by creating policies that favored certain groups. The New Right delegitimated the former view that, in fact, certain social groups had been genuinely disadvantaged in the past and that inequitable patterns still subordinated these groups. Individuals exercising independent choice in a free market came to be the New Right's definition of equity. The New Right insisted that in the marketplace all were equal and rewards in the marketplace went to the best competitors. In some ways, this effort by the New Right represent an attempt to revitalize the individualistic social patterns of the early 19th century.

This same emphasis on viewing social life in terms of a 19th-century individualistic marketplace was shifted to public education. As a result of the civil rights and liberation-oriented social movements, minority and poor student achievement had been seen at least partly tied to social disenfranchisement and deficient educational policies and practices. More funding and improved programs for disadvantaged students were developed in response to these beliefs. However, increasingly, the educational discourse of the New Right argued that minority and poor students' underachievement was due to the inability of each individual student to compete successfully in the academic marketplace. Hence, the poor achievement and lack of future social mobility for minority and poor students was their own fault.

A second key focus of Wexler's (1987) critique of reproduction and resistance approaches was that the United States and other industrialized societies were being transformed into postindustrial societies. Many companies in the United States and the rest of the world have increasingly drawn on the power of the information and communications technologies to produce their goods and services and manage their operations. As a result, occupations that work with and analyze computer-based information or operate and maintain new technologies for businesses have increased considerably. It has also resulted in computers taking over many of the jobs done in the past by human beings Consequently, millions of "human beings are now unemployed or under employed in the world" (Rifkin, 1995, p. xv). Compounding this, many U.S. businesses have moved their manufacturing operations to other countries where labor is considerably cheaper. This is referred to this as deindustrialization. Many U.S. communities and families have been devastated by the consequences of deindustrialization in the form of plant closings and the resulting loss of thousands of jobs. They have been forced to struggle with an economic reorganization over which they have no control. "[F]amilies now survive by piecing together the wages of several family members, exhibiting a sense of bitterness and loss as they try to raise the next generation" (Fine, Weis, & Powell, 1997, p. 255). More recent critical scholarship has sought to address the problems associated with the affects of postindustrial society and the New Right on public schools.

SOCIAL MOVEMENTS, POSTINDUSTRIAL SOCIETY, AND SCHOOLS

The work of Weis (1990) offers an example of critical scholarship that has taken Wexler's concerns about social movements and the postindustrial economy to heart. Weis conducted a year-long study of a high school in the city of Freeway (a pseudonym) to see how the shift to a postindustrial society and deindustrialization were influencing White working-class youths. Freeway had recently experienced an economic downturn when a local steel plant had closed in 1983. In its heyday, the plant employed 18,500 people. By the end of 1983, the plant retained a crew of only 370 workers. Weis wished to know how this powerful social reorganization was influencing the identity of male and female working-class youths. She wanted to explore how working-class youths constructed themselves as individuals in response to these changes and, then, how society was being shaped by their new identities and alignment with current social movements.

During the recent industrial past, White working-class male youths, as we saw in Willis' (1977) study, identified with their male working-class peers in school and eventually in the factory. They shared an oppositional stance toward school authorities and, later, factory supervisors and managers. The intellectual work in school that could potentially move them out of working-class jobs lacked a sense of the physicality associated with masculine work. Willis' working-class boys rejected school knowledge and, therefore, contributed to their own future working-class status.

Weis (1990), however, found that the loss of industrial work in Freeway changed how males' and females' working-class identities took shape in Freeway High School. For example, working-class males in Freeway High did not take nearly as oppositional a stance toward school authorities as the students from Willis' study. Male students grumbled a bit and skipped out of class occasionally, but they generally accepted school rules. They recognized that the traditional manufacturing jobs were gone and that school was an important path toward college and the new work opportunities afforded by a higher education. However, at variance with a desire to go to college, they were not very involved in the process of learning. Freeway males did all of their schoolwork, but just enough to get by. Frequently they just copied each other's work. Weis argued that in doing this they exhibited a contradictory code; they attended to the form of schooling, but not its intellectual substance. There was "some apparent conflict operating within the emerging collective identity regarding the value of schooling" (p. 37) that would, contrary to their stated aspirations for upward mobility, keep them from good colleges and eventually middle-class work.

Surprisingly, given their contradictory code regarding school and the lack of jobs in Freeway, male students still believed they would earn enough to have their future wives stay home and care for the house and children. Apparently, despite changed economic circumstances, they maintained an older, industrial working-class vision of the relationship between men and women; men dominated the public sphere of work and women remained in the domestic sphere of the home; they also believed that men, by virtue of earning the money that paid for the household, should have the ultimate decision-making power over their wives and what happens in the home. In the face of postindustrialization, the identity of Freeway's working-class boys continued to be based on a belief that they were other than and better than women.

Another important aspect of identity for the White working-class males at Freeway High was their intense dislike of racial minorities. This antipathy extended to both male and female racial minorities. A notable element of this prejudice was a fear that Black males would be attracted to White working-class females. (White females seemed far less concerned about this issue.) These views suggested that White working-class boys constructed their identity in relationship to minorities as they had to White females. Working-class boys defined who they were by who they were not. They were not females and they were not racial minorities.

Weis (1990) found that female working-class identity at the high school was moving in a more emancipatory direction. Females saw the importance of education for getting a job to be able to support themselves; jobs would enable them not to be dependent in the future on husbands. They were cultivating a primary identity as wage laborers. This was a change from past research such as Villi's (1983), discussed earlier, that indicated working-class female identity was tied primarily to the domestic sphere and secondarily to the workplace. Freeway High females indicated they would only consider raising families once they were settled and had a career started.

Interviews with female students suggested this desire to develop a primary identity as wage laborers was connected to their awareness of the changing economic and cultural circumstances in Freeway. Their own families, friends, and experience had convinced them that—due to a lack of jobs, insufficient skills for the new technologies, and related problems such as divorce and excessive drinking—men could not be counted on. However, this argued that in many ways females were still identifying themselves in relation to men. It was in response to men not being dependable that they valued education as a path toward future employment. Only a few Freeway females argued for jobs and independence as intrinsically rewarding.

The female students also displayed some contradictory behaviors regarding the importance of education for getting a job. To some extent, like Freeway High males, the females were not fully engaged in their classes with learning. They too occasionally did just enough work to get by, seeming to put more emphasis on the form of school rather than its intellectual and academic substance.

Sadly, Weis (1990) observed that Freeway High School actually played a significant role in transmitting a contradictory attitude toward learning to male and female students. Teachers frequently told students how important an education was for getting a job. However, their classroom processes give little prominence to thinking, discussion, questioning, and the active construction of knowledge. Rather, classroom instruction was highly routinized. Teachers lectured on various topics and students took notes with little interruptions. Teachers even gave students explicit instruction on how to write and organize their note taking. This relationship between teachers and students was mirrored by the manner in which administrators related to teachers. Administrators attended to the form of teachers' lesson plans rather than to the substance of lesson content. In all this, the school communicated a contradictory code about schooling to students that the actual knowledge or substance of education was of little importance. Instead, what mattered was eventually getting a diploma, which would lead to a better economic future. Gaining academic knowledge appeared to be a less important goal for the school staff.

Additionally, the school "served to encourage the creation and maintenance of separatist identities along gender and race lines" and supported the notion that "White-male identity [was] superior" (Weis, 1990, p. 81).

The school promoted this inequality in a couple of ways. First, the school bolstered separatist identities for male and female students through the allocation of distinct spaces for male and female school staff. In the faculty lounge and the lunchroom, males and females sat separate from one another and often discussed stereotypical gendered topics. Also, in keeping with the traditional division of males dominating the public sphere of work and, ultimately, the private sphere of the home, male staff sometimes invaded female space in the lunchroom, faculty lounge, and classrooms, but females never went into male space. Also, female faculty occasionally picked up after male faculty in the lunchroom. Implicitly separate spheres for both sexes were reinforced by the school, as was male dominance. Second, the school reinforced separate, hierarchical identities for Whites and Blacks through segregated seating patterns at lunch, teachers' frequent references during school to racial segregation in Freeway neighborhoods, and explicit racist comments by school staff. In both these ways, females and Blacks were constructed as deviations from an implicit norm of White male behavior.

There were flickers of hope in the school for constructing more emancipatory identities. Female faculty sometimes were critical of males. They discussed male sloppiness and gender inequality. Issues of inequality were especially raised regarding the low pay women received as compared to men. Additionally, the school offered occasional challenges to traditional gender identity. For example, in the guidance office, an article that encouraged female students to be independent was prominently displayed.

By questioning traditional male behavior and dominance at Freeway High, Weis suggested that the women's movement and the postindustrial economy played a role in constructing a piece of the new working-class female identity. In fact, a few of Freeway High's females recognized that their identity was explicitly linked to a larger feminist struggle in the United States. However, most of the girls, although they critiqued the traditional female role, did not see themselves as connected to a broader struggle for women's rights. Theirs was an individual response to a set of problems, rather than a first step toward an identification with women as a group. Weis speculated that in the future these females may come to see the importance of aligning with the women's movement; however, they may also decide, based on the lack of good paying jobs for women and societal pressure to be take more traditional female roles, to align with the New Right.

Regarding Freeway High male students, Weis suggested that they may very well end up aligning with the New Right in the future. The New Right very much supports the traditional separation of spheres for males and

females; work and home. Also, through a variety of implicit communications, the New Right also reasserts White male dominance. Each of these
views are congruent with the identity being developed by White working-
class males at Freeway High. As these students enter the economy and
struggle to get good jobs, they will be thwarted by having attended to the
form of schooling, rather than the substance of learning. Consequently, job
opportunities linked to a quality college education will be beyond their
grasp. The frustration of this experience may very well lead Freeway's White ·
working-class males to align with the New Right. Also, Freeway High's
separate spheres based on gender and race may play a role in supporting
their potential connection with the New Right. However, like many of their
female peers, they still view their problems as individual rather than a
collective issue. It remains to be seen what will happen in the future in terms
of their alignment with different social movements.

SOCIAL MOVEMENTS AND WHITENESS

Other critical scholars have made a shift to looking at the way public
discussions and mass-media presentations outside of schools play an important role in creating an environment that promotes inequitable social
patterns in the United States (Giroux, 1992). By writing about inequitable
patterns outside the school, some critical scholars hope to improve U.S.
society as a whole; they believe this activity will eventually help to change
what happens inside schools. A key focus of this new scholarship is the issue
of whiteness (Fine, Weis, Powell, & Wong, 1997), particularly how the New
Right has strategically played on the growing anxieties of White Americans.
    Other factors beside the postindustrial economy have alarmed some
people in the United States. Starting in the late 1960s and growing over the
last 20 years, many White Americans have come to believe that the flow of
immigrants from Asia and Central American and the swelling of urban areas
with minorities threatens their sense of security and dominance in the
United States (Giroux, 1997). Various members of the New Right have
capitalized on these concerns by suggesting that people of color are to blame
for the country's ills and that Whites now face the kinds of discrimination
once faced by African Americans; some conservatives have even argued
that Whites are, in fact, the group currently subjected to inequitable social
patterns. Popular media outlets often echo these ideas. The New Right as a
social movement has been able to gain a good deal of support through this

strategy. Many critical education scholars have begun to focus on this developing identification for Whites and in doing so hope to understand the "impact that the dominant racial identity in the United States has had not only on the treatment of racial 'others' but also on the ways that Whites think of themselves, of power, of pleasure, and of gender" (Roediger, cited in Giroux, 1997, p. 290).

The work of McLaren (1997) provides one example of how critical educational scholars have started to explore this issue. For McLaren, focusing on whiteness as an ideology and a practice is important because of the historical role, as discussed in chapter 1, it played in the subordination of other races. However, because of its prevalence in our daily lives, whiteness is very difficult to identify and tease out for the purpose of challenging it and reducing its affect on inequitable social patterns. Creating a public space in schools where the problems generated by whiteness can be scrutinized, confronted, and then removed offers a potentially hopeful future.

Taking an activist stance against whiteness seems particularly important, for McLaren, given the growing disparity created by the postindustrial restructuring of the economy in the United States and the rest of the globe. The new economy with its emphasis on high-tech skills excludes many from ever having a chance at a job. Workers find it difficult to organize collectively to oppose certain inequitable business practices because company operations are scattered around the world. Frequently businesses find it cheaper to hire part-time employees because they do not have to provide benefits. This leaves many workers without security and health benefits. Wages for workers have been held down in the last two decades because it would reduce corporate profitability for elites who own and operate these businesses.

These business trends have significantly increased the gap between the poor and corporate owners, managers, and information-technology professionals. Businesses have, in fact, recorded record profits from their current operations, acquisitions, and mergers. In the face of this prosperity, the aforementioned winners in this new postindustrial economy have been unwilling to consider dispersing some of these benefits to workers and the less fortunate. The poor in urban and rural environments have been abandoned to poverty, homelessness, and hunger. The Neo-liberal wing of the New Right has legitimated this inequitable situation through its public defense of market-based ethics as the operative ideology for every sector of U.S. life. Neo-liberalism is another way of labeling the New Right's revitalization of 19th-century individualistic social patterns. Neo-liberals argue that there is an opportunity for all to compete equally in the marketplace for jobs. However, the actual reality is that not everyone is served by the prosperity of the current economy. Whites by and large manage and staff the professional positions of the new postindustrial businesses, gather in the profits, and live sequestered from the problems of the poor and minorities in White suburbs.

Whites are reluctant to grasp their privileged positioned in this situation and its ties to the issue of whiteness. McLaren (1997) used the views of William Bennett (1996), former U.S. secretary of education and a New Right public figure, as a case in point. Bennett argued that getting rid of affirmative action would end racial discrimination. Affirmative action is not in keeping with the spirit of Martin Luther King's vision of civil rights for Bennett because it emphasizes a person's race rather than their merits and morality as an individual. He complained that current civil rights workers have caused unnecessary conflicts and undermined a sense of community that was present in the United States in the past. By focusing so centrally on race, current civil rights leaders have undermined this sense of community.

McLaren (1997) contested this view by suggesting four problems with Bennett's arguments. First, Bennett assumed that all groups currently residing in the United States can compete in the marketplace on an equal basis, so that affirmative action is unnecessary. Second, Bennett did not acknowledge the current advantage and domination of the economy by Whites. Third, he did not see that some Whites in the workplace still have prejudicial racial attitudes toward people of color. Finally, Bennett's vision of community in America's past leaves out the fact that the sense of harmony was enjoyed by Whites only, whereas African Americans and other minorities were largely excluded and silenced. In short, Bennett's proposed wish for a society based on colorblindness is "actually a form of race subordination in that it denies the historical context of White domination and Black subordination" (Gotanda, cited in McLaren, 1997, p. 270).

In contrast to Bennett's neo-liberal notion of democracy, McLaren put forward a vision of democracy that confronts the invisible domination of whiteness in the United States. He argued that by contesting this suprema-cist ideology and practice out in public spheres like schools, people can come together in a social movement based on true justice and democratic citizen-ship. For McLaren, by rising to this challenge, we:

> become agents of history by living the moral commitment to freedom and justice, by maintaining a loyalty to the revolutionary domain of possibility, and by creating a collective voice out of the farthest "we"—one that unites

all those who suffer under capitalism, patriarchy, racism, and colonialism throughout the globe. (p. 291)

MASS CULTURAL FORMS AS EDUCATORS

Mass cultural forms such as movies, television, and advertising have come to play an enormous role in the lives of Americans and other people throughout the globe (Gross, 1992). Wexler (1987) and others argued that these mass cultural forms, to some extent, have become a model for reality and a part of our very identities. This is a result of the considerable time many Americans interact with mass cultural forms like television. Critical scholars are concerned that sometimes this happens to the point that, "non-mass-produced alternative images and understandings, and perhaps even the capacity for interpretation itself, are obliterated" (Wexler, 1987, pp. 158–159). In fact, a number of researchers have begun to focus on the way television and movies play an important role in educating children and youth, often in contradictory ways, about issues of class, race, and gender. What makes it particularly difficult to confront these messages is that television programs and movies are products being packaged to get consumers to like them and spend money on them, earning vast profits for media corporations. And, unfortunately, mass cultural forms rarely call explicit attention to the special communication processes they employ to make them pleasing, consumable products.

Giroux (1994) played a key role in focusing critical educational scholarship on the importance of mass cultural forms. As he noted "The electronic media—television, movies, music, and news—have become powerful pedagogical forces, veritable teaching machines in shaping the social imagination of students in terms of how they view themselves, others, and the larger society" (Giroux, 1997, p. 301). Giroux provided readings of various movies and other mass cultural forms to highlight some of their troubling messages. He also encouraged his education students to do the same. Giroux (1993) saw engaging education students with popular culture as part of a project to develop teachers who have a strong commitment to democracy. Popular culture can be an important vehicle for educators and their students to critically discuss the troubling images and beliefs that pose problems for a democratic society. Engaging with popular culture can also offer students the possibility of generating new knowledge and ethical stances about their own current societal situation and the possibilities for struggling toward a better future. Giroux also strongly believed that the notion of popular culture as simply a form of entertainment needs to be challenged. Undemocratic social visions are promoted by many forms of mass culture regardless of how pleasing and emotionally engaging they may be. Giroux held all forms of popular culture up to scrutiny, asking an important question: Do they promote a vision of an equitable society? If not, they need to be challenged.

Giroux (1993) provided an example of this work with his reading of *Dead Poet's Society* (1989), a movie staring Robin Williams. This movie focuses on an exclusive private boys' boarding school in New England. Williams plays Mr. Keating, a new English teacher at the school who a number of the boys come to admire. The administrator and other teachers at the school emphasize conformity to a strict behavioral code and the rote mastery of traditional high culture knowledge. Mr. Keating encourages his students to be individuals, cultivate their own thoughts and ideas, and not to succumb to conformity. The motto that he passes on to the students is to "Seize the day," to live life to its fullest. Bolstered by Mr. Keating's advice, a group of students form a club, the Dead Poet's Society, that meets after the school's curfew to read poetry and enjoy life. Additionally, a member of the club feels emboldened to court a girl from the neighborhood; another, Neil Perry, contrary to the wishes of his father, acts in a school theater production. Toward the end of the movie, Neil's father finds out about his acting in the play, removes him from the school, and threatens to send him to a military school. In response, Neil commits suicide. Mr. Keating is blamed for setting this chain of events in motion and is forced to leave the school.

Giroux's reading of this movie is complex and nuanced; however, especially notable sections focus on issues of race, class, and gender and offer an interpretation that is quite at odds with readings frequently made by audiences. Regarding race, Giroux noted that "[social identities in this film are constructed within an unspoken yet legitimating discourse that privileges whiteness ..." (p. 42). The film accomplishes this by not allowing any of the problems that grow out of racial and cultural difference in society to be visible in the narrative. For example, during the time period in which the movie is set, the United States was struggling with issues of civil rights for African Americans. Not even a hint of this type of conflict is in the movie. The movie presents an image of life in which there is a certain taken-for-granted homogeneity and consensus in which the characters generally operate comfortably.

Concerns related to social class abound in the movie. Most of the students and the families depicted in the movie come from the ruling class in the United States, but there is not explicit recognition of the fact that the vast majority of children in America would not be able to attend this kind of school. More centrally, Mr. Keating's teaching message about seizing the day and living life to the fullest puts an emphasis on the internal experiences of these students from the ruling class. The students never learn how this individualistic, inward focus keeps them from developing an awareness of the privileged nature of their school experience and their actual connection to a social ranking in which many below them suffer in poverty. Students are being offered a chance at self-empowerment rather than a better understanding of inequitable social patterns in society. This is also evident in the character of Mr. Keating himself. His rebellion against the more traditional teaching at the school is for purely aesthetic reasons rather than political or social reasons. Mr. Keating's teaching of literature focuses solely on the development of the individual, rather than seeking a connection with the wider society and the problems of class domination and subordination. Finally, the only student from a lower social rank, Neil Perry, kills himself in the end, suggesting that Neil was not quite able to handle the demands of living comfortably in the cultural context of the ruling class. To some extent, this seems to communicate that some are born to rule and others are not.

The movie also reinforces gender inequality. Women are frequently objectified in stereotypical ways. Keating tells the students that an important use for poetry is to "woo women." During one scene, boys from the Dead Poet's Society have an excited discussion about a *Playboy* centerfold they pass around to each other. Girls are brought to one of the Society meetings, but do not seem to be treated with much intellectual respect. A neighborhood girl is the object of one of the boy's attention simply due to physical attraction. Little emphasis is put on potential friendship or intellectual companionship between the two. Even the boys' attempts to have females admitted to the school appears to grow from a desire for more opportunities for dating and sex rather than an enriched and humane atmosphere.

PATTERNS OF INEQUALITY
AND TEACHER-INITIATED CHANGE

As we noted in the chapter on reproductionist approaches, critical scholars seek to explain patterns of inequality in schools not only for the purpose of critique but also to help create a more just society. From the beginning of public education in the 19th century and on into the 20th century, schools have been regarded as important institutions to alter the inequality generated by capitalism. Mann, sometimes referred to as the father of public schooling, was very clear about the hope provided by education. "Nothing but universal education can counter this tendency to the domination of capital and the servility of labor" (Mann, cited in Bowles & Gintis, 1976, p. 24). "Education, then beyond all other devices of human origin, is the great equalizer of the conditions of men—the balance wheel of the social machinery" (p. 28). Similarly, a group of educators in the 20th century known as the social reconstructionists urged teachers and administrators during the Great Depression of the 1930s to consider the possibility that schools could empower students from all walks of life to facilitate the creation of a new social order—a social order more equitable than the one generated by capitalism (Giroux, 1988).

Contemporary critical scholars believe schools can still perform this function (Aronowitz & Giroux, 1993) because at any moment educators are in the process of either reproducing or transforming ongoing social patterns in schools (Angus, 1985). Similarly, at any moment educators in schools can play a role in either reproducing patterns of inequality or transforming them. Critical scholars Beane and Apple (1995) believed that schools that fully embody democratic principles can make a difference in transforming patterns of inequality for students. Four alternative public schools, Central Park East schools, in one of the poorest areas in the country, East Harlem, New York, support this contention.

Former public school kindergarten teacher Meier (1995) played an important role in starting the Central Park East schools. During her teaching career, Meier found herself frustrated with trying to educate children in meaningful ways in the standard bureaucratic classroom and school. A district administrator offered her the chance to create an alternative school that operated in the manner she believed was best for children. A key beginning point for Meier in developing this new school was her belief in democracy: citizens of the United States governing their country through active and sustained participation. For her, public schools played an important part in fostering the skills, knowledge, and attitudes needed for citizens to support and nurture democracy. In the chapter on communal patterns, we discussed the notion of democracy as it relates to administrators and teachers. Meier's notion of democracy applies to teachers and administrators working together but also stresses the importance of democracy as it relates to students. She was particularly concerned that children from disadvantaged backgrounds have an equal opportunity to participate as fully as possible in the democratic community of the United States. This played a large part in informing the key organizational features she and her colleagues jointly developed over time for the Central Park East schools.

A key feature for the new schools was the importance of size. At the heart of democracy is a sense of people having greater responsibility in actively guiding the patterns that influence their daily lives. For this reason Meier and her colleagues tried to keep the elementary schools and the secondary school fairly small. Fueled by a variety of grants and special funding, the secondary school has 450 students divided into three divisions that themselves are divided into houses of 75 to 80 students. Each house has four core teachers. Class sizes at both elementary and secondary levels are capped at 20 students. The secondary teachers only see 40 students a day; about 15 of the 40 each teacher "sees daily for an extended advisory period—a combination tutorial, seminar, and study hall—and whose families the adviser keeps informed about how things are going" (Meier, 1995, p. 54). This smallness was thought to be key if students (and teachers) were to have a sense of control and active input into the decisions that affected them on a day to day basis. It also allowed for students and staff to know each other well and develop trust and respect. This meant breaking from the more traditional hierarchical authority patterns in schools among administrators, teachers, and students. It also required leaving behind the anonymity of large elementary and secondary schools.

High intellectual standards set for and with all students is another key feature. Every student at Central Park East engages in a common, rigorous curriculum in Grades 7 through 10 because Meier and her colleagues viewed schools as supplying the habits of mind that all democratic citizens require regardless of their occupational future. Their notion of the ideal citizen was modeled after people who exhibit empathy and skepticism (Meier & Schwartz, 1995). For Meier and the Central Park East staff empathy and skepticism were evident if students were in the habit of approaching different life situations and the curriculum areas with five questions in mind: "How do you know what you know? (Evidence) From whose viewpoint is this being presented? (Perspective) How is this event or work connected to others? (Connections) What if things were different? (Supposition) Why is this important? (Relevance)" (p. 30). The curriculum and the assessments are organized around these questions. This also means that students are not tracked into different types of curriculum. To engage a topic area or problem with these questions in mind means working actively and engaging with the full complexity and ambiguity that each subject area or problem presents. This frequently means covering less material but probing in much greater depth. It also means that there is no tracking into college preparation and vocational levels for students. To reveal the mastery of this type of learning also requires that students exhibit these habits of mind in other than multiple choice and short answer types of assessments. Students exhibit these habits of mind through papers, projects, single and group presentations, experiments, and solution proposals.

A third key feature is that Meier and the Central Park East staff dealt directly and thoughtfully with equity issues (Meier, 1995). The schools have an ongoing Race, Class, and Gender Committee that meets to reflect on different educational practices and problems and how they impact equity for the student body. The committee also sets up workshops and brings in speakers to help the staff deal more effectively with issues of race, class, and gender as it relates to students (and to staff). This has not completely solved problems like racism but it has enabled a continuing dialogue and growing awareness among staff of how better to approach and deal with these issues in classrooms and the school as a whole, and it points to where future growth and discussion still need to occur. This has fostered a climate in which equity issues can be discussed openly by faculty and between teachers and students (see Meier, 1995, for a complete discussion of how the staff developed the skills to obtain these results). Teachers will often present curriculum to students related to patterns of inequality regarding race, class, and gender. Hence, Meier and her colleagues attempted to model democratic practices by ensuring that their own organizational and classroom patterns did not unconsciously promote inequitable patterns. Students are also brought into these democratic practices by making them aware of social inequities and by opening up these problems to be addressed through the empathy and skepticism of thoughtful habits of mind developed in the rest of the curriculum.

A fourth feature is empowering students by honoring significant issues that arise in their home communities or the school itself and making these available for discussion and a part of the educational process. A White jogger was attacked a few blocks from the Central Park East secondary school and the public climate following the event cast the adolescents from the East Harlem neighborhood as a threat to the general well-being of White, middle-class New York. The size and flexibility of Central Park East enable Meier and her colleagues to work with students regarding the assault and to help them deal with intrusive inquiries by the local press. A similar response by the staff was possible in the wake of the Rodney King trial verdict and the ensuing conflicts in Los Angeles.

These features were not implemented overnight, nor were they attained without controversy, conflict, problems, time, and energy. Democracy, as one scholar noted, requires a tolerance of certain amounts of messiness

(Beyer, 1995). Meier and her colleagues started developing the Central Park East elementary schools in 1974. The secondary school was not initiated until 1984. However, these schools have proven to be very successful for students who frequently have not been well served by traditional bureaucratic organizational patterns. Nearly 75% of the students at these schools are African Americans and Latinos from poor or low-income backgrounds. Approximately 20% of the students qualify as handicapped according to state guidelines. As noted earlier, many of these kinds of students drop out and do not finish their high school education. In 1991 the Central Park East Secondary School had a graduation rate of 95%. Additionally, 90% of those graduating went on to some form of college and remained there. The Central Park East schools have continued to maintain these high levels of graduation and college attendance in subsequent years.

THE BENEFITS OF CRITICAL APPROACHES
FOR UNDERSTANDING INEQUALITY

Critical approaches offer a number of benefits to educators that help clarify patterns of inequality. In particular, they make us aware of the importance of the economy in shaping schools and their patterns of inequality. They sensitize us to the possibility that educators themselves may inadvertently play some role in fostering patterns of inequality. They provide some analytic tools to understand the contributions of the capitalist economy to patterns of inequality

We would hardly argue that a student's ability, willingness to work hard, and family background do not significantly affect academic performance. However, there are other factors that make a difference. Similar to our reluctance to view politics as important to schools, we as educators have an identical reluctance to view economics as important to schools. Critical approaches highlight for us the important role of the economy in shaping patterns of class inequality in schools and society at large. More recent critical approaches also accent race and gender dynamics as they relate to schools and the economy.

We do not believe that any educator consciously attempts to reinforce existing patterns of class, gender, and racial inequality with their students. Critical approaches do, however, give us pause to rethink some of the unexamined patterns in schools such as the hidden curriculum, the formal curriculum, and tracking. We may inadvertently structure relationships between teachers and students and administrators that perpetuate stratification based on class, race, and gender. We may not provide certain kinds of curricular experiences for some groups of students that result in inequality. We may even allow less funding for other people's children in poor urban and rural areas because those children are not our own (Kozol, 1991). Critical approaches bring these unexamined practices to the forefront.

Before the Cold War with Soviet Russia following World War II, there was a long-standing critique of capitalism in the country (Noble, 1985). U.S. citizens frequently vocalized concerns regarding how the intense competitiveness of capitalism and its unceasing grasp for profits eroded a sense of morality, stability, and community (Pocock, 1975). Many Americans also worried about large business corporations wielding inequitable amounts of power and influence. The fear of communism from the 1950s until the recent fall of the communist-based governments tended to create a political climate in which criticizing capitalism became highly suspect and in some cases nearly a treasonous act. These older critical traditions were silenced as a consequence. The renewal of critical scholarship in the last 25 years has provided an important service by restoring these arguments to the public debate about inequality, pointing out that capitalism is not perfect; it has problems and these problems impact schools.

THE LIMITATIONS OF CRITICAL APPROACHES

Like anything else, critical approaches have drawbacks as well as benefits. One problem is that they tend to focus on broader societal patterns that impact school organizations and, as a result, tend to have underdeveloped discussions of the detailed particularities that constitute school organizational processes. A related criticism is a lack of detail about how daily school organizational processes foster inequalities for students from different backgrounds.

Although some critical education scholars have focused on school organizations as the primary unit of analysis (Anderson, 1989; Angus, 1985; Bates, 1987; Foster, 1982), these efforts have not been built on and expanded nearly to the extent that they might be. New critical work has been done in looking at business organizations (Aktouf, 1992; Alvesson & Willmot, 1994), but little has been done recently regarding schools. The images presented of schools by critical scholars tend to be somewhat sketchy and not fleshed out with much detail of the daily goings-on between teachers, teachers and administrators, students and administrators, and school staff and parents. There is a framework for analyzing schooling in general but not really one for understanding what goes on in a specific school. Work still needs to be done on creating a richer, more complex picture of individual school organizations from a critical perspective (Angus, 1985).

This limitation is very much related to the one described earlier. Because critical approaches lack a rich, complex picture of school organizational processes, many of the important details that clearly explain how inequality is sustained and/or transformed on a daily basis are lacking. This makes understanding the claims of critical scholars regarding inequality difficult to envision sometimes and it detracts to some extent from their believability. More work needs to be done on explaining the small, subtle, everyday interactions between all the participants in school organizations that result in patterns of inequality based on class, race, and gender being sustained. This needs to be done for the purposes of understanding inequality and also for providing educators the insights to change their classrooms and schools.

SUMMARY

In this chapter we discussed how more recent critical approaches can offer the organizational literacy to understand inequitable social patterns in U.S. schooling. Looking at resistance provided insights into how working-class students struggled against capitalism in schools but at the same time played a role in reproducing their working-class future. The concept of contradiction offered an understanding of how the imperatives of both capitalism and democracy structured the State's allocation of resources to public schools as well as conflicts in the reproductive processes and educational processes of schools. A focus on race and gender highlighted the significance of other dynamics, besides social class, that influence inequitable social patterns.

New critical scholarship has challenged different aspects of the reproduction and resistance approaches. This scholarship offers an organizational literacy that emphasizes the importance of social movements in the dynamic changes and shape of the United States and its schools. A social movement called the New Right has played a particularly important role in the last two decades in shaping public discussion and policies about schooling and its relationship to patterns of inequality. Additionally, new critical scholarship calls our attention to a shift in the United States and other large countries from an industrial economy to a postindustrial economy. The use of information and communications technologies has significantly altered how businesses operate. In this transition, millions of jobs have been eliminated, leaving many people unemployed or underemployed. The New Right and the shift to a postindustrial economy has had an important influence on working-class students, schools, and patterns of inequality. It has also affected the sense of identity and dominance of White Americans in the United States. Currently, mass cultural forms such as television and movies seem to be playing a more significant role in our society in educating youth. The messages communicated about race, class, and gender in these mass cultural forms are often contrary to a vision of democratic community.

PRACTICE CASE—STRUGGLING
IN FELTON'S SCHOOLS

In the last 30 years Felton had been transformed just like many other northern cities by a series of large-scale social and economic changes. Following World War II and moving into the 1950s, large numbers of African-Americans emigrated to the city from the south. They moved to escape discrimination, low wages, and little hope for future social and economic opportunity. Felton, although still highly segregated in its residential patterns, offered a range of freedoms and possibilities many Blacks only dreamed of in the South. Felton's booming factories also provided plenty of employment with relatively high wages. The city's population swelled in response.

The federal courts mandated the desegregation of Felton's public school system during the late 1960s. Bussing was one of the key practices adopted by city officials to meet the demands of the court for racial balance. However, bussing appeared to exacerbate the growing flow of Whites out to the new suburbs surrounding Felton. White families reported a range of motives for leaving: concerns about deteriorating city schools, the safety of family members, and decreasing property values. Many meetings were held across the city to quell people's fears. However, little seemed to alter the exodus to the newly developing suburbs such as Highland Hills and Galdonia. By the middle of the 1980s, a city that had once been 70% White and 30% African American had nearly reversed to 60% Black and 40% White. In conjunction with this demographic shift a considerable number of White-owned businesses and service professionals also relocated to the suburbs. Many of those remaining in the city were poor and struggling financially to maintain their families and neighborhoods. Their plight was not made any better by other changes in Felton.

Like many once heavily industrialized cities, Felton had been devastated by economic trends during the 1970s and 1980s. To compete in the new global economy, Felton's largest employers argued they could no longer profitably maintain their locally based operations. They closed their doors and moved their companies to the south or overseas. Seemingly overnight, thousands of Felton's citizens were unemployed. Many families already struggling were devastated. Hope for recovery of the city's once prosperous economy began to dwindle.

These changes shook Felton's public school system as well. With significantly less wealth in the community from affluent residents, businesses, services, and especially large industrial concerns, Felton's property tax base shrank dramatically. There were now scant tax dollars to pay school staff, replenish dwindling supplies, replace out-of-date textbooks and library holdings, and particularly to maintain and fix Felton's crumbling school buildings, most of which had been built at the turn of the century. Felton residents overwhelmingly voted to tax themselves at higher rates than many of the affluent suburbs, but the city simply did not have enough property wealth to change the grim financial picture for its schools. Felton's public schools squeaked by each year, but barely.

The new city administration headed by Mayor John Connelly worked vigorously to bring large businesses back into Felton. Initially this held out the promise of a growing property tax base to help the schools out, but that promise was short-lived. To compete with neighboring cities in attracting large businesses back into Felton, Connelly was forced to offer substantial tax abatements to nearly all of the newly arriving businesses. Abatements let the new businesses off the hook with sizably reduced tax bills that historically had helped pay for the city's schools. Felton residents now had more jobs and unemployment went down, but most of these jobs paid much lower wages than those in the past. Consequently, Felton's schools still continued to spiral into debt and provide a lower quality of education compared to the surrounding suburbs.

One of the few recent glimmers of hope for Felton's schools was that Standish Company, a large and successful food products firm, decided to form a partnership with Dawson High School. Standish Company helped set up a new computer lab (albeit with older, used computers) and pumped a little money into the school's academic and vocational offerings. Standish was particularly generous in supporting Dawson's food services cooperative education program. Many of Dawson High School's food services students like Tyrone Wheeler also received job placements at Standish Company.

For Tyrone, the Standish job in the afternoon was the best part of his day. He liked the hands-on nature of working with the food production machines. He even did not mind working on the assembly line. He could operate the hopper that sprinkled sugar on products that rolled by on the conveyer belt below him and still find time to think about his life and especially Dawn Bledsoe, his girlfriend. Tyrone also liked the older Black brothers he could hang with during breaks and lunch. They never let a chance go by during breaks and lunches to crack jokes about the managers and scientific staff who paraded around the building acting important and telling everybody else what to do.

Tyrone had started to form a friendship with one of the older brothers, Maleic. Maleic ran the large candy ovens, a job he had moved up to after working the assembly line for a number of years. Maleic had a great car and great clothes.

Clearly pay checks got a lot bigger when you moved up to the kind of job Maleic had. Although currently Tyrone had absolutely no complaints about his own his pay check. Getting paid every two weeks made every hour at work interesting and compelling somehow.

The second best part of the day for Tyrone was the food service classes at Dawson just before going to work. His teacher, Mr. Tyler, gave him lots of good information about possible food service careers. Mr. Tyler also regularly dispensed practical tips about getting along with coworkers and supervisors and avoiding conflicts and problems. There was also a solid feel to the class. All the students liked Mr. Tyler, and he liked them as well. Everyone joked with everyone else. Nobody got uppity or too serious, not even Mr. Tyler. You could talk to him like a friend and not worry about being misunderstood. It was nothing like the worst part of Tyrone's day.

Tyrone intensely disliked his college-prep U.S. literature and geometry classes in the first part of the morning. He found the information in these classes completely irrelevant to his life. The teachers droned on and on in endless lectures or crammed all three blackboard with enormous amounts of notes, outlines, and homework. Even the few Blacks in the class were dull. They just sat there, obediently listening, taking notes, or occasionally discussing. To bring a little excitement to his morning, Tyrone frequently hassled the instructors and the students with jokes and put downs. Not surprisingly, he found himself frequently referred to the vice principal's office.

The only reason he the took the classes in the first place and stayed with them was that Dawn hounded him repeatedly in the last year about the importance of going to college. She had even said something about his chances for mobility, a word she picked up in history class. Where did she get off telling him about mobility? She had been changing lately. Even her girlfriends in the cosmetology cooperative education program noticed it and were beginning to talk. Other new words had been creeping into her spoken language and her tone of voice had changed. She had seen him going into the vice principal's office again. Later that night when they got together, she had gotten all uppity about working at Standish for the rest of his life. What was wrong with Standish?

Dawn was tired of the stares and the whispers when she raised her hand in class. "some people think they better than other people, " she heard somewhere in the back of the room after Mrs. Ryan, the cosmetology teacher, praised her for answering a question. And, once again, she found herself wishing for the bell to end cosmetology class so she could make her way to the next class, college-prep English. No one bothered her in this class when she raised her hand or offered an opinion. Most of the White students pretty much ignored her except when everyone was placed into small discussion groups. Then they listened to her and shared their own reactions to the assigned stories.

Strangely last spring, Dawn had found herself caring about the things they talked about in English class. She had an especially strong reaction to Alice

Walker's *The Color Purple*. The book spoke to her. The character Celie seemed to know her inner-most secrets. She never realized a book could do that to you. She found herself alert in class after that in a way she had not been. This alertness spilled over into a history class. Mrs. Thompson, her only African-American teacher, started to show her a lot more attention. At the close of the school year, Mrs. Thompson asked her if she was considering going on to college. Dawn felt like the wind had been knocked out of her. She and Tyrone had talked about getting married after their senior year. They had even started to plan their lives together. Tyrone would work at Standish and she would continue to work at Bellini's Beauty Shop, her cooperative education placement, until they started having children. At that point she would quit and stay home to raise Ty's children. Mrs. Thompson's question had begun to slowly draw her inner thoughts away from these careful plans. She even found herself more distracted at Bellini's in the afternoon.

Mr. Bellini tapped her on the head and she came out of her reverie with a jolt. "Mrs. Polina deserves to have your full attention when you wash her hair," said Mr. Bellini in a loud, impatient voice. Dawn realized that she had been daydreaming while shampooing a client's hair. Mr. Bellini stared at her with angry eyes and she quickly moved to rinse the shampoo out of Mrs. Polina's hair. However, she still continued to be distracted by Mrs. Thompson's question. What would it be like to go on to college? What would Ty think? What would that character, Celie, from *The Color Purple* do?

EXERCISES

1.   What characteristics of the critical approach do you find present in this case? Create a concept map or word web to explore the conflicts that are present. Using the map or web as your guide, link each of the characteristics of the critical approach to the specific action or event in the case that exemplifies those ideas.

2.   If you were to design a school program to address the concerns about education the critical approach raises, what would you include? How would you design professional development and educational opportunities for faculty to explore these themes? Is it possible to organize a school according to these themes? What difficulties might you face if you were to choose to implement some of your ideas in your current educational setting?

3.   The critical approach challenges many of the ideas and ideals we hold for schools. One example would be the idea that kids from poor or disadvantaged homes have parents that just don't care or don't have time to attend to their child's learning. What are your ideas and opinions on such statements? How would the critical approach challenge you to think differently about statements such as these?

READING YOUR OWN SCHOOL

Consider your own school. How are the ideas and concepts presented in this chapter present in your work setting? How might these ideas help you to make sense of your school and the events that occur there? List five examples of how you see these concepts in practice at your school; examples might include the actions of administration, staff, faculty, students, or parents; or specific issues or events such as a curriculum adoption or annual school celebration. Link each event to an idea or concept presented in this chapter. Do you think these actions or events facilitate student growth and learning, faculty and staff efficacy, and sense of well-being? Or do these actions or events create barriers to student growth and learning, faculty and staff efficacy and sense of well being? Finally, how could you use these ideas to initiate positive change within your school setting?

RECOMMENDED READINGS

Apple, M. (1993). *Official knowledge: Democratic education in a conservative age.* New York: Routledge. This book provides a very useful discussion of the New Right and the reasons for its recent social and political ascendance. The book also discusses the various ways the New Right has sought to influence public schooling in the United States.

Fine, M., Weis, L., Powell, L., & Wong, L. (Eds.); (1997). *Off white: Readings on race, power, and society.* New York: Routledge. This edited work offers a range of thoughtful discussions about the role of whiteness in the United States and its schools. The book also offers an opportunity for someone new to critical scholarship to be exposed to many different authors working in this area.

Macleod, J. (1995). *Ain't no makin' it: Aspirations and attainment in a low-income neighborhood.* Boulder, CO: Westview Press. This is a very readable study of poor African-American and White male students and the process by which many of them end up later in life in the same social class as they started life. The author also provides a very clear overview of different theories that attempt to account for the boys' lack of social mobility.

McLaren, P. (1997). *Life in schools: An introduction to critical pedagogy in the foundations of education* (3rd ed.). New York: Longman. This book was one of the first introductions to critical education scholarship in the United States. It offers a helpful overview of some of the major concepts for critical educators and their application to issues of inequality.

Storey, J. (1996). *Cultural studies and the study of the popular: Theories and methods*. Athens: University of Georgia Press. This text provides an exceptionally readable introduction to the study of popular culture. The author describes a range of different theoretical and methodological approaches to popular culture.

Weis, L. (Ed.); (1988). *Class, race, and gender in American education*. Albany: State University of New York. This edited work was one of the first books to look comprehensively at issues of class, race, and gender and their influence on schools. The book also offers specific qualitative and quantitative studies of these issues, and exposure to some of the theories that guide critical scholarship and discussions of inequality.

7

Patterns of Inequality: Feminist Approaches to Schooling

◆◆◆

It is generally acknowledged that teaching is a woman's profession (Apple, 1982, 1985; Benz, 1996; Regan & Brooks, 1995; Stone, 1994). Since the 1960s, the context of education has been one of various functional approaches toward persistent problems in public education: problems of instruction and curriculum; of classroom and schooling organization; of relationships of teachers, students, parents, and the larger community; of positionings of race, class, and gender; and so forth. The lives of women are related to all of these. What underlies these considerations is that in spite of continual efforts at reform (some with considerable effect on improvements in student achievement and teacher empowerment), educational patterns of inequality continue. Some students learn and some do not, some progress and some do not, some earn diplomas and other credentials of schooling and some do not. Although many students do prosper as scholars and human beings, many more do not. Many who do not are girls and women. This chapter continues the focus on patterns of inequality begun in the last chapter by using the work of feminists as another form of organizational literacy to read and interpret these patterns. Feminists argue for school organizations to be founded on an ethic of care for all members of the school community. As the following story illustrates this is not an easy task—gender role socialization runs deep in our culture.

One of eight high schools in a southwestern school district, Howell High School is located within the boundaries of a large urban center. Howell is a large school with 2,700 students from an ethnically and culturally diverse student population. The school is the newest of the eight in the Allyn district and was designed to focus on a multicultural curriculum. In an effort to create a learning environment that would support rather than detract from the multicultural focus, student-focused education has become a cornerstone of the school's scheduling plans, instructional focus, and curriculum planning. In the principal's words: "We wanted Howell to be a school in which each student finds a home, a family to support their learning, where they can focus on academics and not have to move around in a mad scramble to establish themselves socially before being able to attend to their school work."

The school has embraced block scheduling and thereby reduced the number of teachers students see daily to only four each semester. Furthermore, the block teachers are teamed, allowing for interdisciplinary planning opportunities and more flexibility in class scheduling. In practice, a student taking physics is concurrently enrolled in a complementary mathematics class that uses a problem-solving approach to create an opportunity for real-world application of the course skills. Although this does occur at some times, the reality is less glowing. Teachers already stressed by trying to squeeze a full year of study into a semester attempt rarely have time to follow through on such interdisciplinary units.

The most successful of these teams is that of Brian Chavez and Abilene Walsh. Brian, an English teacher, and Abilene, a social studies teacher, work together on the 11th-grade team devoted to developing a curriculum attentive to the incorporation of current events in the surrounding community in the daily study of students. The charge is a cumbersome one. Teachers can rarely plan lessons more than 1 week in advance and often are left scrambling for supporting materials from the local library or the county courthouse. Yet students appreciate and support their efforts. Research into local history and culture has become a commonplace addition to many student assignments Additionally, students have been able to draw on their own family history and biographical stories to enrich the school's academic focus.

So when a news story devoted to the presence of a glass ceiling for women in the local industrial plants became an important news story, Brian and Abilene took the opportunity to develop and discuss issues of equity and equality in the larger historical and current culture of society. The news report was in many ways typical of the kinds of stories many local stations often run. Promoted as investigative journalism, the story highlighted the struggles of seven female plant workers to obtain management level positions and salary increases equal to that of men. Each woman featured in the story was interviewed from behind a glass partition, thus increasing the drama of the news report while protecting the women from possible repercussion. The stories the women told were poignant. Predictably, management's response to the series was to create a task force to study the matter while proclaiming to the media that equality has always been a focus of the plants.

Brian and Abilene showed the series in its entirety to the combined classes and invited the reporter in to discuss the making of the story as well as to provide background for the study of women's issues in history and the surrounding communities. The discussion progressed well and students asked thoughtful questions of the reporter. The conversation quickly become one of the males questioning the real needs of the women in the story.

Many cheered when a male student from the back of the class suggested that the women "shouldn't be promoted to management since they'll just quit to have babies anyway." Another heatedly decried the whining of the women in the story, stating, "I don't see the problem here. They shouldn't expect the same jobs that men get. Men should be able to be men and that means getting more money than women." Finally, an outspoken female student loudly suggested that the problem was, "Guys are used to getting all the attention and they just think that they deserve everything. Look at how this school is—the guys get football and all the sports attention and the girls get nothing." Another girl quickly added that, "Even in the classroom the boys get most of the attention." A boy countered with, "Yeah, all the punishments."

At this point, Abilene jumped into the conversation and suggested that research in schools did support both of those points. She cited some research from a study she recalled that suggested boys got called on more often and did receive more attention than girls in similar instructional settings. At that point, Brian suggested the classes might want to study the issue. He suggested keeping track of the number of times students spoke in class and creating a series of projects designed to focus on the equity issue in schools. Among his suggestions for projects were counting the number of references to women in the history books they used, developing a study of prominent women in the local area and doing their own home follow-up interviews with some women in their families. The ideas were not met with great enthusiasm. The male members of the class laughed loudly and the female members seemed to "shrink into their seats," Abilene later recalled. The discussion continued until the period ended and the students were dismissed for the day.

Dejected, the two teachers discussed the class. They were both amazed by what they viewed as the lack of empathy by the male members of the class and the lack of spunk demonstrated by the female members in the discussion. They decided that the only way to create a sense that this was an important issue was to "drive the point home and not retreat." As Abilene noted:

> It would have been really easy to just forget it. To say we missed on this topic and move to another. But my gut told me we hadn't missed. That we had hit a major important point here and we needed to pursue it.

The question remained how to do so.

GENDER IN SCHOOLS AND SCHOOLING

Any understanding of the significance of gender in our school organizations is based on information about where men and women and boys and girls are located in that system and the wider society. Historically, when public schools began in the 19th century in the United States, women were generally relegated to the private sphere of the home, responsible for a variety of domestic tasks such as raising children (Allison, 1995; Evans, 1989). The public world of work and, especially, politics was the place of men. This meant women were excluded and invisible in the key arena in which the collective fate of the U.S. people was debated and shaped. The history of women in the United States as a narrative story details the active struggle of women to enter the public sphere and visibly partake of the social, economic, and political opportunities in the country and to stand as equals with men in deciding the policies and practices that guide daily life (Evans, 1989).

There have been barriers along the way in the course of this struggle. In the first half of the 19th century, girls and boys attending the rural schools that dominated the educational landscape were very much taken for granted (Tyack & Hansot, 1992). However, there were clear differences regarding the particular spheres and future roles boys and girls were to be socialized to play later in life. One 19th-century educator spoke for many when he wrote about the desired outcomes of public schooling: "Useful. Not a piano, French, Spanish or flower daub education, but one that will make the men scientific farmers and mechanics and the women fit to become ... husband-honoring wives" (Robinson, cited in Allison, 1995, p. 93). The belief that education should prepare girls for domestic roles and boys for the public world beyond the home continued to shape educational practice into the 20th century. A teaching manual from the early 20th century informed new educators that girl students "are not expected to choose trades or professions for life. Every moral girl should look forward to homemaking and be fitted for domestic duties" (Dinsmore, cited in Allison, 1995, p. 207). Current educators struggle with the historical legacy of domesticity and the public invisibility of girls and women. Feminism has provided an important body of thought to aid educators in this struggle.

Feminism, like most broad categories of study, accommodates several varieties of thought under the term. No short chapter can be exhaustive in its discussion of the competing theories feminism offers us for study. However, we can begin to develop the ideas that inform the greater body of knowledge on feminist thought. The presentation here provides only a partial answer to the question, "What would a feminist school organization look like?" However, what continues to fascinate us is the way in which even these partial answers intersect with ideas our students already hold about the development of school as places of caring and concern for all its members.

Here, we try to explain and develop the ideas included in the broader discussion of feminist thought and place those ideas directly within the walls of our nation's school organizations. This chapter tackles those ideas in four ways: First, we begin by discussing the foundational ideas of equity and equality; second, we create an argument for the need to focus on the development of girls and women in school organizations; third, we describe and examine two forms of feminism—liberal and psychoanalytic; and finally, we discuss the development of feminist school organizations where caring and relational leadership can be established.

EQUALITY AND EQUITY

As we work to define feminism and the related ideas of a feminist school organization, it is important to develop two concepts that affect discussion in these areas. Although many teachers, administrators, parents, and students use the terms *equality* and *equity*, few understand the distinction between them. It is important that the two are distinguished from each other in that they provide very different approaches to solutions for gender-based inequality in schools.

As with many terms, stories provide the best definitions. Imagine you are heading for a visit to the doctor's office. Your ear has been bothering you for a week and you decide it is best to see a professional to determine if you are in need of treatment. On arriving at the doctor's office you find a close friend sitting in the waiting area. Her leg is propped up on a pillow and a bag of ice sits atop her ankle. She fears it is sprained or perhaps broken. The doctor is running late and offers to chat with you both briefly to determine who should be seen first and who can wait a while longer. Together the three of you determine that your friend should be seen first—her pain is greater. The doctor treats your friend and then calls you into the office. She mentions that your friend has been sent for x-rays and proceeds to check your ear and write a prescription for an antibiotic for a possible infection. Finally, you leave to get your prescription filled at the local pharmacy.

In this example, both you and your friend have been treated equitably—that is, you both received treatment commensurate with your illness or injury. Had you both received the same treatment, either you both were written prescriptions for antibiotics or you both had your ankle x-rayed, you would have been treated equally yet one of you would not have had your needs met. Equal treatment is just that; the same treatment; equitable treatment means giving attention to individual needs.

Schools are often faced with the equality and equity dilemma. Providing programs that treat boys and girls equally is difficult enough but finding programs that treat them equitably is even more difficult. In fact, as teachers work to develop classrooms that embrace issues of equity for previously neglected students, they often encounter resistance from students who previously have enjoyed an unequal share of the attention (Lundeberg, 1997; Orenstein, 1994).

SHORTCHANGING GIRLS

In a landmark study, the American Association of University Women (AAUW; 1992) brought to the nation's attention issues of gender inequity in our schools. Their efforts resulted in the publication of *How Schools Shortchange Girls*, a lengthy meta-analysis of current research on girls' development through their school years. The meta-analysis of published research was supported by more than 3,000 responses by both boys and girls to survey items as well as focus group interviews. The study is notable in that the AAUW set out to determine what the research suggested about equality almost 20 years after Title IX legislation. The hopes of the AAUW were to report the gains and progress girls had made since the landmark ruling. Instead, their findings suggested that although some changes had occurred in our nation's schools, the majority of girls in this country are still educated in systems that cannot or do not attend to their educational and social needs. We discuss the major findings of the AAUW report as they relate to the development of gender roles in schools and the formal and hidden curriculum of our classrooms.

Findings of the AAUW Study

The report resonated with girls and women nationwide. As described by Orenstein (1994) in her year-long journalistic study of girls in middle schools in California, the passage for many girls from childhood to adolescence is marked by "a loss of confidence in herself and her abilities, especially in math and science [and] a scathingly critical attitude toward her body and blossoming sense of personal inadequacy." The AAUW study suggests that although, or in spite of, the changes in women's roles in society, many of today's girls fall prey to sagging self-esteem as they are judged not by their academic confidence but by their ability to be silent and pleasing. The AAUW discovered that the most dramatic gender gap in self-esteem is centered in the area of confidence. In the survey findings, the study reported that boys are more likely to say they are "pretty good at a lot of things" and are twice as likely to name their talents as things they like about themselves. Girls, not surprisingly, cite their physical appearance (AAUW, 1992). Girls are also less likely to believe they are smart enough to achieve their academic and life goals.

The work of Sadker and Sadker (1980) supports the conclusions of the AAUW study. Using interview and classroom observation data they asserted that teachers encourage more assertive behavior in boys—calling on them in class more often and engaging them in conversation that lasts longer than that of the girls. The result is that boys feel more comfortable speaking out in class and challenging a teacher's actions or comments. Meanwhile the same research suggests that as girls lose confidence in speaking out and in their abilities, they lose confidence in their ability to do well in classes. These findings are meaningful in that a loss of confidence is most often followed by a drop in academic ability. The Sadkers' work contends that the loss of confidence precedes a drop in achievement rather than the reverse. Their work suggests that it is the confidence gap rather than the ability gap that offers the best explanation as to why girls score more poorly than boys in academic situations and testing.

Furthermore, the AAUW study suggests that the gender-role typing that exists in schools also results in the misidentification of girls for special education courses. The study's findings cite a 1988 report by the U.S. Department of Education that states that boys outnumber girls in all special education courses by one third. They suggest that school personnel do poorly at identifying girls' learning disabilities, mistaking learning problems for shyness or lack of effort. Whereas boys' problems maybe overidentified, placing boys who have behavioral problems in special education classes they may not require, girls' problems are often overlooked because it is assumed they will naturally do worse in areas such as math. Their problems are ignored because of gender-role stereotyping rather than by evidence of ability.

The study also finds that as boys and girls grow they have different experiences in classes such as math and science. Orenstein (1994) documented such differences in class experience. She observed that even when science teachers created lessons designed to provide hands-on experimental practice, the girls were less likely to use the equipment than the boys in class. In her observations she found that girls would play with the materials provided for scientific investigation, waiting until male lab partners would complete the tasks at hand. When Orenstein inquired about their behavior, the girls responded by saying that if they did not behave as if they needed the boys to complete the lab they would be labeled as brains and ostracized by the other class members. Orenstein concluded that in the race for social standing, the girls felt academic achievement could be sacrificed. Yet, although the construction of a gendered identity affects how girls respond to school activity, it does not predict equitable outcomes for girls.

Although conventional wisdom suggests that girls do better at language activities and readings and boys do better at math and science, the research does not support such conclusions. Two major surveys have tracked the scoring in reading sections of national tests. On the National Assessment of Educational Progress (NAEP; 1988) and the National Education Longitudinal Survey (NELS; 1989), girls were found to outperform boys on reading tests. However, the gender differences were rather small. Even in these test results, the performance of boys relative to girls varied depending on the type of reading experience. AAUW reported that, "Boys did as well as girls on the expository passages and were most disadvantaged relative to girls in the literary passages." They continued to report that, "boys do slightly better than girls on other NAEP tests in subjects requiring good skills in expository reading and writing: civics, history, and geography" (p. 37).

However, if, as it has been suggested, fiction reading is more popular among girls and that expository reading is more routine among boys, the findings underscore the cultural biases of children's reading material rather than a gender-based ability difference. Furthermore, the findings of the test results are encouraging when the eye is turned to differences in mathematical and scientific content. In recent years gender differences on the SAT mathematics sections have decreased; however, males still outscore females 498 to 455. Course enrollment data supports the decrease in scoring differences as well. Girls' enrollment in higher level mathematics courses has increased steadily since 1982.

Additionally, science course enrollment by girls has increased in the freshman and sophomore years of science education. Enrollment in Biology I and Chemistry I has held steady over the last decade. Only when upper level courses in biology and chemistry and physics at all levels are compared do girls demonstrate losses in academic opportunity. Here again, the findings support the notion that ability in these areas is not genetic or biological but founded on cultural differences in treatment of students in schools. It has been reported in a number of studies that girls are systematically discouraged from choosing upper level math courses and upper level science courses (AAUW, 1992; Orenstein, 1994; Sadker & Sadker, 1980; Shakeshaft, 1989). Discouragement from enrollment paired with a lack of attention within the courses them-selves result in girls who begin to doubt their abilities to master difficult content.

When boys begin to do poorly in upper level courses, they are more likely to receive tutoring, mentoring, and verbal encouragement designed to address a lack of ability. On the other hand, girls and their teachers are more likely to assume that it is not ability but personal failure at a male subject that has led to their poor performance. When girls are discouraged from the career and academic goals they hold, their confidence lags. It has been argued that encouragement by teachers and other meaningful adults can increase the confidence levels of girls and thus increase enrollment and academic skills for girls (Sadker & Sadker, 1994).

However, the story of inequity does not end here. Even when girls are placed in classrooms that do nurture their confidence and academic ability, they face additional gendered issues at the hands of curriculum and content. As we discussed in the chapter on critical approaches, curriculum can be considered as formal—the different subject areas schools teach—or hid-den—the messages about hierarchy, authority, work, rules, and power. Each is equally problematic for girls as they try to navigate the halls of our schools.

Formal Curriculum

The formal curriculum has been the focus of many criticisms of late. It has been suggested to be found lacking in both representations of women and minorities. Heilbrun (1988) suggested that girls cannot find themselves in traditional texts because they have been left out and ignored. She continued by suggesting that the lives told in traditional stories of history, English, and civics are lives of service rather than lives of adventure, lives of cooking and child rearing rather than lives of construction and creativity. Heilbrun asserted that the lives portrayed in these traditional texts provide few choices for girls, portraying life opportunities as in service to those of adventurous men. Heilbrun suggested that these visions of women's lives provide no mirrors in which girls can see themselves as productive members of society but offer instead many windows to passively view the lives of others. She also said the formal curriculum must change to include the lives of women and minorities much like the lives of men have been for many years.

Textbooks

Textbook publishers have responded by adding sections to texts about these previously neglected groups. However, women and minorities have often been added to the texts in ways that still marginalize their contributions to the field of study. They become the added biography at the end of the chapter, an addition to the story problem's list of characters. Their stories are rarely featured as the major focus of a section or chapter. Women's lives and writing are still secondary to the lives of men when it comes to the telling of historical events, scientific discovery, or civic adventure (Belenky, Clinchy, Goldberger, & Tarule, 1986; Heilbrun, 1988; Henry, 1996; Houston, 1996; Orenstein, 1994). In short, scholars suggest that women and minorities have been left out of the official stories of schooling. As many women have suggested, when they looked for themselves in the pages of their texts, they could not find even a shadow, much less an exemplar. The formal curriculum omits women and girls, sending the hidden messages that their accomplishments are less than those of men. Girls respond by absenting themselves from classroom discussions, eager involvement with their study, and silencing their confusions (AAUW, 1992; Henry, 1996; Orenstein, 1994). They learn to be passive recipients rather than active constructors of knowledge.

Gender-Fair Curriculum

Wilbur (1991) suggested another approach. Her work suggests that a gender-fair curriculum has six attributes. The first allows for variation between groups of people, focusing on how we may be alike but also including our differences. The second attribute is inclusion, allowing both females and males to see themselves and to identify with positive messages about themselves. Wilbur's work suggests that girls need to see themselves in roles other than passive. The curriculum is also accurate, presenting information that is data-based, verifiable, and able to withstand critical analysis. A story must hold together under a critical reading providing both mirrors and windows for all students. Fourth, a gender-fair curriculum is affirmative—valuing the worth of all members. Fifth, is balanced and representative including multiple perspectives and the reading of an event, telling, or finding. Finally, it is integrated, weaving together the experiences, needs, and interests of both males and females.

THE UNDERREPRESENTATION OF WOMEN
IN SCHOOL LEADERSHIP

The educational system of the United States consists of a hierarchy of levels of schooling. One often begins the school years in a preschool, moves on to elementary and secondary schools, and matriculates into higher educational settings. For most students, movements between grades and levels of schooling is marked by the earning of diplomas and degrees—a hierarchy of levels that one moves up and then out of. For teachers and administrators, a similar hierarchical structure exists as teachers earn graduate degrees and gain certifications allowing them to take on more responsibilities and job roles. It is assumed that power, salary, and prestige grow with each move up the educational or career ladder.

Although nationally, the sexes' national distribution is relatively equal among students across educational levels, faculty tend to distribute themselves along distinct gender lines. Women are mostly likely (87%) to be teaching in an elementary school and least likely (27%) to be teaching at a postsecondary level (Bell & Chase, 1992). At the administrative levels, the story is similar. Although women comprise a majority—70%—of the nation's public school teaching force, most school administrators (63% in elementary schools and 70% in secondary schools) are men (NCES, 1996). This is the case even though school administrators rise from the ranks of teachers. The highest positions of school leadership are the most telling; nationally only 6% of school superintendents are women (NCES, 1996).

Typically, the absence of women in both the principalship and superintendency has been explained away by suggesting that women do not want those positions or suggesting that women make clear career choices to not aspire to positions of power because they are not interested in the responsibility serving in those positions would entail (Shakeshaft, 1989). This is often not the complete story. Surely some women have chosen to remain in the classroom to remain working with children and to do the important work of teaching. As one teacher recently said, "I'd miss the classroom; in my mind, it's where life is really lived." Personal growth and experience, strong ties to teaching teammates and families provide for many women a reason to remain in the classroom. In many ways, personal development and a focus on teaching practice can substitute for movement up an organizational hierarchy.

Many others do find an institutionalized form of discrimination. The historical record has shown that women have traditionally been the second choice when hiring school administrators (Spring, 1997; Tyack & Hansot, 1982). A wide array of reasons have been offered in the literature to explain the underrepresentation of women in administrative positions. First, gender stratification in schools is maintained by lack of access to opportunities for advancement. Although most school administrators rise from the rank of teachers, elementary teachers have less opportunity than secondary teachers to participate in the activities that result in vertical promotion. Opportunities such as coaching, directing special programs, and chairing departments or curricular committees are rarely granted to elementary teachers. Instead, they are offered to secondary teachers under the reasoning of special skills, knowledge, or ability. Yet, secondary teachers are predominately male. Finally, the assistant principalship, the stepping stone to higher positions of authority, is often absent in elementary schools, providing fewer opportunities for women to advance through close mentoring relationships (Shakeshaft, 1989). Thus, the women who teach in elementary school often remain teachers not because they lack the ambition to become administrators but because they lack an appropriate mechanism to rise from the classroom.

Second, the gatekeepers—those who influence hiring and placement of future administrators—are largely still White males. The network that becomes established through internships, screening, interviewing, and eventual hiring remains closed to women and especially minority women. Career opportunities for women aspiring to upper administrative positions, such as the superintendency, are limited as a form of occupational segregation occurs—prestigious suburban districts are seen as the province of experienced high school administrators who are presumably male. Therefore, women who do become principals remain clustered in the elementary schools from which few upper administrators are drawn. Valverde and Brown (1988) identified a pattern that is particularly concerning. They asserted that for women of color the rise is doubly hard; minorities are shunted to districts with large concentrations of minority students and inadequate financial resources. They are often placed in situations in which it is difficult for anyone—male or female—to succeed. Limited success translates into limited opportunity when one seeks a new or more prestigious position.

Third, women report that fewer opportunities are presented to them as they return to graduate school to gain certification. Chase (1995) reported women's experiences of being ignored in classes similar to those reported in kindergarten through Grade 12 education. Men speak more in class at the graduate level as they do when they enter professional conference situations. Tannen (1990) suggested that although women are highly visible in both conference settings and present 40.7% of papers at academic conferences they only account for 27.4% of questions. On average those questions took less than half the time to ask as the questions men proffered—23.1 seconds to 52.7 seconds for men. Tannen reported the similar results when classroom interactions are studied. Men ask more questions than women, five men to every three women ask questions that challenge the professor or speaker. Women are more likely to ask for clarification in their questions. Although both forms do elicit additional information concerning the subject at hand, challenging questions often engage the speaker in more exchanges of information, take more time, and are more likely to result in positive memory on the part of the professor. Tannen argued that when a superintendent calls to ask for an up-and-coming go-getter, it is the man who is remembered and his name is passed along for the position. As women become invisible in class, they then become invisible when opportunity presents itself.

Finally, issues of equity have lost favor with policy makers in the call for excellence that characterized educational reform efforts of the 1980s. Quite simply, policy standards became the focus of national reports, starting with *A Nation At Risk* (1983) and the debate about equity issues' lost voice and momentum. Underrepresentation of women on national policy boards has remained problematic as well. Recently, three major national task forces were established to study the effects of schooling on the youth of our nation, the Task Force on Education of Young Adolescents (1989; 10 males, 7 women); the Carnegie Council on Adolescent Development (1989; 22 males, 3 women) and the Carnegie Forum on Education and the Economy (1986; 11 males, 5 women). When women do not serve on national boards of policy, policy issues related to equity are ignored.

The preceding sections have demonstrated that girls' and women's lives in schools differ from those of men. The profiles of girls and women in schools differ in important ways from those of boys and men. Furthermore, a legacy of discrimination and exclusion has shaped a world in which girls' and women's experiences and behaviors are unlike those of boys and men. Yet the world of theory about women and women's views can offer much to an inclusive study of schools and schooling in this country. In the following sections, selected issues are examined in an attempt to add a feminist perspective to the organizational literacy needed to read and interpret patterns of inequality in school organizations.

THEORIES OF FEMINISM

It is often thought that the inclusion of feminist theory in a course or set of readings only addresses the issues we have previously discussed—lack of equality, unfair or unjust treatment in school and work organizations, and discrimination in hiring practices. Although these are important issues for educators to address, they are informed by a larger body of thought on issues considered feminist. Feminism, like many other comprehensive philosophical perspectives, includes several branches or families of thought under its broad umbrella. Feminism is not simply the cataloging of injustices and inequity. It includes several analytic frames by which women's lives can be examined, explored, and explained. These analytic frames or theories combine description, explanation, and prescription as they attempt to address the important issues women face in schools and other workplaces. The theories we present here include liberal feminism—based on the rules and roles of women and men in society—and psychological feminism—rooted in distinctly different notions of moral reasoning for both sexes. Although these are by no means the only forms of feminist theory in the literature, they do offer an organizational literacy that uniquely addresses the issues of women and girls in schools. Finally, we end this section of the chapter by discussing the application of an ethic of care as an example of organizational practice based in feminist theory.

Liberal Feminism

Liberal feminism takes as its emphasis the notion that female subordination is rooted in a set of customs and legal constraints that block women's entrance and success into the world of school and work. Liberal feminists argue that, as a culture, society holds notions that females are considered intellectually and physically less capable than men. Therefore, excluding women from the public spheres that have been traditionally dominated by men is justified. The exclusion of women from schools, political forums and discussion, and the marketplace is justified because the assumptions of the argument begin with the belief that women are, in fact, less capable than men in these areas. Liberal feminists argue that what is traditionally defined as male and female in society is, in fact, a set of carefully constructed social rules that ascribe gender-based roles to members. Such rules and roles are constructed in ways that disadvantage women and advantage men.

Liberal feminism challenges these ideas and asserts that women are equal to men in every way. They assert that if given equality of opportunity, women would achieve at equal levels with men. Liberal feminism also asserts that the development of gender equity requires us to first make the playing field level. None of the participants in the marketplace, workplace, or the schoolyard should be systematically disadvantaged

(Tong, 1989). What liberal feminists wish to do is to free women and girls from oppressive, gender-bound roles.

Psychological Feminism

As we have seen, liberal feminism focuses its study on the identification of the rules and roles women are bound by in today's society. Psychological feminism differs as a theory of feminist thought in that its focus is on the development of a theory of reasoning that includes women's ways of knowing and women's voices (Belenky et al., 1986; Gilligan, 1982). Popularized by the work of Gilligan (1982), psychological feminism asserts that the traditional psychological literature on moral development judges women as deficient. Her distinction between a male ethic of justice and a female ethic of care is rooted in an argument that suggests men tend to see the self as an autonomous, separate being, whereas women tend to see themselves as being interdependent beings whose identities depend on others. She asserted that these different views of self account for at least three major differences in the moral reasoning of men and women.

First, she asserted that women tend to stress the importance of a continuing relationship among all members of an exchange, assuming that such bonds will be an ongoing part of one's life. Gilligan contended that women consider the possibility that the members of social, economic, or political exchanges will become meaningful human contacts in their lives. Men, Gilligan suggested, are more concerned with notions of formal abstract rights when considering social, economic, or political exchanges. Thus, a woman may forsake some of her rights if by doing so she will cement an ongoing human relationship. Second, Gilligan's theory posits that women espouse a more consequentialist point of view, considering the results of a decision on all those who may be touched by it, whereas men will uphold certain moral principles even if people might get hurt in the process. Finally, Gilligan argued that women will interpret a social, economic, or political choice in terms of the historical circumstances that produced it, whereas men will consider a moral choice in terms of the rightness or wrongness of the choice as if it lay outside of any circumstances beyond it. Psychological feminism contends that it is important to recognize that women think and reason in ways different than men. Consequently, they are not intellectually deficient compared to men.

AN ETHIC OF CARE

Gilligan is not the only feminist researcher to focus on an ethic of care in schools. Caring as a critical component of all human interaction has been explored in many fields, including education. Family policy studies, social policy work, welfare work, and social work are all areas of study that have recently included a focus on caring in their research (Beck, 1992). Following in the steps of Noddings' 1984 work, Beck's work focuses on the development of caring as a component of reformed school settings. She defined caring as more than a sense of emotion or an illusionary mission. In her research, she asserted that practicing an ethic of care involves an understanding of the goals, context, and activities of caring.

Beck (1992), basing her analysis on Noddings (1984) and Mayerhoff (1971), suggested that the chief goal of caring is human growth and development. She asserted that as children learn to care, they develop needed skills to become contributing members of a communal society. Similar claims can be made for adults. As children are educated in schools that develop challenging academic programs, battle social problems in schools, and re-create school organizations into places where all members are valued, those who work in those schools benefit as well.

Another goal of caring and developing caring in schools is that of responding to the needs of others. In part, this discussion is based in responding equitably to children's needs. Based on Mitchell's (1990) work, Beck suggested that among the tasks of caring individuals is that of alleviation of needs from illness, poverty, disrupted families, and other situations that threaten the personal and societal well-being of children. Mitchell looked at specific ways of life in the last decade and suggested that humanity may be at a crossroads. Mitchell challenged educational leaders to seek to change and to reform schools for the good of children and adults by encouraging activities that support caring in classrooms and schools.

Caring depends on the relationships of the people involved in relationships characterized by some measure of commitment. The context of caring relationships relies on the development of interdependent relationships within a social community. Although caring relationships do exist in family units, they prosper when placed within environments that stress a sense of larger community, such as schools can do. In a similar argument, Bellah et al. (1985) contended that the development of community is important for caring relationships to be formed. School organizations can model themselves on a more communal form and, in turn, develop into more caring, interrelated organizations focused on children's needs.

The development of caring in schools relies on a series of activities related to receiving another's perspective, responding to this perspective in a caring manner, and remaining in the caring relationship for appropriate lengths of time. The first activity, receiving another's perspective, involves an "openness and a willingness to accept another's reality" (Beck, 1992, p. 462). Such a disposition may be defined as the ability to make oneself available to another's sense of the world with an intention to care. By creating a regard for another's well-being (Noddings, 1984), one begins the activity of caring. Once open to or aware of another's state of being, one can then develop skills to respond to the situation: the second activity of caring.

As such, caring begins with an attitude of openness and receptivity to another. However, as Beck stated, "Most scholars agree that caring also includes some kind of action on behalf of the one cared for" (p. 465). She added "that these actions begin with a willingness on the part of one person to assume responsibility for another" (p. 466). Researchers stress that the activities of caring are made of equal parts responsibility and responsiveness to others. Thus, as one begins to care by being open to another's experience, it is reinforced by a response to the caring act and to others who care in similar ways, such as teachers in schools.

Finally, the caring act is reinforced by remaining. Examples of remaining can include a parent's devotion to a child, or as in the case of schooling, a teacher's insistence that her students learn and learn well. Sticking with a difficult topic until children master the ideas, creating activities that let children learn in authentic ways, or providing after-school tutoring programs are all examples of school-based efforts to remain within the caring relationship.

As schools develop into more caring places, attention must be placed on actions that encourage student learning rather than contrived efforts to make students feel good about themselves. Caring takes at its essence the notion that providing programs that improve academic performance will provide for children in meaningful long-term ways. The caring research (Beck, 1992; Bellah et al., 1985; Noddings, 1984) emphasizes that students, teachers, and administrators deserve a supportive educational environment simply because they are people. If accepted, such a view would put at the center of teaching and learning questions concerning the development of personal habits of learning and instruction rather than the development of questions related to competition for grades or test scores. In fact, an ethic of care is in itself antithetical to the development of competitive schooling systems such as those based on proficiency testing. The development of an ethic of care in schools is based on the development of relationships among and between those who work and learn in schools.

FEMINIST APPROACHES
AND TEACHER-INITIATED CHANGE

The development of a gender-fair classroom is not an easy task. It requires challenging both the traditional educational structure and deeply ingrained societal norms. Many teachers nationwide have taken up this challenge and have responded in ways that produce classrooms of equity and reform (Cohen, 1994; Linn, 1994; Linn & Hyde, 1989; McIntosh, 1983; McKenna & Oritz, 1988; Orenstein, 1994) On the national level, the Gender Equity in Education Act, implemented in 1995, included provisions for improved data gathering, for the development of teacher training programs, for programs to encourage girls in math and science, and for programs to better meet the needs of girls of color (Orenstein, 1994). However, there is no single magic formula that will help create classrooms that help girls retain their self-esteem and boys become aware of their privileged status. These are difficult issues. This next story tells the tale of one successful teacher.

Norma Higgins credits a student essay as the motivation that thrust her into the serious study of gender-fair teaching. The essay, one of many she regularly assigned in her sophomore-level history class, was to research and report on the life of an outstanding woman in American history. Although many of the essays she received recounted the lives of well-known women—Clara Barton, Amelia Earhart, Margret Sanger, and Harriet Tubman were among the favored—the paper that caused her to think focused on a relative un- known—Lucy Stone. The report emphasized her efforts in the suffragist movement as well as her then-radical stance on marriage (she married yet kept her own name and with her husband, Henry Blackwell, issued a joint statement protesting the crippling legal effects of marriage on women.) Although the report was unremarkable in many ways, its ending statement was one that caused Norma pause. Unlike the others, this student ended with a personal statement: "I am saddened that even though many women like Lucy Stone exist in our history they receive no attention in our text or classroom studies. It is a sad statement that their important work still goes unnoticed. It is even sadder still that the inequality she fought against still exists in our society today."

It was then that Norma decided that if she were to include the efforts of women in her curriculum, she might then be providing an education that includes all students. She went about her task quietly at first, reading and collecting examples of lesson formats, possible reading lists, and developing course assignments that would truly focus on women and their accomplish-ments. It proved to be a difficult task, requiring that she look for materials out of the mainstream texts and sources. During this period, Norma became frustrated with what she described as the "add women and stir" philosophy of textbook inclusion. Her study suggested that although textbook publishers had made an effort to include the biographies of women (and minorities) and their accomplishments over the past years, they had "added them on to the end of the chapter in those final few pages before the activities." The material was "both easily skipped and not integrated into the story of history or science or whatever." It was "an addition, not an integral part of the whole telling." Norma also realized that although she had worked to add women into the curriculum, she, too, had fallen into the trap of making the study an addition rather than an integral part of the subject matter. She set out to create a classroom that would not fall prey to the same faults again.

When school opened in the fall, Norma'a classroom had been transformed. The walls of her room were lined with posters of women. Some famous, some not; some sports heroes, some scientists, some current figures, some mythical heroines, and some artists figures. Her bookshelves had changed radically as well. They were now lined with biographies and autobiographies of women and stories written by women. She began her year with a discussion of the hidden curriculum, centering on the notions of socialization and proper roles for boys and girls and moved forward into the study of early American history. Here she included a study of the legal rights of the colonists—who could hold property, who could vote, who could attend meetings. Considerable time was spent on the writings of Abigail Adams and her efforts to persuade her husband John to remember the women.

As the year progressed, she included aspects of women's lives at every point she could. Her approach to teaching changed as well; rather than allowing some students to dominate discussion, she worked to balance who spoke and when. She introduced topics directed to provide opportunity for all students to participate. Her assignments changed as she realized that if she allowed students to choose the topics of their reports—male or female—the boys would always choose the men and the girls might choose the women but were equally likely to choose a man to report on. One student, opened her eyes when she told Norma, "If you choose a woman, you have to work harder since there's less stuff out there to read." To remedy the situation, she began to assign reports on both a man and a woman of the period. This "forced the boys to research the women and begin to see how they contributed to history as well as the more prominent men." It also allowed the girls to "feel supported in the choices they saw as more difficult to research."

As her year went on, she found that her philosophies of teaching a gender-fair curriculum evolved. By January, Norma was able to articulate both for herself and her students how she believed this teaching differed from other more traditional forms of social studies instruction.

She said:

I've abandoned the ideas that history is about truth and how things occurred. I now focus my teaching much more around the idea of careful listening—when you hear this telling whose voices are present and whose are absent? I prod students to look for the other side of the story—we work to hear the voices that weren't included. I also work to have students reflect on what we do know, especially to try and locate it in a larger political and social world. We spend time struggling with the issue of power—who has it and who doesn't and when they hold it and when it is challenged. Finally, I try to develop a classroom that generates a sense of care for each student and try to develop it for all students—not only for them but for each other.

Her efforts received mixed reviews. For some students, the work was interesting and welcome. For others, it was described as a big deal about nothing. In a discussion in early February, Norma brought up the subject of the class with her students to ask how they experienced the new focus on women in the curriculum. Many students were quick to say they liked it—not so much the study of women but the fact that to study them they had to leave the boring texts and look at more real documents and sources. It made history more interesting and real, a focus students liked. Norma did not stop there. She pushed on to the subject of the focus on women. Later, she reflected: "If I'd stopped there, they would have gotten away with not confronting the issues of power and the real curriculum. They gave the safe answer first. That's okay, but I couldn't let them stop there."

After Norma's pushing, a blond girl finally added: "Well, it really makes you notice what isn't happening in other classes. Like the other day in English, I gave an answer to a question, my opinion you know, and then everyone ignored it, but later a boy said the same thing and four other kids agreed with him. That would have never happened in here." A boy jumped right on the comment, saying, "Yeah, but in here we aren't listened to enough. If a boy speaks, then a girl must speak also so it's like we don't get the same amount of attention we get in other classes." Another girl added, "But, that's equal treatment. You're just used to more than you really deserve." This opened up the dam that had been holding the students quiet and the discussion really took off. First, students complained about how they experienced the fairness of working in a class so different than others they attended. They commented on the uncertainties it caused them. As one student said: "In other classes, I know what to do. I go in, take notes, and then take the test. In here I have to talk, to defend my ideas, and work at understanding two sides to everything we study. It's harder and I don't always like that."

A small girl from the back of the room jumped into the discussion: "It's like here the learning is better because I feel I can talk and do things that I cannot do in other classes. I know if a boy laughs at me in here you won't let him get away with it. But the price I have to pay for that is to work harder on the projects and things because to be equal takes effort you know. It's okay for me if it's that way."

Following the discussion, Norma commented:

I know the eventual goal here is to change the organization, to challenge how girls are treated in all classes. They're right. Yet, I feel that I have to start that challenge with a small step forward. I have to learn how to do it here first and then bring it out large. In a sense it is already happening, they're going out and demanding more from these teachers. They're gaining a sense of their own power and that's how the change will really occur, as they see the difference and respond to it themselves. I know that their voices will carry, in many ways louder than mine. The change has begun you know. Already, other teachers are asking me how I do this. I see it like the women's movement itself—it had to start small to gain voice. I can do that here also. School organizations start in the classroom and so change must start there as well.

THE BENEFITS OF FEMINIST APPROACHES

At the end of the 20th century we have become aware, often painfully, of a multitude of issues related to power and privilege that affect all of us in educational settings. Certainly among these are issues of gender and equity. However, these issues do not stand alone as important issues for educators to be concerned about if they are to create schools that provide caring and nurturing learning environments for children. Issues of class and race are equally important. However, issues of gender cannot be dismissed as less important or placed on the back burner to be addressed at an often undetermined, later date. As we saw in earlier parts of this chapter, young women and girls in schools often experience gender-related types of oppression. They are judged by their looks and weight, their ability to be passive and pleasing (AAUW, 1992; Orenstein, 1994; Pipher, 1994). The politics of appearance has crippled many a young girl. Women are also systematically disadvantaged in educational systems as they search for employment and long-term job satisfaction (Bell & Chase, 1992; Chase, 1995; Shakeshaft, 1989). Such inequities are allowed to continue because they find their foundation in the deeply held cultural systems of our society. Our society, at least when it comes to issues of gender, is a society in which privilege has allowed domination to flourish. Privilege involves the power to systematically dominate those who hold less power. Such domination is at once ideological and material, institutional and personal. Yet as troubling as these issues are, more troubling is the idea that even as we strive to obliterate a culture of inequity in our schools, we ourselves perpetuate the very systems we hope to dissolve.

So how do we, each, at once work to develop educational systems that are better places for girls and women and yet continue to work in those systems? Can we in reality expunge issues of gender from the curriculum and the organizational structure? The answers to these questions are not easy. In order for us to each become fully aware of the power hierarchies in which we participate, we must strive for both awareness and honesty with regard to our own positioning on these issues. Only in this way can we avoid replicating and mimicking in our own behavior that which we find troubling.

Schools do exist that provide some positive examples for study. In a 1996 *American Educational Research Journal* article, Louis, Marks, and Kruse argued that gender composition in schools is a contributing factor in the development of a teacher's professional community. They contended that elementary and secondary schools differ in their gender composition. Elementary school faculties are predominately female (NCES, 1996). They posited that, "Given the salience of gender as a mediating characteristic in schools, greater proportions of female teachers may account, at least partially, for documented differences in elementary and secondary school organization, as well as the development of professional community" (p. 765).

They continued to argue that when women constitute a social group, its culture differs from that of a mixed group. Hofstede's (cited in Louis, Marks, & Kruse, 1996) work concurred:

> On average, men have been programmed with tougher values and women with more tender values, but the gap between the sexes varies by country … individual women can learn to function in a masculine way and individual men in a feminine way. Where men are together masculine culture is likely to dominate; where women are together a feminine culture. Calling these differences "cultures" stresses their profound and emotional nature. (p. 766)

They suggested that women pay greater attention to work environments and interpersonal relationships than men typically do, and that women are more likely to cooperate and help each other with difficult tasks, leading to greater development of professional and communal work environments. The work is not merely speculative. Based on quantitative data from 24 schools in a national sample, they concluded:

> Our findings invite further attention to the rarely addressed issue of gender in the school workplace, both in larger sample studies and more detailed case analysis. The topic, in our view, should be examined not as a Thurberian war between the sexes but in conjunction with the emerging research on cultures of caring and support in schools. (p. 785)

Additionally, individual teachers can create nurturing environments for students in their classes. In Noddings' (1986) article, "Fidelity in Teaching, Teacher Education, and Research for Teaching," she clarified the ways an ethic of care can become an integral part of even traditional academic teaching. She provided an example in which a math teacher reflects on whether to give new exams to a number of students who have failed a previous unit test. The teacher considered providing remediation only without a chance to retake the exam, therefore assuring that the students know the material but are not given an opportunity to raise their grade. She decides that although this approach would guarantee a positive learning outcome, it would not be the most caring way to approach the problem. The teacher decides that the bad grade on the test is itself a hindrance. It makes the students feel dejected and scared. The teacher then decides the students need both remediation and a chance to be examined again over the material. By focusing on nurturing and caring for students, pedagogical method can gain clarity. What becomes important is not the competition of a grading curve but the goal of learning for all students.

Caring, then, simply becomes a form of pedagogical practice. It becomes a concern equal with subject context attainment and other important school goals. Examples such as those given by Louis et al. (1996) and Noddings (1984) suggest that the development of feminist forms of organizational systems and practice can enhance our ability to provide such learning and working environments in our schools for the betterment of all students and teachers.

THE LIMITATIONS OF FEMINIST APPROACHES

There are dangers in assuming all women (or men) act in particular ways. To suggest that a feminist ethic encompasses all women is to fall prey to the same false generalization proposed by the theory feminism attempts to critique. It essentializes one experience by placing it in a superior position to other theories. It perpetuates dangerous generalizations. The critique of such thinking falls along two distinct lines. The first suggests that feminist thought as it is discussed in the literature is based on a White, middle-class notion of feminism; the second suggests that by essentializing women into caring and nurturing roles, they are still unable to resist and challenge the status quo. We shall consider each critique separately.

The work of hooks (1989) and other African-American female writers reminds us that, in the United States, White womanhood is often defined as a cultural universal. hooks suggested that when women's issues are discussed, it is the White woman that comes to mind. Thus, the critique of feminist thought suggests that "White and middle-class are the hidden transcripts of femaleness, the womanhood invariably and historically repre-sented and celebrated" (Fordham, 1993). Such normalizing of the White woman's experience removes Black women from the focus of conversation and study, reducing their experience to the margins—the very place from which White women have struggled to remove themselves. Likewise, Rich's (1986) work has exposed a heterosexual bias present in much mainstream feminist theory. Thus, feminism as is currently understood can be critiqued for not being as inclusive as some feminists might themselves imagine.

A second critique suggests that even as women work to develop a sense of self separate from those identified in the male-focused academic litera-ture, that voice is at once different yet still prescribed to be a single voice (Houston, 1996). By prescribing feminist thought as a different voice (Gilligan, 1982), the critique suggests that women become essentialized and minimized by such a limiting description (Fraser & Nicholson, 1990). Houston (1996) suggested that when theory is created that emphasizes the caring and nurturing nature of women as a measure of femaleness, the theory will always fall short in that "it is not an ethic that will help women to resist and challenge their own oppression" (p. 79). Thus, as feminist theory offers possibilities for teachers to create classrooms that may be more nurturing and better places for children to learn, it also comes with its own dangers. Such dangers exist when any one theory is used to describe a complex and changing system such as schools. We call for the reader to consider devel-oping a personal awareness of these issues and to examine their own thoughts and concerns. As Alcoff (1988) reminded us, "a movement cannot be only and always against. It must provide alternatives, a vision of a better future that can motivate people to sacrifice time and energy towards its realization" (p. 272). We suggest careful consideration of one's own position on issues such as these can provide a thoughtful beginning.

SUMMARY

In this chapter, we argued that schools as organizations and classrooms as subunits of the school organization are not places of equality and equity. In fact, we argued that in many cases, public educational institutions replicate, generate, and strengthen the patriarchal domination of women and girls by their ingrained practices and processes. We attempted to address the tran-sitional problem of moving from a gender-biased curriculum in a (perhaps) sexist school culture to a gender-fair curriculum. We argued that the most effective way to deal with these biases is to adopt a gender-sensitive and caring perspective that fundamentally encourages a critical and constant review of the meaning attached to decisions in schools as they relate to texts and tests, employment and empowerment, hiring and promotion. Furthermore, by discussing these arguments and providing alternative organizations goals and values, we suggested that schools can create the kinds of environments that do foster more equitable environments for all members of the school organization.

PRACTICE CASE—SINGLE SEX EDUCATION AT LA SALLE MIDDLE SCHOOL

Gayle Mathers had taught math for more than 11 years at La Salle Middle School. During her time at the school, she had seen many improvements in her teaching. She felt that the introduction of problem solving into her curriculum had greatly helped many of her students learn more complicated processes and ideas. She also felt that the introduction of cooperative groups had helped her meet the learning needs of many more of the students than traditional lecture styles of instruction. In all, as she considered her career, Gayle felt she had grown as a teacher and was ready to assume a leadership role in the department. She would definitely accept the department chair position that had been offered to her the previous week. The position had become open when the long-standing chair had decided to take early retirement. She had been pleased when the principal had extended the offer of the chair to her, yet at the time had not been sure she wanted the added responsibility. But now, after a weekend of consideration, she could accept the job with confidence.

Monday morning, she entered the principal's office and told him she was excited to begin work as chair. He scheduled an appointment for them to discuss goals for the department later in the week. In preparation for the meeting, Gayle reviewed the department curriculum, test scores for the last few years, and the supplies and inventory of her fellow teachers. She also asked each teacher what they would like to see changed in the department. Although most of the teachers asked for predictable items—more textbooks and manipulatives—one teacher, Pat Connelly, suggested that she take a look at the differences between the test scores of the girls and the boys over time.

She had been concerned that over the years, many of her girls had lost confidence in their abilities and had decided to drop her upper level course in favor of business-level mathematics or the extremely popular Mathematics in Everyday Life. In previous years, she had seen girls who had come in as bright, eager learners in seventh grade lose interest in math by the time they reached the end of the eighth grade. The girls, at least the ones who would talk with her, often said that math had become boring or that they wanted to spend more time working on other stuff. However, Pat suggested that rather than a loss of interest on the girl's part, it was instead a social phenomena that kept the girls from doing well. Pat suggested that being bright and working hard was not the image the young girls wanted to project. Popularity was based on not doing better than others, she argued. Pat wanted Gayle to look into what the department could do about her concerns. Gayle promised to consider her request and get back to her following her meeting with the principal.

At home that evening, Gayle considered Pat's comments. She had to agree that in her classes she had noticed a similar pattern. Girls tended to come in as willing, attentive seventh graders only to slip as the year went on. They would arrive at the middle school, pencils sharpened, and as the year progressed they would raise their hands less, and when they did offer answers, their voices were more tentative, the answers less complex. Although a few girls were able to continue doing well, the majority's grades fell and confidence waned. She considered her options as the evening wore on.

The next morning during her meeting with the principal, she shared Pat's concerns and her new suspicions. She suggested a number of options: tutoring programs, special meetings with the counselor, and finally piloting a girls-only class for eighth graders the following year. Gayle had heard about other schools who offered single-sex math classes. She offered to check into the success of such programs and report back as soon as she had sense of their success. The principal was mildly supportive—he suggested that if perhaps she could demonstrate an increase in test scores he might consider such an arrangement.

Gayle considered how she might create a course for girls only. First, the students enrolled needed to be representative of the larger student body for any results to be convincing. Second, she decided that the first year the course would be open to volunteers only. She and Pat would hold a parent meeting and explain the course as an option for the incoming eighth-grade class. Third, she or Pat would teach the class according to the same lesson plans as their other courses. Finally, she looked at the numbers and decided that if necessary she would bear the burden of teaching a boys-only course as well. Besides, it might provide an interesting comparable group for her study. Perhaps the boys might score better if they were in a course of their own as well. The idea troubled her but she decided to suppress her concerns and plunge ahead.

The night of the parent meeting, both Gayle and Pat were nervous. They spent the day checking in with each other, sharing their concerns: What if no one came? What if they were hostile to the ideas? What if their questions were ones they had not considered? At 6 p.m. they entered a crowded cafeteria. Above the din, they exchanged tense wishes of luck.

As Gayle approached the podium, she reviewed her note cards for the speech that explained the program. The principal introduced her and Pat and they proceeded to share their concerns about the failure of girls to continue to do well as they progressed through middle-school math courses and their suspicions that an all-girl math course might provide them a learning environment more conducive to their needs. At the end of her speech, she introduced Pat as her choice as teacher for the program and then invited questions. Inquiries were sparse. The few parents who asked any questions were more concerned about how their daughters would fare if they chose to place them in the course. They were concerned about their children being labeled different or at risk. Pat and Gayle assured the group that the material would be the same and the focus of the course would remain mathematical. The course was only to provide a more supportive learning environment for girls. They also promised that if at any time they chose to remove their child from the program, they could.

As the parents filed out, a few made it a point to stop and talk with Pat or Gayle. A few shared stories of older daughters who had suffered the drop in math scores and confidence they had mentioned and pledged to enroll their daughters. A few continued to press for assurance that this was not a course that would place their children at a disadvantage later in their schooling. The major fear was that the course material would be taught more slowly and perhaps the material would not be fully covered. Gayle and Pat seemed to be able to assure the curious parents that the course would be taught exactly the same as the others and the material would be identical. Finally, around 8 p.m., the last parent left the room. Together they counted 10 parents who seemed definite, about 6 who seemed adamant they would not include their daughters, and the rest uncertain. The evening was deemed a successful start for a fledgling program.

As eighth-grade registration proceeded, registration for the girls-only course was steady. It seemed they would obtain the necessary student count to declare the course a go. Eagerly, they began plans to keep careful records for the project. Each eighth-grade student would take a pretest in September to determine math ability, confidence in completing the course with a passing grade, and a general attitude toward school inventory. The pretests were scored and a posttest would be administered in June.

September came quickly. Pat started her teaching year and the girls-only course began uneventfully. At first Gayle dropped in on occasion to check if there was greater participation in discussion than in her mixed-sex courses and tried for a bit to count responses. But such data collection proved difficult because she could not participate on a daily basis. At the fall grading period, grade point averages and overall test scores were compared—the girls-only students seemed to do slightly better than other girls in the school yet the differences seemed insignificant and difficult to trace directly to the single-sex nature of the course. At the semester, Gayle and Pat decided to readminister the attitude survey to determine if perhaps the differences were more subtle than grades alone.

The findings surprised the two. Not only did the girls-only students rate their math experiences as significantly better than other eighth-grade girls, they also reported a greater sense of confidence in their math ability than other eighth-grade girls. In fact, when the two compared the girls-only students with the top boys, they found similar confidence ratings even if the girls were not receiving grades as good as the top boys. Gayle and Pat were ecstatic with the results. They quickly moved to share them with the principal. Although he was encouraged, he reminded them that, in the end, test scores would determine the overall success of the program. Gayle and Pat entered the second semester with renewed confidence.

EXERCISES

1. Using the case as your data bank, identify the features of feminist organizational theory and practice that are present in the case. List these. How do these features affect the professional or scholarly interactions between the members of the case? How do these features affect social interactions between the members of the case?

2. Consider your own teaching or schooling experiences. From your experiences, do the conditions that concerned Gayle and Pat exist in other schools? Is the creation of single-sex courses a viable option for schools to address the concerns of equity and equality in schools? Would your school consider such courses? Would you consider either teaching such a course or sending your student to a single-sex course?

3. As teachers and curriculum directors attempt to create schooling experiences that provide opportunities for students who may be experiencing inequity do they create greater inequities, for other students? How can schools address both the social and learning needs of all students?

READING YOUR OWN SCHOOL

Consider your own school. How are the ideas and concepts presented in this chapter present in your work setting? How might these ideas help you to make sense of your school and the events that occur there? List five examples of how you see these concepts in practice at your school; examples might include the actions of administration, staff, faculty, students, or parents; or specific issues or events such as a curriculum adoption or an annual school celebration. Link each event to an idea or concept presented in this chapter. Do you think these actions or events facilitate student growth and learning, faculty and staff efficacy, and sense of well-being? Or do these actions or events create barriers to student growth and learning, faculty and staff efficacy, and sense of well-being? Finally, how could you use these ideas to initiate positive change in your school setting?

RECOMMENDED READINGS

Belenky, M. F., Clinchy, B. M., Goldberger, N. R., & Tarule, J. M., (1986). *Women's ways of knowing: The development of self, voice, and mind*. New York: Basic Books. Based on in-depth interviews with 135 women, this book chronicles the feelings and experiences of women who feel silenced in their families and schools. A classic in feminist study, this book describes the multitude of obstacles women feel they must overcome in developing the power of their minds and convictions.

Gilligan, C. (1993). *In a different voice: Psychological theory and women's development*. Cambridge, MA: Harvard University Press. Perhaps the second classic on this recommended readings list, *In a Different Voice* first burst on the scholarly scene in 1982. Since then, the book has continued to create controversy and discussion. Gilligan argues that women's moral development differs from that of men and offer distinctive ways of understanding and representing what the moral may be and may become.

Heilbrun, C. G. (1988). *Writing a woman's life*. New York: Ballantine. Drawing on the life experiences of several celebrated women, from George Sand to Adrienne Rich, Heilbrun examines the struggles that made it possible for them to follow different life paths from that of the traditional narrative. The book examines the scripts traditional biography and autobiography offer for women's lives and suggests more inclusive courageous texts for women.

Sadker, M., & Sadker, D. (1994). *Failing at fairness: How America's schools cheat girls*. New York: Scribners. The Sadkers argue, through first-hand observation and analysis, the finding that nationwide classrooms lack equal opportunities for boys and girls, men and women, to learn. The book offers a comprehensive examination of the history of women's education and continues by critiquing classroom, texts, and tests in today's schools.

Shakeshaft, C. (1989). *Women in educational administration*. Newbury Park, CA: Sage. Shakeshaft comprehensively explores the paths of women into the ranks of school administration and concludes not nearly enough women complete the journey. The author argues from document analysis, personal experience, and interview data the difficulties women face as they enter the administrative ranks, and the struggles they engage in to continue to hold positions of power in schools.

8

Complexity and School Organizations

◆◆◆

In the preceding chapters, we attempted to teach the organizational literacy needed to read social patterns common to school organizations. In this chapter, we explore the social patterns collectively to develop an understanding of the overall complexity of school organizations.

At first glance, the notions of reading organizations and using those readings to create school change and a pedagogy of promise may seem to have a great deal in common with the tale of the neighbor, the young boy, and the ax. In short, the Taoist tale goes something like this:

> Once a man found that his ax was missing and suspected his neighbor's son of taking it. Observing the youth walking around, the man became convinced that his was the walk of a thief. The youth looked like a thief and talked like a thief; everything he did pointed to his having stolen the ax. A few days later, the man happened to find his ax leaning up against a tree in a far orchard on his property. After that, he noticed that his neighbor's son was not behaving like a thief anymore.

There can be little doubt, as with the owner of the ax, that our actual experiences of organizations differ depending on who we are in the organization. Our sense of experience varies dependent on our role, task, years of service, and sense of how things should be. Our experience of schools is, in part, based on our own sense of what we define as the purposes of schooling. Thus, as a traditional stand-up-and-lecture teacher, we may find nothing wrong with a system that sorts and classifies students by test scores into those who excel and those who fail. Others may question the purposes of such a grading system, citing unequal opportunity to learn the material as reason for their opposition. Neither is right and neither is wrong in a conventional sense. No amount of discussion, research, or investigation will bring either side to an understanding of the issues based on a correctness of facts. We all experience each event differently. Instead, one may convince another that, given a certain set of assumptions about teaching and learning, their position may better serve the students of the school at this time. Developing such an understanding around the assumptions one holds about schools and teaching and learning requires a focus on schooling as a cooperative venture rather than a competitive arena. It requires an understanding that certainly is rare. We need to be able to realize that we have lost our ax and that the reason it is missing may not be immediately apparent.

Similarly, different aspects of an organization can be present at once. An organization can be political and communal. Most family systems stand witness to such a statement. Planning who brings what to the Thanksgiving table can seem more complicated than planning an entire high school schedule. Aunt Bea always brings her cranberry ice, even though half the family would rather eat cranberry sauce. Yet, to introduce cranberry sauce to the table would be to risk real and lasting insult on Aunt Bea. The stuffing is traditionally made with walnuts, although the kids all pick the nuts out and most adults would prefer a vegetable side dish. Yet, to change the stuffing would be to risk the scorn of grandmother Kate. The pies are always pumpkin, apple, and mince. Any change would require at least 14 phone calls to the great aunts, grandparents, and siblings. The politics of dinner are enough to bring many an innovative cook to their knees. Miss it? Never. The communal nature of the event is more than enough to bring each family member back year after year.

DETAIL AND DYNAMIC COMPLEXITY

As we previously noted, all organizations are deeply complex. Schools are no exception to this rule. Senge (1990) offered two ways to consider the complexity within organizations. First, he suggested organizations have detail complexity. Detail complexity includes the sum of the daily variables that must be attended to if the organization is to operate on a day-to-day basis. For schools, these include the ordering of lunches, counting pupil attendance, scheduling students semester to semester, planning meetings and assemblies, bus schedules, field trip forms, and so on. Detail complexity, although overwhelming at times, is fairly easy to attend to. It responds well to bureaucratic forces. People can be assigned the tasks of coordinating the daily details of running a school building.

However, Senge suggested there is a second type of complexity, dynamic complexity. Dynamic complexity suggests that at times events occur in organizations where the effects are subtle and where the effects of a decision over time are not obvious. When the same action has dramatically different effects in the short and long runs, there is dynamic complexity. Dynamic complexity asks that we view our school organizations as influenced by multiple forces: that we consider the bureaucracy of schooling as part of the issues concerning race, class, gender, teaching, and learning.

When the organization is viewed only as a bureaucracy, conversation about change focuses only on the detail complexity. The systemic forces at play, the roles and rules rather than the community or politics become the focus. Issues of equality and equity are often shunted to later conversations. This occurs because most organizations lack a vocabulary for dealing with dynamic complexity. Learning about dynamic complexity is limited by language. If one member sees a problem more systematically than others, that person's insight will get sanctioned—if for no other reason than the biases we hold toward linear explanations in our daily language. As a society we tend to give credibility to explanations that suggest causality. That is, if X occurs then Y will predictably follow. Yet, as we all know, X does not always predict Y. Decisions made on the presumption of causality appear, at first glance, to hold great promise. Yet they often fail because the assumptions about teaching and learning that underlie them are not brought forth.

For example, one of us has recently worked with a local high school in developing a new school attendance policy. An urban school, the faculty is concerned about their low daily attendance rate—about 73%. Discussion among the faculty predictably focused on the issues of how to entice more students to attend. Calling parents of absent students had been tried with little success. Increasing the detention time for unexcused absences had been tried with little success. A policy that excused students from final exams if they have less than five absences for a semester had been tried and it did increase the attendance of those students who already missed five or less days but was not effective for those students who were chronic absentees. Yet, discussion after discussion, policy after policy, the faculty has never addressed the issues of what kinds of instruction and learning opportunities are provided for students when they are present. Every time a causal explanation was offered, the faculty jumped at the chance to develop a new "if X then Y" solution. They lacked the vocabulary to have a conversation that encompassed ideas beyond those of detail complexity.

On the other hand, the benefits of developing fluency in other forms of discourse are enormous. We can begin to develop new social patterns that address dynamic complexity in our school organizations. Language is part of our collective social patterning. By learning to converse (and listen) more effectively, we can then learn to address the complex issues of our organizations more clearly. We are able to develop styles of conversation that see interrelationships rather than linear cause–effect chains. Furthermore, we are able to see organizational change as a series of incremental shifts rather than change as a single event. When we consider the dynamic complexity of an organization as well as attending to the complex details of a school, we can then focus our efforts in more meaningful ways. Focusing our efforts in more meaningful ways requires that we consider new ways to think about our approaches to the issues of inequity and social patterning in our schools.

SOCIAL PATTERNS AND SCHOOL CHANGE

Thinking about schools from different theoretical perspectives on organizations, this text affords educators new ways to deal with the detail and dynamic complexities of schools. These theoretical ideas provide educators the ability to consider changes in the systemic patterns of schools. For example, Fullan (1991) suggested that we currently search for solutions to the systemic problems of schooling in the wrong ways. He called this the "if-only" phenomena: "If only parents would be more involved"; "If only our students would wear uniforms to school"; "If only we could guarantee homework would be completed"; "If only our daily attendance would increase. Although all these ideas may help to create a more focused school environment, they cannot, in Fullan's estimation, result in lasting and effective reform. He said, "If only statements beg the question, externalize the blame, and immobilize people" (p. 351). If-only statements suggest that the solutions to school-based problems lie outside the ability of teachers, administrators and parents to solve. Fullan suggested instead that educators should consider an "if I" or "if we" approach to problem solving by changing the patterns with which we think about school problems, we can effect meaningful change efforts.

Changing the social patterns that exist in schools is an exercise in pursuing new meanings for why inequities, stagnation, and hopelessness occurs in schools. Opportunities for school reform and change are abundant. Yet opportunities can be overlooked or wasted when school personnel do not choose to meet the challenges of schooling today. In part, as we suggested, change is often accompanied by political tensions. However, political tensions can be mitigated by a continuing focus on shared goals. Tensions can be productive if managed properly.

To do so, we suggest a focus on four interrelated principles. First, we must learn to count on ourselves to raise important questions concerning issues of organizational change. Second, small changes in our daily patterns of interaction can add up to large-scale systemic change. Focusing on dynamic complexity can lead schools to large-scale change. Third, we must remember that systems cannot change by themselves. People change systems by their altering their actions, attitudes, and assumptions. Finally, if a focus on the social patterns of schools is to result in improved educational outcomes, school change must be deliberate in the context of goals for educational purpose and progress.

PRINCIPLES OF CHANGE

The principles of change that follow are compatible with the theories discussed throughout the book. Because schools are organizations, and we are suggesting that educators can learn to read their school organization to produce schools that are more responsive to the learning needs of students and the workplace needs of faculty, these principles can be viewed as an extension of those ideas. The application of these principles will need to be adapted to fit your school organization. Feel free to consider each in turn and the possibilities they suggest together.

- We must learn to count on ourselves to raise important questions concerning issues of organizational change.

Establishing new patterns of involvement in schools requires an extended focus on questions of importance. Research by a variety of scholars (Fullan, 1991; Hargreaves, 1994; Louis & Kruse, 1995; Newmann, 1996; Rowan, 1991) suggested that teachers and administrators will engage in greater innovative efforts and change in their classroom practices when they perceive that risk-taking and personal reflection on practice is encouraged and expected. By creating environments in which faculty and staff consider their personal and group efforts important and meaningful, risk taking and reflection on the tasks of schooling can be fostered. Once nurtured, risk taking and reflection can lead to changes in the patterns of interaction in our schools.

So what does this mean for educators? First, these ideas suggest a resounding call for action. No matter who they are or from what position they write, researchers can agree that reflective practice and organizational risk taking denotes the need to address and relate thought about teaching to action within the classroom (Beck, 1992; Benz, 1996; Chase, 1995; Little, 1990; Shakeshaft, 1989). Expressed is the need for both focused goals and meaningful strategies in pursuing school improvements. The idea of schools developing focused goals recognizes the essential nature of organizational knowledge appropriate to the content, tasks, and skills of teaching. Once such knowledge is obtained and shared within the school organization, meaningful strategies for action can be addressed. Meaningful strategies are not isolated, random actions but carefully coordinated and independent tactics designed to achieve important and valued goals by the participants in the action.

Second, teachers must act on what they have decided and, under the best circumstances, act in concert with other practitioners. Although individuals can and must be introspective, responsible, and rigorous in order to contribute to reflective processes and organizational risk taking, the highest potential of such practice can be realized only through the collegial efforts of the varied members of the school community. Collegial practice is essential for a holistic effect. However, action in any form is necessary for the completion of the risk-taking and reflective process.

- Small changes in our daily patterns of interaction can add up to large-scale systemic change. Focusing on dynamic complexity can led schools to large-scale change.

School change takes time. At the end of each chapter, we have purposely chosen to highlight the change efforts of individuals and groups of teachers. We have done so for two reasons. First, we are strong believers in the importance of providing examples in which our readers can, perhaps, find themselves and their schools. Second, we have done so to highlight the point that small changes can result in systemic change. Individuals can serve to fly test balloons and develop pilot projects that can result in systemic reform.

Cross-case analysis of these chapter-ending change cases suggests that, at the individual level, what separates these teachers' practice is their focus. Some teachers appear to be able, in a consistent and sustained manner, to focus their teaching activity on one aspect of their work, curriculum, instruction, students or interpersonal work skills. The teachers' stories who provide the examples of focused action suggest a greater sense of efficacy in their work as well as greater ownership in their classrooms and school goals and missions. These teachers look for innovations and new pedagogical forms of practice with a specific purpose in mind. In contrast, teachers who are less focused in their activity concentrate on the enduring dilemmas of classroom practice. They focus on issues of control as it relates to student conduct, time management, and school politics. In each case, the small changes these teachers began resulted in attention to these issues at a schoolwide level. As a consequence of their individual action, systemic patterns were altered throughout the school system.

- Systems cannot change by themselves. People change systems by changing their actions, attitudes, and assumptions.

All people living in schools inhabit their own place in the bureaucracy. Imagine, if you will, a series of fault lines that divide the school into departments, grade levels, tenured and untenured teachers, students who are in or out, and predictably, administration and faculty. Some live above a fault line of privilege; they have the good assignments, the upper level classes, a planning period with their peers, or the ability to earn good grades easily. Some live below the fault line of privilege; they struggle to achieve, teach or learn in isolation, or fail to accomplish at a level equal to that of their peers. Participation in this system of fault lines is, in a sense, assumed to be normal, predictable, the way things are supposed to be. It is far easier not to challenge the system than it is to change the system. It is far easier not to see than to see the inequalities that exist in the bureaucracy. After all, the system moves on daily seemingly without our participation. We are socialized to believe that the patterns we see are part of the bureaucracy, separate from ourselves and our actions.

Yet, as we have suggested in this text, that does not have to be the case. Among all of us are people who persevere through the hard questions to arrive at a place where together we can constructively work for change. The place allows for the fault lines to become a focus of discussion, a place where members can collaborate. Collaboration among members of the school organization can result in a joint vision of how schools can be organized differently. We are encouraged about the possibilities for educators to administer change. From the beginning, we have asserted that knowledge created from a study of organizational literacy is assessable to all members of the school organization. This is not knowledge solely for administrators, for teachers, or for parents. It is knowledge for discussion, knowledge to help create school change. We encourage our readers to reach out and begin the inquiry that will lead to understanding, developing, and teaching and leading on behalf of themselves and the students entrusted to them.

- If a focus on the social patterns of schools is to result in improved educational outcomes, current practices must be deliberated in the context of the purposes and goals for educational progress.

Although much of the restructuring movement has focused on the daily interactions of students in classrooms, little of it has resulted in systemic change. For example, the assumption that schools are competitive arenas has yet to be challenged in most of our school communities. Furthermore, many educational reforms have done little to affect student outcomes (David, 1990; Newmann, 1996). Without focusing on student outcomes one might ask, why bother? Yet schools consistently have adopted reform agendas that do little to meet the needs of students. Our favorite example is site-based management (SBM). Hailed as one of the most promising reform efforts of the 1980s, SBM has stalled in many schools that have adopted it. In part, it has stalled due to lack of understanding about mission and purpose. In part, it has stalled due to an inability of faculty to move beyond surface politics. Yet, in many schools SBM has stalled because faculty have become bored with seemingly endless discussion about issues unrelated to their daily life in classrooms. In the end, many site teams have failed to focus on issues of teaching and learning, students and instruction.

If you come away with no other memory of this text, we would hope you come away with the memory that school change and reform efforts must be directly linked to student growth, progress, and instructional goals. However, we feel clarification is needed here to explain the kinds of foci we believe are important to achieve these goals. Since A Nation at Risk in 1983, educators have been overwhelmed by the call for excellence in schools. Implicit in this call is a strong emphasis on production. Demands for more academically engaged students, quality workers, and effective team members for a changing workplace have dominated both the political and business literatures as they promote their vision for schools. Educational leaders are repeatedly called on to focus their efforts on the goal of producing students who embody these attributes.

Such a focus suggests that economic utility and global competition are the primary purposes for schooling in America (Beck, 1992; Postman, 1995). Simply put, schools exist to train and educate a workforce so America can compete in a global marketplace. Relying on the notion of a competitive ethic, success is achieving more, faster, than others. Educators are forced into the position of scampering for programs that can deliver the goods. Thus, strategies for improving schools include improving basic skills (i.e., a core curriculum), more class time devoted to instruction (i.e., time on task), longer school years, and higher and stricter graduation standards (i.e., proficiency testing). Yet, rarely, do we ask if the purposes of these programs align with the democratic values we hold for students and schools. We assert that a competitive economic model falls short of providing educators a satisfactory model for school reform.

The competitive economic model falls short for two reasons: It fails to provide direction for educators whose work asks them to make hard choices on a daily basis concerning students, and it assumes that strategies that have worked in businesses are both appropriate and feasible in schools. In Postman's (1995) words, "the [model] of economic utility fails to provide adequate purpose for students and teachers to complete the necessary daily tasks of schooling" (p. 31).

Uncritically accepting the competitive economic model has resulted in the adoption of many unconnected, directionless, short-term solutions to what remain complex and challenging problems in today's schools. Like back-to-basics curriculum or proficiency testing, we adopt a series of programs and policies designed to mitigate our failings without challenging the identification of those failings as accurate or just. Therefore, our reform agenda addresses failings, focusing on the insufficiencies of students to produce, rather than the possibility of creating open, trusting, professional communities of learning. What we have lost in our emphasis on competition and economic utility is a sense of the intrinsic value of students as people (Beck, 1992; Noddings, 1984). Development of an expanded conception of educational values allows educators to develop an expanded perspective of the purposes of schooling. Examination of the values and purposes of education, schools and schooling are important foci if we are to promote human growth and community development.

To begin focusing on possibilities rather than insufficiency, we offer a series of simple, yet orienting questions to be used in formal and informal meetings:

1. Does this discussion focus on students in ways that suggest positive change?
2. Does this discussion focus on instruction? Do we continue to challenge the status quo?
3. Does this discussion reflect our instructional goals for individual student progress and growth?

4. In what ways can we challenge our current understandings of learning?
5. In what ways can we challenge students' beliefs about their own capacity to learn?

By focusing on students and instruction, in the spirit of school reform, we suggest that attention to the social patterns that exist in schools will then result in meaningful, lasting change.

SUMMARY

We argued throughout this text that school improvement efforts have little chance of succeeding without an expanded understanding of current social patterns coupled with a thoughtful focus on the purpose of new patterns. To improve school and student performance, professional and public involvement in our educational systems must be strengthened. The ideas in this book have focused on developing mutually reinforcing theories and strategies that build knowledge and skills, broaden information about the current practices in schools, and provide direct rewards for neglected members of school organizations. Applying these ideas requires that all members of the educational effort develop a shared understanding of the hidden ways schools reinforce societal inequities as well as a commitment to continuous examination and improvement of teaching and learning.

As educational systems move in the direction of challenging the traditional and creating schools that benefit all members of the community, we can move away from service models that focus only on the detail complexity or bureaucracy of schools. We can create school organizations that focus on dynamic complexity; hopefully, what will emerge is a variety of school organizations, each focused on the learning needs of the student population they are designed to serve.

Knowledge of organizational literacy serves many purposes. However, without effort and focus, knowledge alone cannot ensure systemic change. We agree that redesigning schools into places where social patterns are identified and addressed will be extremely challenging. We believe that such efforts can result in the creation of schools that are better places in which to work and learn, places that are deserving of our attention and labor as well as places where students and faculty feel valued and hopeful. Places we would be proud to be a part of.

9

Cases for Analysis

◆ ◆ ◆

In the spirit of constructivist teaching, learning, and analysis we offer five cases for discussion and further study. Constructivist teaching practices help learners to internalize and reshape new information. We believe that oftentimes the best and most authentic learning occurs after the text has been consumed and digested. In our teaching we have learned that the provision of final projects, narratives, and case study often provide students the ability to synthesize information in new and creative ways. Such study seeks the long answer, the application of life story and theory, and then uses these tellings to develop how a student's ideas are constructed, authored, owned, and interpreted by themselves. Attention is paid to how analysis and evaluation are constructed and represented.

The cases are provided to allow students of organizational literacy an opportunity to hone their skills of analysis and evaluation and to apply the ideas presented in the text in more holistic ways than the chapter cases provide. As with all of the cases in this text, the foundation for the case stories are based on either schools we have visited or schools in which our students teach. The cases are followed by activities designed to create discussion and strengthen the ideas presented in the previous chapters. We would encourage you to move beyond our suggestions and to incorporate your own activities and discussion topics as you proceed through the study of these case vignettes.

CLOSING LAKE HIGH SCHOOL

Lake High School occupies a full block in a medium-sized midwestern city. Built in the late 1920s, the brick structure is home to 2,800 students in Grades 10 through 12. Students move from class to class through their seven-period day and enjoy a full complement of extracurricular activities. The building opens at 6 a.m. for staff and faculty. Students can take a zero-hour class—jazz band and aerobics are popular offerings—and they begin to arrive around 6:30. The school is open late as well. Extracurricular sports begin after the last bell rings, as do many clubs and rehearsals for several musical and drama groups.

The faculty at Lake High School are proud of the school's academic tradition. Over the years, the school has produced a number of National Merit Scholars and 85% of the students go on to a 4-year college. Many of these students are the first in their family to attend a 4-year school; a source of pride for the faculty and parents in the community. Members of the faculty often comment on their ability to engage their students in higher order thinking and cooperative activities. They credit the efforts of the junior high and elementary schools in the district with setting the stage for the success of students at Lake High.

Faculty also enjoy a liberal policy for professional development. Faculty often take time from their classroom duties to attend workshops and plan curriculum. They enjoy the freedom to experiment with creative instructional forms and are often seen demonstrating new ideas for their peers. Although there is not much interdisciplinary study at Lake High, teachers often work to coordinate schedules so similar topics share top billing for students. Notable examples of such coordination include the study of probability in mathematics before science students begin genetics as a topic of study, and the study of novels in English to complement social studies content.

Faculty are also quick to credit the administration for the strong support they lend to the efforts of the staff in the area of academics. Teachers comment that the work they do is respected by the administrative team in many ways. For example, announcements occur at the beginning and end of the day and never interrupt classes except in case of emergency. Another source of pride for the faculty is the presence of the administrative team in the halls, lunchroom, and classrooms. They believe that as the principal and many assistant principals walk the halls of the building, they get to know students in ways that they could not if they stayed in the office. The principal prides himself on knowing many students' names and personally calls parents to share the successes of students.

Students like attending Lake High because they enjoy the high energy level of the staff and the focus on their academic growth. Students often comment that they believe teachers care about them as people, not just as students. Students also remark on the many after-school activities available to them, allowing them to extend friendships beyond the lunchroom.

So when the district announced plans to close the aging building after the construction of a new school was completed, a sense of excitement quickly moved through the faculty, community, and students. This excitement was quickly dampened when the staff and students learned that included in the closure plans were plans to reorganize the district to so that the new school would hold only a fraction of the students currently attending Lake High. The remaining students would be attending other high schools in the district. The reorganization of the boundary lines in the district would cause many students and faculty to be forced to move to new schools.

The faculty were stunned. Teachers believed the environment that had been created at Lake would be difficult to re-create elsewhere. They noted that although none of the staff would miss the leaking roof, clanging radiators, and lack of air conditioning, they would miss the closeness among the staff and the camaraderie they felt with the parents and students who attended Lake. Privately, they wondered if another school would provide the level of support they had enjoyed for professional development and growth. Publicly, they wondered what would happen to the friendships they had developed with other members of the faculty.

Furthermore, many of the faculty had taught their entire career at Lake High. As veteran teachers, they now looked forward to a certain predictability in their work. They knew they would be assigned to teach certain courses each year and could count on the regularity of the school calendar at Lake High. They also could rely on their colleagues to provide assistance in times of need and capable support for instructional and classroom issues.

The teachers' union also publicly voiced their concerns about the nature of the upcoming transfers of high school faculty. To date, a large-scale transfer of faculty had not occurred in this community and the union was attentive to issues of seniority and teacher preference. The union president, a high school teacher herself, set forth a legal inquiry into the processes other districts had used to protect the rights of the membership.

Parents also had concerns. Many parents had attended Lake High themselves and liked knowing that their children were going to the same community school they had attended. Over the years, the building had come to represent the success that had come to the neighborhood families. Furthermore, they doubted that the teachers in another school would care as deeply for their students as they had been cared for at Lake.

The students had mixed feelings. Many of those who were most upset over the closure were the students involved with athletics. They had lived their lives waiting to become Lake High Tigers and felt that opportunity had been unjustly taken away from them. Student athletes were concerned that their ability to gain playing time on new teams with new coaches would be limited. Because the opportunity to obtain an athletic scholarship is based in part on the availability of large amounts of guaranteed playing time, they worried about their futures as students beyond high school.

The same worries concerned many of the upcoming graduating senior class. As current juniors, they believed the relationships they had forged with the faculty would provide a stable base for letters of recommendation to college. They had also looked forward to continuing their studies with teachers they had grown to know and admire.

However, there was a segment of the student body that welcomed the closing of the school. The size of the student body at Lake had been a source of frustration for many students. Although the staff had strived to create many activities for student participation, it was impossible to provide opportunity for all the students who wanted to play football, basketball, and hockey or hold the leading role in the school play. By moving to a smaller school, some students hoped they would have greater opportunity to participate in high profile extracurricular activities.

Similarly, newer faculty felt a professional move might prove interesting. As in many high schools, newer faculty were often assigned to teach the more basic classes while the veteran faculty enjoyed the opportunity to teach the more advanced sections. Perhaps in a district reorganization they might find themselves offered an exciting new teaching opportunity.

Everyone at Lake High waited with great anticipation to discover how the district would proceed. The school board called a series of community meetings designed to provide an opportunity for teachers, parents, and students to voice their concerns and learn about the new school their children would attend. The union held a number of breakfasts and after-school events to inform the high school faculty of the union's stance toward the transfers.

Over the next year, the district worked closely with the community, teachers, union, and students as the closure of Lake High neared. Early in the year, buried time capsules were opened, exclaimed over, and resealed to be included in the foundation of the new building. As the winter progressed, the faculty were advised of their new position and placement. Although a few faculty members chose to seek employment in neighboring districts, many cheerfully participated in the retreats and inservices offered by the district to orient the newly formed faculties. The spring of Lake's final year was marked by a series of celebrations as previous graduating classes held reunions and parties to remember their years at Lake High. Textbooks were packed to be shipped to the new high school and individual teachers boxed their personal belongings for the district to move to their new assignment. Although the neighborhood would have liked to see Lake High remain the centerpiece of their community, they reluctantly resigned themselves to the school's closure. Amid tears, the building closed for its final time as a high school in early June. For many community members, the symbolic meaning the high school held for them was lost.

In September, the new high school opened and the community, students, and teachers began the process of creating a new shared meaning for themselves in a new setting.

Activities

1.   Using the case as your data bank, identify the social, cultural, and historical patterns and practices that are present in the case. List, chart, or web these. How do these patterns affect the professional or scholarly interactions among the members of the case? How do these patterns affect social interactions between the members of the case?

2.   How could solution(s) be found using the social, cultural, and historical patterns discussed in this book to continue to create a school in which high quality learning is present as well as quality staff relations?

3. Consider your own high school experience. What different meanings were held in that organization? Identify four or five distinct groups that existed in your school. Describe what meanings school life may have held for the members of those groups.

EQUAL TIME

It was late afternoon at Adams–Ashton Study Center. Most of the teachers had gone home for the day with the exception of a few newer teachers who were known for working late into the evening. They had all been hired in the previous 2 years and formed a supportive group—always ready to help each other out with a lesson idea or a willing ear for discussions about shared management problems. Today, a Tuesday, was no different. As Alan Marshall, Adams–Ashton's principal, walked the halls he saw a tightly gathered group in Talisha's room.

Adams–Ashton Study Center was a unique concept in this urban district. Housed at two sites, the primary building, Adams, was home to 15 kindergarten through Grade 3 classes and a teaching staff of 20. The intermediate site, Ashton School, contained an equal number of classes and teachers of Grades 4 through 6. Both schools had a history of low test scores, high staff turnover, and high absenteeism rates. Until recently, the schools had been separate buildings with separate principals and separate concerns. However, in a recent downsizing move, the upper administration had decided to merge the two buildings creating separate primary and intermediate sites. The move had been popular with parents. The two sites were within blocks of each other and the boundary lines had always seemed to blur. Additionally, parents had liked the separate site idea. The district had sold the plan by stressing the ability for teachers to work together at the study centers and the ability to provide special early start services at the primary building.

Early start included three separate components. The first was a comprehensive kindergarten program that began when the child turned 5. The district had abandoned the idea that children should start school only in September. Instead, children started at their fifth birthday, effectively eliminating the birthday cutoff for kindergartners. Promotion to the first grade was then based on the mastery of entry skills from the reading, writing, and mathematics areas. Students could be enrolled in kindergarten for as long as 2 years or as short a period as 6 months. It was district policy that children had to complete at least a semester of kindergarten before they could be considered for promotion to the first grade.

Early start's kindergarten program received national attention. Hailed as an innovative way to met the intellectual and social needs of young children, by all accounts it was a success. Teachers enjoyed teaching in the program. It was especially rewarding in those cases where children who had been considered not quite ready could enjoy an extra year of school preparation and skill development. The downside was the constant entry of new students; yet, an effective peer mentoring and buddy system had been implemented to bring new students up to speed as quickly as possible.

The second and third components of the early start program were popular as well. The school literally had an early start. The doors were open at 6 a.m. and a breakfast program was in place for the primary students. Staffed by para-professionals, the morning time allowed students to be dropped off when their parents left for work and therefore avoided a second day-care switch. Parents and students alike enjoyed the ability to have a one-stop morning. Finally, early start provided pre-K screening for learning problems and strengths as well as medical check-ups and vaccination programs.

When the district had merged Adams–Ashton, they had promised the community cutting-edge education and by all accounts appeared to be making good on that promise. The program also was cost efficient. By merging the two staffs, the district had managed to cut a principal's position and make better use of the music and physical education teachers as well. The total savings to the district had been approximately $100,000. This saved money had then been used to support the early start program. Alan Marshall, originally the principal at Adams, now found his time split between two buildings but nonetheless enjoyed some personal benefits in the job. Because the school sites had been marked as innovative schools in the district's restructuring program, he had been allowed to hire several new staff positions, mostly in the primary school. He had also been allowed to create an agreement with the local university to provide an internship site for the development of new school administrators. So even though officially he had sole responsibility for two school sites, in practice, each site always had a second administrator present. This allowed Alan freedom from many daily tasks that could eat at an administrator's time. For example, his intern administrators handled most of the day-to-day discipline as well as much of the teacher supervision load. This afforded Alan time for the work he loved best—school reform and change programs.

As part of his reform program, he had centered much of his energy on the development of new teachers like the ones he now saw huddled in Talisha Wren's room. In fact, he was glad to see many of his newer teachers gathered this afternoon because he had good news to share with them. In the past year, Alan had worked toward the development of a special fund of money to provide teachers with extra time for extra work. Similar to a coaching stipend, Alan saw the money as a way to support his new teachers in the development of their skills. The money, most of it donated by a local industry grant program, was to provide new teachers with tuition dollars for college coursework related to their teaching area. However, Alan had held aside some of the money to provide for what he called reflective days. His idea was to provide substitute time for teachers who wanted an extended period of time to develop new programs and units. It was this plan he shared with his new teachers.

As promised, Alan announced the reflective time program at the next faculty meeting. The new teachers were excited and began making plans for their day off. Talisha was the first to use her day and came back to school excited about the unit she had begun to work on for her reading students. She had used her day to make an appointment with a friend who was a children's librarian and had returned with a long list of source material she could use to help her class develop research skills. Her excitement was infectious.

Alan headed back to his office pleased his program seemed to be headed for instant success. Yet, as he entered his office, he was greeted by two veteran Ashton teachers with yellow legal pads in hand. They expressed immediate concern over what they called an unfairness between the treatment of the two buildings. All the programs that gained attention were at Adams, they charged, as well as most of the improvement money. Accusing Alan of favoring the Adams staff, they pointed to reflective time as the ultimate example. Alan tried to explain his desire to support the development of new teachers, but was met with anger. "Our school thinks you're allowing these primary teachers to take days off to shop. We heard that Talisha went to the bookstore and out to lunch with a college buddy."

Alan quickly responded, first explaining how Talisha had used her day and secondly by attempting to explain the program and put it in a better light. Calling it a pilot for new teachers, he promised that if it resulted in better planned, more interesting learning opportunities for students, he would expand the program to the full faculties at Adams–Ashton next year. The teachers seemed calmed. Alan felt that he had settled what could have potentially been a crisis situation.

Activities

1.   Alan Marshall developed a plan that he thought could provide much needed time for new teachers to reflect and develop new teaching skills. Was this a good idea? How might he had handled the situation differently to provide for more equitable allotment of resources in the two buildings?

2.   Does Alan seem to be favoring the new faculty and the Adams school? How could he create opportunity for programs at both schools while still favoring the development of new teachers?

3.   Comment on the early start program. Is this an example of providing programs that count for minority children? Could this kind of program help to level the playing field for other urban children?

GRADING AT WASHINGTON MIDDLE SCHOOL

Jessie Pender was proud to walk the halls of Washington Middle School. She saw before her the kind of school of which she never believed she could be principal. The brand new, state-of-the-art school had opened only months before. Landing the job had not been easy. She had to interview on three separate occasions, each more stressful that the last. Her final interview had been a community forum. She was asked to answer questions from an audience of concerned parents and business leaders. It had been tough. On several occasions during the interview, she had thought she had lost her shot at the job. Her no-nonsense approach to discipline and school governance had taken a number of community members by surprise. She left feeling they were looking for a more laid-back kind of person, not someone like herself who knew what she wanted in a school faculty and how she expected children to behave. When the call came to offer her the position, she was truly excited and surprised. The personnel director assured her that it was exactly her style that had won her the job. The parents had loved her take-charge attitude and were anxious to support her commitment to excellence. Her newly acquired doctorate in educational administration had not hurt either, he confided. Many parents in the upper middle-class community Washington served were pleased to have a doctor for a principal. They felt it offered the school a sense of prestige.

In her new role as principal, the first meeting Jessie called was held during the month of July. Although the final touches had not been finished in the new building, she took her staff on a tour, instructing them on how final work would complete the structure and what rooms they could expect to call home. She assured them the building would open on time and they would have plenty of time to prepare for the new student body. Finally, the meeting ended over a barbecue in the parking lot. She felt the staff was off to a good start. She felt strongly that she had assembled the best teachers she could find to fill the positions at Washington. The district had been experiencing amazing growth over the past few years as the urban center moved east toward old farmland. Housing had boomed and many new families had followed the prosperity east as well. Jessie had been able to choose from a long list of teachers already employed by the district as well as hiring about 20 new teachers—a mix of transfers from other districts and new, fresh faces. She felt the staff were a good combination. Not too many old timers and just the right mix of new blood. Jessie had hoped to avoid the problems some principals had when they took over a building run by someone else. By staggering her hires, she hoped that the staff from other buildings in the district would provide her needed insight into how things were traditionally handled in the district, and the new faculty would temper their sense of having a home court advantage.

As the summer neared its end, Jessie began putting in longer and longer hours at the school site. She began to fear that the building would not open on time, that school would have to be delayed, and that her teachers would not have enough time to move their materials into their new classrooms. When the carpet failed to arrive at 9 one morning, she was on the phone with the distributor, demanding the crew work the weekend to complete the task if necessary. Similar problems arose with the paint crew and again she found herself negotiating extra hours and overtime so the job could be completed. She viewed these tasks as necessary to the smooth opening to a new school year. Close friends reminded her that things would settle down after the students and faculty were in place. Word spread around the community about her demands. Reaction was split. Some teachers and parents were impressed by her decisive action, imagining their concerns would be treated as swiftly. Others questioned her impulsiveness.

The building nearing completion, Jessie called a staff meeting at the new site. The faculty crowded into the media center amid boxes of library materials, computers, and school supplies. Jessie introduced herself formally to the faculty, reminding them that she preferred to be called Dr. Pender and added that in the interest of professionalism, all staff require students call them by their last name as well. Introductions accomplished, she began to orient the faculty to her vision for the middle school and outlined several programs she hoped to develop, including extensive foreign language offerings and several advanced placement or honors courses. Jessie then explained how she had arranged for these courses to be taught by faculty shared with the high school but promised the staff that, if successful, the middle school would begin hiring their own staff to fill these positions as early as January.

Several of the staff were shocked. They had expected to be a part of decisions such as these. Previously, the district had worked to include teachers in all decisions considered part of the instructional program. Although not quite site-based managed, the district negotiated as part of the last union contract a clause allowing teachers input as necessary into all program planning. Several faculty vowed to keep their eyes on this new doctor. Still others were happy to be working for an administrator as dedicated as Jessie. In the past, a few teachers had worked for principals that had not seemed to accomplish anything and they welcomed Jessie's take-charge attitude and spunk.

Finally, Jessie distributed the new faculty handbooks and a special gift to each faculty member—a desk set and school stationary imprinted with each teacher's name and position. "For writing notes home or other professional correspondence," Jessie added. She asked each faculty member to read the handbook carefully and dismissed the hour-long meeting, allowing teachers to begin the task of moving in and setting up for the new year. For most teachers, the handbook sat unread as they attended to more pressing issues. In fact, it was not until a month into the school year that the handbook would be mentioned again.

The October faculty meeting was progressing well. The faculty had celebrated the birthdays of the month and had taken part in a long discussion concerning the use of playing fields during lunches for intramural activity. The faculty appeared to be coming together intellectually and socially. Jessie was beginning to feel successful. Just as the faculty was leaving the meeting, Jessie called out, "Just a reminder, your mid-term grades are due to me by the 15th." The faculty stopped short. Mid-term grades? What had they missed? John Lammont, a tall, outspoken math teacher asked for the group, "Mid-terms? When was this decided?" Jessie looked up from her papers and answered quickly, "It's in the handbook, under the section on grading policy. I'd assumed you'd all read it."

The staff felt caught. Admitting to not reading the handbook was one thing, but their concerns ran deeper. What else was in that book? The meeting adjourned and the teachers fled the room, heading back for a look at the long-forgotten handbook. Pockets of staff members collected in the open hallways as they riffled through the pages, looking for the section on grading. To their chagrin, the section was plainly written. It called for a midterm report of all students who might receive a grade lower than a C and instructions on providing parents information concerning all missing assignments. The section also outlined the all school grading policy; it was a typical grade distribution; As would be given for all students with 90% or above in any subject area, Bs for 80% and above, and so forth. "Standard stuff," as one teacher put it. The teachers seemed relieved and vowed to read the handbook lest they be caught by surprise again.

However, a small group of teachers was concerned. They had transferred together, an intact eighth-grade teaching team of six members, and had taken a string of policies from their previous middle school with them to Washington. Traditionally, they had graded on improvement and student achievement on set skills. In fact, they prided themselves on giving almost all As and Bs as students progressed through the curriculum. Retests and redos were their motto and they believed that teaching to mastery served their students well and prepared them for their high school experience. Because mastery was their goal, Cs did not exist in their grading policy. Students either mastered the material at the A or B level or received a grade of IP (in progress) for their efforts. Collectively, they decided not to submit any names to the office at mid-term time.

The remaining staff submitted student names of those at risk of Cs or worse and the front office responded by sending a range of materials designed to help parents provide better study environments for their children as well as providing homework help tips. Parents were encouraged to contact their child's teacher if they were interested in a conference to discuss their student's progress. The eighth-grade team waited for a response. The response finally came on Wednesday afternoon. The team was called down to the office. Jessie was wondering if their lists had gotten lost in the shuffle. "No," the team responded, "the lists had not been lost." They simply did not have any students who would be receiving a C or worse. Jessie was concerned. Her first thoughts leaped to the notion that these teachers were easy graders and she began stressing her concern for excellence and high standards. The team assured her they did hold high standards and in fact they believed that their policy held all students accountable for achieving because they were not allowed to take a C and move on. Mastery was expected and the team believed they were providing an excellent education.

Jessie said she would consider their response. Relieved that the team had not just ignored her request, she left for the day, wondering if perhaps this was a better plan. She decided to schedule a discussion of the idea for an upcoming staff meeting. She asked the team for help in developing a position statement with which she could open discussion. On what ideas had they based this grading policy and on what ideas did they carry it out?

For the November staff meeting, Jessie scheduled an open forum on the grading issue. Prior to the meeting, she distributed the eighth-grade policy as well as a few other statements about grading to the faculty. She also copied a recent article on grading from a professional journal to provide even more information for discussion. Her idea was to hold a discussion in which all sides could state their ideas and perhaps by December a schoolwide policy could be developed.

The faculty entered the meeting with concern. Their previous experience had told them that Jessie was not the kind of administrator whom one could expect to change easily. A few expected a floor fight over the grading issue and others did not seem to understand why the issue was even being discussed. Policy was, after all, policy; wasn't it? The discussion opened easily enough. Jessie introduced the issue and offered an apology of sorts by saying, "It has come to my attention that although I had published a grading policy in the handbook, I had not, perhaps, been open to alternative ideas concerning the subject. I would like to hold that discussion at this time." John was out of his seat at once. "I would like to speak to holding the policy as it stands. Students need to learn responsibility for their own learning. A clear grading policy supports that."

Anna Straught responded, "As a foreign language teacher I have always supported a policy that lets children be rewarded for their improvement. I teach a subject that takes time to master and if I were to grade from the start I would discourage many of my students from taking a second class."

"You're just too nice." It was John again. "I think it's possible to keep kids motivated by grades. My class works to do better. I think a strong grading policy supports kids trying. You just want to praise all the kids all the time. This isn't elementary school anymore. The world's a competitive place. We have to prepare them for it."

Joanne, a new teacher who had been quiet from the start of the year, brought up another concern:

> I'm worried. I grade according to the policy. I give weekly quizzes to see if they're learning the material. I only gave 55% As and Bs at mid-term. I'm worried my reputation will be hurt if others grade easier. I don't care what the policy looks like, but I do think we should be together on whatever it is.

Anna spoke up again:

It's not fair to compare elective classes with academic classes. If I were to give out Cs and Ds the language department would be decimated—no one will support the new program. You have to choose. If you want kids to take risks and try new ideas we cannot be standing over them with a grading policy. You tried but didn't measure up ... sorry.

At this time, Jessie stepped in to the discussion. Flustered, she stated:

This is an issue I had not expected this much discussion on. I really had not considered many of these points. I was seeking to develop a program devoted to excellence. I still think we can get there. However, these issues won't be solved here today. I suggest we form a task force. After the meeting I'll take the names of those who are interested."

Although nothing was resolved at the meeting, Jessie felt relieved. Her faculty had proved itself to be thoughtful and genuinely concerned about the progress and learning of the students. She had entered administration believing that an iron hand was the best was to manage a staff. Perhaps she could trust her staff more. Perhaps it was time to change. She hoped her trust would not prove to be misinformed. She looked forward to the task force meetings and hoped the grading issue would unite rather than divide her new faculty.

Activities

1. Is anything problematic about Jessie's leadership of Washington Middle School?

2. Is anything problematic about the current grading policy at Washington Middle School? Should one team be able to create its own policy? What about the elective departments? Should they have to conform to the same grading policy as the academic teams?

3. Describe the argument between the two teaching interests. With which would you agree, and why? Reflect on the role of mastery learning in your analysis.

4. In analyzing this case, on which theoretical ideas did you draw? From which theoretical perspective would you think this situation is best analyzed and evaluated?

SITE-BASED MANAGEMENT
AT FOREST GLEN ELEMENTARY

In the spring of 1995, contract negotiations were progressing well in the City School District. The recent hiring of a new superintendent had proved to be an excellent decision. The new superintendent, Bill Johnson, had been brought in from a smaller, nearby district. As was popular in this east coast community, he had made a series of moves in his career. Starting as a teacher in a suburban district, he had jumped districts five times in his career. Each transfer had been a promotion for him, both in position and salary. Obtaining the superintendency of City Schools was his crowning achievement.

Located in an urban metropolitan area, City Schools was floundering between the past and the present. The prior superintendent had served the community well for the last 20 years although the district was considered well behind the times in terms of technology and other curriculum innovations. The former superintendent had managed money well and the district could boast that it was one of the few urban districts in the nation not anticipating a crippling debt load in the coming years. Bill counted this as good news. In fact, had he discovered that the district had substantial debt, he would not have taken the position. Here he felt he had a wonderful opportunity to create a new vision for City Schools. His agenda included updating many of the aging buildings, creating technology centers in every school and providing teachers with ample professional development opportunities. Moreover, he was excited to implement a school governance plan for each of the 50 schools in the City District.

Bill viewed the union contract negotiation process as an excellent opportunity to implement some of his ideas. Reasoning that if the administrative position was to offer the teachers more in the way of responsibility for the management of their own buildings, teachers would see by this effort that he meant to treat them as equal in the educational process. He believed that offering opportunities to develop site teams at each school in the contract language itself was a public display of his support for a professionalized teaching force. The union was excited by the administration's offer. Just the previous year, a nearby district had refused to allow contract language concerning the composition of a site team into the contract. Union leadership viewed this move as a positive start with the new superintendent.

The reminder of the negotiations went smoothly. The teachers received a 4.1% raise, extended contract time for curriculum planning during the summer months, and the right to 2 personal days during the school year to be taken at their discretion. The site team language went through as well, stipulating, "Each building may create a site-based governance council consisting of six teachers, the principal or his/her designee, two parents, and one student as appropriate." Principals and teachers, excited by the notion of creating councils, read the language as supportive of shared governance initiatives and those uninterested in site-based governance pointed to the word *may* as assurance that they would not be "forced into a system of governance we didn't want in the first place." The contract was signed in record time—teachers voted and approved the new agreement by a 92% margin by July 1. All parties agreed that the cooperative relationship established through negotiations was a positive sign of things to come for City Schools.

Shortly after the contract was signed, Bill attended to the hiring of new administrators. In a district the size of City Schools, there were at least a few openings every year and this year was no exception. In particular, Bill was interested in hiring a dynamic principal for Forest Glen Elementary School. Forest Glen Elementary served a small population of students in the northeast corner of the city. Forest Glen's attendance rate was among the best in the district, more than 95%, almost 10 full points above the district average. Seventy-two percent were African American, 10% were White, and the remaining students were of Asian or Hispanic decent. Fewer than half of Forest Glen's students came from homes in poverty, as compared to 75% for the rest of the city. However, as one teacher put it, "Our families have gone from blue collar to no collar in a short period of time—we're worried." It was, in short, a school with a solid reputation.

Prior to the coming school year, Forest Glen's principal had been ill, causing the school to be in the position of running itself for most of the year. The principal, a well-loved woman, had decided to retire and left the opening Bill was eager to fill. Because Forest Glen had a reputation for an excellent faculty and a supportive community base, Bill felt with the right principal it could become a model site-managed school. He sought to hire a principal who met those expectations.

When Sandy Ford walked into the personnel office for her interview, Bill knew he had found his principal. Sandy had relocated from the midwest, having followed her husband to his new position. Her experience included working in a school that had established a site council 5 years prior and her references were excellent. Bill virtually hired her on the spot and provided her with a set of keys to the building to check the place out.

Sandy toured the building and met with the former principal to gain insight into the staff she would inherit. She, too, was impressed by the professional culture and academic climate described at Forest Glen. However, despite the glowing reports, Sandy was convinced improvements could be made. An important innovation, she believed, would be to change the perception of the principal's role in the school. Unlike a traditional principal, Sandy viewed herself as a leader of curriculum and instruction, a cheerleader for a focus on teaching and learning. She believed that given the excellence of the staff at Forest Glen, she could easily slide into the role of head teacher and allow most of the management decisions to be made by the site council, much as she had done in her prior position. Sandy also wanted to update the school's evaluation and supervision procedures, instituting a peer-coaching model instead of the outdated checklist-style evaluation the school had used previously. She planned to take these ideas to the site council in early fall.

From the outset, the staff liked and admired Sandy's style of leadership. She made it clear there were changes she wanted to make in the school but approached them from the position of wanting input from all the members of the school community before any real changes would be implemented. Furthermore, she often talked about piloting any new plans to assess the fit with the existing climate at Forest Glen. Teachers felt they could trust Sandy and she felt the teachers would respond well to the new changes she had planned.

At the first meeting of the newly designed site council, Sandy spoke up immediately, asking for assistance in designing a survey to determine the concerns and needs of the school community. Instead of the eager response she had expected, the site council backed down from her idea, suggesting that perhaps they could wait until spring to survey the community and use the first 6 months of the year to get to know one another and develop a mission statement for the team. Sandy pushed her position, reflecting that waiting until spring would waste the year. The council offered a compromise: Sandy could begin plans on her survey but it could not be distributed until the mission statement had been approved. The council successfully argued that without a clear mission their actions might be misunderstood but the community.

Sandy worked closely with Bill over the next month on the survey. He was supportive of her efforts and offered to accompany her to the October meeting to support her plan, the survey and the council's efforts. Part welcome, and part business, was how he described his upcoming presence at the site council meeting. Sandy was grateful for his involvement. Privately, she hoped that with Bill's support, the council would see how important the survey could be to the direction of the school and they would take action on distribution of the document more quickly.

The meeting began uneventfully. Bill offered his welcome to the newly formed site council and made a few remarks about visiting all the teams over the next few months. The minutes from the last meeting were distributed, coffee was served and Sandy spoke up, "I have here the draft of the community/school survey for your review." She distributed the five-page document and waited as the members read the sample items provided in the packet. After 10 minutes had passed, Hal Resman put down his copy and carefully stated, "I think there's been a misunderstanding. I thought we had tabled this until the mission statement was finished." Sandy quickly responded, "My understanding was we were to develop the two simultaneously." Quick glances between the other members on the committee reinforced Sandy's sense that she had overstepped the boundaries established by the new site council and needed to reconsider her actions.

Sandy said:

> I'm concerned I have lost your trust here, I only wanted to begin a process I see as important to the growth of our school. I realize that site-based decision making can stretch the decision-making process out over several months and I felt that I could take some initiative on my own and then seek your approval. I'll be honest with you. I had also asked for Superintendent Johnson's help on the document in front of you. Again, I only wanted to begin, to take action, to start a new initiative for Forest Glen. I only hope you can see past my eagerness to begin and allow us to work on creating a school-based governance system that can work.

Activities

1. What skills are necessary for members of site councils to operate effectively?

2. Site-based management is often seen as a vehicle to influence relationships among staff, parents, and community as well as to enhance student learning. Do you see evidence of this happening at Forest Glen?

3. If you were to remedy this situation, from which theoretical notions would you draw? How is this problem influenced by feminist theory? Critical theory? Political? Bureaucratic?

4. Is it possible to exercise leadership while building consensus?

SUBSTITUTE WOES

The following memo has appeared in your mail box:

October 29, 1995
To: Terry Smith, school principal
From: Tim Brown, substitute teacher

You don't know me but I have been a substitute teacher in this school from time to time over the last several years. I don't like to complain because I'm not that kind of person and because I think this is a good school. However, I (and others) are considering asking not to be placed in this building again and thought you should know why I/we feel this way. I/we offer these comments in the spirit that improvement can result from your attention to these matters.

First, rarely have I (and others) found an up-to-date lesson plan from a teacher who is absent. I understand that on occasion it is impossible for a teacher who is ill to provide a full plan, but I often find no plans, even in cases where the teacher knows he or she is to be absent. In these cases, if I know about the meeting several weeks in advance, I assume they must know as well. Not providing a detailed plan in that case is deplorable. A substitute teacher's job is hard enough, but without lesson plans it is terrible.

Second, along with the absence of lesson plans there is often an absence of other, more procedural, kinds of information. Seating charts, discipline procedures, fire drill information, etc., are often unobtainable. The absence of these kinds of information put your students and me in an untenable position as to classroom management and safety issues.

Third, I often try to eat my lunch in the staff room. I find this helps me to get to know the climate of the building and allows me to ask questions of other teachers. Often the discussion in the room is less than professional. Student names are often tossed about and rather nasty or personal things are said. As a parent in the district, I find it distressing that students appear to be so ill-treated and disrespected by faculty. This lack of professionalism is discouraging, as I would like to believe that the teachers really do care about kids, as your school slogan states.

I/we would be happy to meet with you about these issues. Thank you for your prompt attention to this matter.

cc: Cindy Jones, assistant superintendent for personnel

Activities

1.   The involvement of the parents and substitutes can have a strong impact on the image of a school. To what degree should community members, such as parents and substitutes, have a say in school affairs?

2.   What would you do in this case? How could these relationships be managed differently?

3.   From what arena is the letter writer operating? How else might he have shared his concerns? Do you think this was an appropriate memo?

4.   Substitutes often comment that their work is difficult because they rarely get to develop a lasting relationship with the students they contact. They remark on the difference in their daily experience when they work regularly with one school or class, stating that it is easier to work in buildings they know well. Which ideas from the organizational theory and practice would help to explain why this is so?

References

◆◆◆

Abas, K. K. (1997). Neglected aspects of the liberal–communitarian debate and implications for school communities. *Educational Foundations, 11,* 63–82.

Abrahamsson, B. (1993). *The logic of organizations.* Newbury Park, CA: Sage.

Aktouf, O. (1992). Management and theories of organization in the 1990s: Toward a critical radical humanism? *Academy of Management Review, 17*(3), 407–431.

Alcoff, L. (1988). Cultural feminism versus post-structuralism: The identify crisis in feminist theory. In E. Minnich, J. O'Barr, & R. Rosenfeld (Eds.), *Reconstructing the academy* (pp. 257–288). Chicago: University of Chicago Press.

Allison, C. (1995). *Present and past.* New York: Peter Lang.

Allison, L. (1996). Power. In I. McLean (Ed.), *The concise Oxford dictionary of Politics.* New York: Oxford University Press.

Alvesson, M., & Willmot, H. (1994). Making sense of management: A critical analysis. Thousand Oaks, CA: Sage.

Amato, J. A. (1982). *Guilt and gratitude: A study of the origins of contemporary conscience.* Westport, CT: Greenwood.

American Association of University Women. (1992). *The AAUW report: How schools shortchange girls.* Washington DC: The AAUW Educational Foundation and National Education Association.

Anderson, G. (1989, April). *The management of meaning and the achievement of organizational legitimacy.* Paper presented at the annual meeting of the American Educational Research Association, San Francisco.

Angus, L. (1985, April). *Human action and social structure in the study of schools as organizations.* Paper prepared for the annual meeting of the American Educational Research Association, Chicago.

Anyon, J. (1995). Social class and hidden curriculum. In E. Stevens & G. Wood (Eds.), *Justice, ideology, and education* (pp. 162–178). New York: McGraw-Hill. (Original work published 1980)

Apple, M. (1979). *Ideology and curriculum.* Boston: Routledge.

Apple, M. (1982). *Education and power.* Boston: Routledge.

Apple, M. (1985). Teaching and "women's work": A comparative historical and ideological analysis. *Teachers College Record, 86*(3), 445–473.

Apple, M. (1993). *Official knowledge: democratic education in a conservative age.* Boston: Routledge.

Apple, M. (1996). *Cultural politics and education.* New York: Teachers College Press.

Appleby, J. (1992). *Liberalism and republicanism in the historical imagination.* Cambridge, MA: Harvard University Press.

Arnett, R. C. (1986). *Communication and community.* Carbondale & Edwardsville: Southern Illinois University Press.

Aronowitz, S., & Giroux, H. (1993). *Education still under siege* (2nd ed.). Westport, CT: Bergin & Garvey.

Ayres, J. (1984). Four approaches to interpersonal communication. *Western Journal of Speech Communication, 48,* 408–440.

Ball, S. J. (1987). *The micro-politics of the school: Towards a theory of school organization.* London: Metheun.

Ball, S. J., & Bowen, R. (1991). Micropolitics of radical change: Budgets, management, and control in British schools. In J. Blase (Ed.), *The politics of life in schools: Power, conflict, and cooperation* (pp. 19–45). Newbury Park, CA: Sage.

Ballantine, J. (1997). *The sociology of education* (4th ed.). Upper Saddle River, NJ: Prentice-Hall.

Bates, R. (1987). Corporate culture, schooling, and educational administration. *Educational Administration Quarterly, 23*(4), 79–115.

Beane, J., & Apple, M. (1995). The case for democratic schools. In M. Apple & J. Beane (Eds.), *Democratic schools* (pp. 1–25). Alexandria, VA: Association for Supervision and Curriculum Development.

Beck, L. G. (1992). Meeting the challenge of the future: The place of a caring ethic in educational administration. *American Journal of Education, 100*(4), 454–496.

Beck, U. (1992). *The risk society: Toward a new modernity.* Newbury Park, CA: Sage.

Belenky, M. F., Clinchy, B. M., Goldberger, N. R., & Tarule, J. M. (1986). *Women's ways of knowing: The development of self, voice, and mind.* New York: Basic Books.

Bell C., & Chase S. (1992). The underrepresentation of women in school leadership. In C. Marshall (Ed.), *The new politics of race and gender: The 1992 yearbook of the politics of education association* (pp. 141–154). Washington, DC: Falmer Press.

Bellah, R. M., Madsen, R., Sullivan, W. M., Swidler, A., & Tipton, S. M. (1985). *Habits of the heart: Individualism and commitment in American life.* New York: Perennial Library.

Bellah, R. N., Madsen, R., Sullivan, W. M., Swidler, A., & Tipton, S. M. (1991). *The good society.* New York: Knopf.

Bennett deMarrais, K., & LeCompte, M. (1995). *The way schools work.* White Plains, NY: Longman.

Bennett, W. (1996, August 13). Civil rights is the GOP mission. *Los Angeles Times*, p. B5.

Benz, C. R. (1996, October). *Feminist pedagogy: A model for classrooms in educational administration.* Paper presented at the University Council of Educational Administration, Louisville, KY.

Bercovitch, S. (1993). *The rites of assent: Transformations in the symbolic construction of America.* New York: Routledge.

Berger, P. L., & Berger, B. (1979). Becoming a member of society. In P. Rose (Ed.), *Socialization and the life cycle.* New York: St. Martin's Press.

Beyer, L. (1996). *Creating democratic classrooms.* New York: Teachers College Press.

Blase, J. (1984). A data based model of how teachers cope with stress. *The Journal of Educational Administration, 22*, 173–191.

Blase, J. (1985). The socialization of beginning teachers: An ethnographic study of factors contributing to the rationalization of the teacher's instructional perspective. *Urban Education, 20*, 235–256.

Blase, J. (1987). Political interactions among teachers: Sociocultural context in the schools. *Urban Education, 22*, 286–309.

Blase, J. (Ed.). (1991a). *The politics of life in schools: Power, conflict, and cooperation.* Newbury Park, CA: Sage.

Blase, J. (1991b). The micropolitical perspective. In J. Blase (Ed.), *The politics of life in schools: Power, conflict, and cooperation* (pp. 1–18). Newbury Park, CA: Sage.

Blase, J. (1991c). Everyday political perspectives of teachers toward students: The dynamics of diplomacy. In J. Blase (Ed.), *The politics of life in schools: Power, conflict, and cooperation* (pp. 185–206). Newbury Park, CA: Sage.

Bolman, L., & Deal, T. (1991). *Reframing organizations: Artistry, choice, and leadership.* San Francisco: Jossey-Bass.

Bourdieu, P. (1986/1997). The forms of capital. In A. H. Halsey, H. Lauder, P. Brown, & A. S. Wells (Eds.), *Education: Culture, economy, and society* (pp. 46–58). New York: Oxford University Press.

Bowles, S., & Gintis, H. (1976). *Schooling in capitalist America: Educational reform and the contradictions of economic life.* New York: Basic Books.

Brinkley, A. (1982). *Voices of protest: Huey Long, Father Coughlin, and the Great Depression.* New York: Vintage Books.

Brinkley, A. (1998). *Liberalism and its discontents.* Cambridge, MA: Harvard University Press.

Brown, C. T., & Keller, P. W. (1973). *Monologue to dialogue.* Englewood Cliffs, NJ: Prentice-Hall.

Brown, R. (1976). *Modernization: The transformation of American life, 1600–1865.* Prospect Heights, IL: Waveland Press.

Bryk, A. S., & Driscoll, M. E. (1988). *The school as community: Theoretical foundations, contextual influences, and consequences for students and teachers.* Madison, WI: Center for Effective Secondary Schools, University of Wisconsin.

Bryk, A. S., Lee, V. E., & Holland, P. E. (1993). *Catholic schools and the common good.* Cambridge, MA: Harvard University Press.

Buell, F. (1994). *National culture and the new global system.* Baltimore: Johns Hopkins University Press.

Bull, B. L., Fruehling, R. T., & Chattergy, V. (1992). *The ethics of multicultural and bilingual education.* New York: Teachers College Press.

Caldwell, B. J., & Spinks, J. M. (1992). *Leading the self-managed school.* Washington, DC: Falmer Press Education Policy Perspectives Series.

Carnegie Council on Adolescent Development. (1989). *Turning points: Preparing youth for the 21st century.* New York: Carnegie Corporation of New York.

Carnegie Forum on Education and the Economy. (1986). *A nation prepared: Teachers for the 21st century.* New York: Carnegie Corporation of New York.

Carnoy, M., & Levin, H. (1985/1993). Contradiction in education. In H. Shapiro & D. Purpel (Eds.), *Critical social issues in American education* (pp. 5–29). New York: Longman.

Carroll, P. (1982). *It seemed like nothing happened: The tragedy and promise of America in the 1970s.* New York: William Abrahams.

Carroll, P., & Noble, D. W. (1989). *The free and unfree: A new history of the United States.* New York: Penguin.

Carter, L. (1985). *Contemporary constitutional lawmaking: The supreme court and the art of politics.* Cambridge, MA: Harvard University Press.

Chase S. (1995). *Ambiguous empowerment: The work narratives of women school superintendents.* Amherst, MA: University of Massachusetts Press.

Cohen, E. G. (1994). *Designing group work.* New York: Teachers College Press.

Corbett, H. D. (1991). Community influence and school micropolitics: A case example. In J. Blase (Ed.), *The politics of life in schools: Power, conflict, and cooperation* (pp. 73–95). Newbury Park, CA: Sage.

Corcoran, T., Walker, L., & White, L. (1988). *Working conditions of urban teachers.* Washington DC: Institute for Educational Leadership.

Coser, L. (1977). *Masters of sociological thought* (2nd ed.). New York: Harcourt Brace Jovanovich.

Cremin, L. (1970). *American education: The colonial experience, 1607–1783.* New York: Harper & Row.

Cremin, L. (1988). *American education: The metropolitan experience, 1876–1980.* New York: Harper & Row.

Crowley, B. L. (1987). *The self, the individual and the community.* Oxford, England: Clarendon.

Dahl, R. A. (1967). *Pluralist democracy in the United States: Conflict and consent.* Chicago: Rand McNally.

Darling-Hammond, L. (1984). *Beyond the commission reports: The coming crises in teaching.* Santa Monica, CA: RAND.

Darnell, D., & Bruckriede, W. (1976). *Persons communicating.* Englewood Cliffs, NJ: Prentice-Hall.

David, J. (1990). Restructuring in progress: Lessons learned from pioneering districts. In R. F. Elmore (Ed.), *Restructuring schools: The next generation of educational reform* (pp. 209–250). San Francisco: Jossey-Bass.

Dewey, J. (1944). *Democracy and education.* New York: The Free Press. (Original work published 1915)

Downing, L. (1981). Teaching in the little red schoolhouse. In N. Hoffman (Ed.), *Woman's "true" profession* (pp. 27–36). Old Westbury, NY: The Feminist Press. (Original work published 1951)

Dworkin, R. (1977). *Taking rights seriously.* Cambridge, MA: Harvard Press.

Dworkin, R. (1989). Liberal community. *California Law Review, 77*(3), 479–504.

Etzioni, A. (1991). *A responsive society.* San Francisco: Jossey-Bass.

Etzioni, A. (1993). *The Spirit of community: Rights, responsibilities and the communitarian agenda.* New York: Crown.

Evans, S. (1989). *Born for liberty: A history of women in America.* New York: The Free Press.

Fine, M., Weis, L., & Powell, L. (1997). Communities of difference: A critical look at desegregated spaces for and by youth. *Harvard Educational Review, 67*, 247–284.

Fine, M., Weis, L., Powell, L., & Wong, L. (Eds.); (1997). *Off white: Readings on race, power and society.* New York: Routledge.

Finkelstein, B. (1979). Reading, writing, and the acquisition of identity in the United States: 1790–1860. In B. Finkelstein (Ed.), *Regulated children/liberated children: education in psychohistorical perspective* (pp. 114–139). New York: Psychohistory Press.

Firestone, W. A., & Bader, B. D. (1992). *Redesigning teaching: Professionalism or bureaucracy?* Albany: State University of New York Press.

Firestone, W. A., & Rosenblum, S. (1988). Building commitment in urban high schools. *Educational Evaluation and Policy Analysis, 93*(4), 285–299.

Fischer, A. (1978). *Perspectives in human communication.* New York: Macmillan.

Fiske, J. (1989). *Understanding popular culture.* London: Routledge.

Fitzgerald, F. (1979). *America revised: History schoolbooks in the twentieth century.* Boston: Little, Brown.

Fordham, S. (1993a). Racelessness as a factor in Black students' success: Pragmatic strategy or pyrrhic victory? In H. Shapiro & D. Purpel (Eds.), *Critical social issues in American education* (pp. 149–178). New York: Longman. (Original work published 1988)

Fordham, S. (1993b). Those loud Black girls: (Black) women, silence, and gender: Passing in the academy. *Anthropology and Education Quarterly, 24*(1), 3–32.

Foster, W. (1982, April). *Toward a critical theory of educational administration.* Paper presented at the annual meeting of the American Educational Research Association, New York.

Franklin, J. H. (1976). *Racial equality in America.* Chicago: University of Chicago Press.

Fraser, N., & Nicholson, L. (1990). Social criticism without philosophy. In L. Nicholson (Ed.), *Feminism/postmodernism* (pp. 19–38). New York: Routledge.

Friedman, M. (1992). Feminism and modern friendship: Dislocating the community. In S. Avineri & A. De-Shalit (Eds.), *Communitarianism and individualism* (pp. 101–119). New York: Oxford University Press.

Fullan, M. (1991). *The new meaning of educational change.* New York: Teachers College Press.

Fuller, W. (1982). *The old country school.* Chicago: University of Chicago Press.

Gamson, W. (1968). *Power and discontent.* Homewood, IL: Dorsey Press.

Geertz, C. (1983). *Local knowledge.* New York: Basic Books.

Gerstle, G. (1989). *Working-class Americanism: The politics of labor in a textile city, 1914–1960.* Cambridge, England: Cambridge University Press.

Gilligan, C. (1982). *In a different voice: Psychological theory and women's development.* Cambridge, MA: Harvard University Press.

Giroux, H. (1981). *Ideology, culture, and the process of schooling.* Philadelphia: Temple University Press.

Giroux, H. (1983). *Theory and resistance in education: A pedagogy for the opposition.* South Hadley, MA: Bergin & Garvey.

Giroux, H. (1988). *Schooling and the struggle for public life.* Minneapolis: University of Minnesota Press.

Giroux, H. (1992). *Border crossings: Cultural workers and the politics of education.* New York: Routledge.

Giroux, H. (1993). *Living dangerously: Multiculturalism and the politics of difference.* New York: Lang.

Giroux, H. (1994). *Disturbing pleasures: Learning popular culture*. New York: Routledge.

Giroux, H. (1997). Rewriting the discourse of racial identity: Towards a pedagogy and politics of whiteness. *Harvard Educational Review, 67*, 285–320.

Grant, G. R. (1983). The teacher's predicament. *Teacher's College Record, 84*(3), 593–609.

Greene, M. (1997). A philosopher looks at qualitative research. In R. M. Jaeger (Ed.), *Complementary methods for research in education* (2nd ed., pp. 189–207). Washington, DC: American Educational Research Association.

Grimmett, P. P., & Crehan, E. P. (1992). The nature of collegiality in teacher development: The case of clinical supervision. In M. Fullan & A. Hargreaves (Eds.), *Teacher development and educational change* (pp. 56–85). New York: Falmer Press.

Gross, D. (1992). *The past in ruins: Tradition and the critique of modernity*. Amherst: University of Massachusetts Press.

Gusfield, J. R. (1975). *Community: A critical response*. New York: Harper & Row.

Gutman, A. (1987). *Democratic education*. Princeton, NJ: Princeton University Press.

Haft, S., Witt, P., & Thomas, T. (Producers), & Weir, P. (Director); (1989). *Dead poet's society* [Videotape]. Burbank, CA: Vista Home Video.

Hargreaves, A. (1994). *Changing teachers, changing times: Teachers' work and culture in the postmodern age*. New York: Teachers College Press.

Heath, S. B. (1983). *Ways with words*. New York: Cambridge University Press.

Heilbrun, C. G. (1988). *Writing a woman's life*. New York: Norton.

Henry, M. (1996). *Parent–school collaboration: Feminist organizational structures and school leadership*. Albany: State University of New York Press.

Herzberg, W. (1955). *Protestant, Catholic, Jew: An essay in American religious sociology*. Garden City, NY: Doubleday.

Hoffman, N. (1981). *Woman's "true" profession*. Old Westbury, NY: The Feminist Press.

Hofstadter, R. (1955). *The age of reform*. New York: Random House.

Hofstadter, R. (1969). *The idea of a party system*. Berkeley, CA: University of California Press.

hooks, b. (1989). *Talking back: Thinking feminist, thinking black*. Boston: South End Press.

Houston, B. (1996). Theorizing gender: How much of it do we need? In A. Diller, B. Houston, K. Morgan, & M. Ayim (Eds.), *The gender question in education: Theory, pedagogy, & politics* (pp. 75–88). Boulder, CO: Westview Press.

Hoyle, E. (1986). *The politics of school management*. London: Hodder & Stoughton.

Hurn, C. (1993). *The limits and possibilities of schooling*. Needham Heights, MA: Allyn & Bacon.

Johnson, S. M. (1990). *Teachers at work: Achieving success in our schools*. New York: Basic Books.

Johnstone, H. W. (1981). Toward an ethics for rhetoric. *Philosophy and Rhetoric, 20*(2), 129–134)

Kaestle, C. (1983). *Pillars of the republic: Common schools and American society*. New York: Hill & Wang.

Kanter, R. M. (1983). *The change masters: Innovation for productivity in the American corporation*. New York: Simon & Schuster.

Karl, B. (1983). *The uneasy state*. Chicago: University of Chicago Press.

Karp, D., & Yoels, W. (1993). *The sociology of everyday life*. Itasca, IL: Peacock.

Kazin, M. (1995). *The populist persuasion: An American history*. New York: Basic Books.

Kozol, J. (1991). *Savage inequalities: Children in America's schools*. New York: Crown.

Kruse, S. D. (1995). *Professionalism as the foundation for community: Case studies of middle school teachers*. Unpublished doctoral dissertation, Minneapolis, MN: University of Minnesota.

Kruse, S. D. & Louis, K. S. (1997). Teacher Teaming in middle schools: Dilemmas for a schoolwide community. *Educational Administration Quarterly, 33*, 261–289.

Kushman, J. W. (1992). The organizational dynamics of teacher workplace commitment: A study of urban elementary and middle schools. *Educational Administration Quarterly, 28*(1), 5–42.

Kuzmic, J. (1993). A beginning teacher's search for meaning: Teacher's socialization, organizational literacy, and empowerment. *Teaching and Teacher's Education, 10*, 15–27.

Kymlicka, W. (1991). *Contemporary political philosophy: An introduction*. Oxford: Clarendon.

Lamdin, D. (1995). Testing for the effect of school size on student achievement within a school district. *Educational Economics, 3*(1), 33–42.

Lee, V. E., & Smith, J. B. (1993). Effects of school restructuring on the achievement and engagement of middle grade students. *Sociology of Education, 66*(2), 164–187.

Lee, V. E., & Smith, J. B. (1995). Effects of high school restructuring and size on early gains in achievement and engagement. *Sociology of Education, 68*(4), 241–270.

Leithwood, K., Dart, B., Jantzi, D., & Steinbach, R. (1992). *Fostering organizational learning: A study of British Columbia's intermediate developmental site initiatives.* Final report of research to the British Columbia Ministry of Education: Victoria, B.C.

Leithwood, K., Jantzi, D., & Steinbach, R. (1993). *Sutton District High School: A case study of how one school transformed itself into "An oasis of safety, sanity, and stability."* Ontarion: Centre for Leadership, Ontario Institute for Studies in Education.

Lears, T. J. J. (1983/1993). *No place of grace.* Chicago: The University of Chicago Press.

Levine, S. L. (1989). *Promoting adult growth and schools: The promise of professional development.* Boston: Allyn & Bacon.

Lewis, R. W. B. (1955). *The American Adam: Innocence, tragedy, and tradition in the nineteenth century.* Chicago: University of Chicago Press.

Lieberman, A., & Miller, L. (1992). *Teachers, their world and their work: Implications for school improvement.* New York: Teachers College Press.

Linn, M. C. (1994). Gender and school learning: Science. In T. Husen & T. P. Neville (Eds.), *The international encyclopedia of education.* New York: Pergamon Press.

Linn, M. C., & Hyde, J. S. (1989). Gender, mathematics and science. *Educational Researcher, 18*(8), 17–27.

Little, J. W. (1990). The persistence of privacy: Autonomy and initiative in teachers' professional relations. *Teachers College Record, 91*(4), 509–536.

Lortie, D. C. (1975). *Schoolteacher: A sociological study.* Chicago: University of Chicago Press.

Louis, K. S. (1992). Restructuring and the problem of teachers' work. In A. Lieberman (Ed.), *The changing contexts of teaching* (pp. 138–156). Chicago: University of Chicago Press.

Louis, K. S. (1994). Beyond managed change: Rethinking how schools change. *School Effectiveness and School Improvement, 5*(1), 2–24.

Louis, K. S., & Kruse, S. D. (Eds.). (1995). *Professionalism and community: Perspectives from urban schools.* Thousand Oaks, CA: Corwin Press.

Louis, K. S., Marks, H., & Kruse, S. D. (1996). Teachers' community in restructuring schools. *American Educational Research Journal, 33*(4), 757–798.

Louis, K. S., & Smith, B. (1992). Student engagement and achievement in American secondary schools. In F. Newmann (Ed.), *Cultivating teacher engagement: Breaking the iron law of social class* (pp. 119–152). New York: Teachers College Press.

Lundeberg, M. A. (1997). You guys are overreacting: Teaching prospective teachers about subtle gender bias. *Journal of Teacher Education, 48*(1), 55–61.

MacIntyre, A. (1981). *After virtue: A study in moral theory.* Notre Dame, IN: University of Notre Dame Press.

Macleod, J. (1995). *Ain't no makin' it: Aspirations and attainment in a low-income neighborhood.* Boulder, CO: Westview Press.

Makay, J. J., & Brown, W. R. (1972). *The rhetorical dialogue.* Dubuque, IA: Brown.

Malen, B. (1994). The micropolitics of education: Mapping the multiple dimensions of power relations in school politics. *Journal of Educational Policy, 33*, 147–167.

Mann, D. (1986). Authority and school improvement: An essay on little king leadership. *Teachers College Record, 88*(1), 41–52.

Mayeroff, M. (1971). *On caring.* New York: Harper & Row.

Mazzoni, T. (1991). Analyzing state school policy making: An arena model, *Educational Evaluation and Policy Analysis, 13*, 115–138.

Mazzoni, T. (1994). State policy-making and school reform: Influences and influential. *Journal of Educational Policy, 16*, 53–73.

McIntosh, P. (1983). *Interactive phases of curricular re-vision*. Wellsey, MA: Wellesley College Center for Research on Women.

McKenna, T., & Ortiz, F. (1988). *The broken web*. Berkeley, CA: Floricanto Press.

McLaren, P. (1997). *Life in schools* (3rd ed.). New York: Longman.

Meier, D. (1995). *The power of their ideas: Lessons from a small school in Harlem*. Boston: Beacon.

Meier, D., & Schwartz, P. (1995). Central Park East Secondary School: The hard part is making it happen. In M. Apple & J. Beane (Eds.), *Democratic schools* (pp. 26–40). Alexandria, VA: Association of Supervision and Curriculum and Development.

Metz, M. (1988). "Phase I" of the teacher working conditions study (final report). Madison, WI: University of Wisconsin, Center for the Study of Effective Secondary Schools.

Meyer, J., & Rowan, B. (1983). The structure of educational organizations. In J. V. Baldridge & T. Deal (Eds.), *Dynamics of organizational change in education*. Berkeley, CA: McCutchan.

Miller, G. (1985). Work, rituals structures, and the legitimation of alternative communities. *Work and Occupations, 12*(1), 3–22.

Minow, M. (1990). *Making all the difference: Inclusion, exclusion, and American law*. Ithaca, NY: Cornell University Press.

Mitchell, B. (1990). Loss, belonging and becoming: Social policy themes for children and schools. In B. Mitchell & L. L. Cunningham (Eds.), *Educational leadership and changing contexts of families, communities and schools*. Chicago: National Society for the Study of Education.

Mittroff, I. (1981). *Creating a dialectical social science: Concepts, methods, and models*. London: Reidel.

Mohrman, S. A., & Wohlstetter, P. (1994). *School-based management: Organizing for high performance*. San Francisco, CA: Jossey-Bass.

Morgan, G. (1986). *Images of organization*. Beverly Hills, CA: Sage.

Muncey, D., & McQuillan, P. (1992). The dangers of assuming a consensus for change: Some examples from the Coalition of Essential Schools. In G. A. Hess (Ed.), *Empowering teachers and parents: School restructuring through the eyes of anthropologists* (pp. 47–70). Westport, CT: Bergin & Garvey.

Murphy, J. & Louis, K. S. (1994). *Reshaping the principalship: Insights from transformational reform efforts*. Thousand Oaks, CA: Sage.

National Assessment of Educational Progress. (1998). *The science report card: Elements of risk and recovery*. Princeton, NJ: Educational Testing Service.

National Center for Educational Statistics (NCES). (1996). *American education at a glance*. Washington DC: U.S. Department of Education.

National Commission on Excellence in Education. (1983). *A nation at risk*. Washington, DC: U.S. Government Printing Office.

Nelson, J. I. (1995). *Post-Industrial capitalism: Exploring economic inequality in America*. Thousand Oaks, CA: Sage.

Newmann, F. M. (1991). *What is a restructured school? A framework to clarify ends and means* (Issue Rep. No. 1). Madison: Center on Organization of Schools and by the National Association of Secondary School Principals, University of Wisconsin.

Newmann, F. M., and Associates (1996). *Authentic achievement: Restructuring schools for intellectual quality*. San Francisco: Jossey-Bass.

Newmann, F. M., & Rutter, R A. (1987). *Teachers' sense of efficacy and community as critical targets for school improvement*. Madison, WI: University of Wisconsin Center for the Study of Effective Secondary Schools.

Noble, D. W. (1965). *Historians against history: The frontier thesis and the national covenant in American historical writing since 1830*. Minneapolis: University of Minnesota Press.

Noble, D. W. (1980). *The progressive mind, 1890–1917* (rev. ed.). Minneapolis, MN: Burgess.

Noble, D. W. (1985). *The end of American history*. Minneapolis: University of Minnesota Press.

Noble, D. W., Horowitz, D.,& Carroll, P. (1980). *Twentieth century limited*. Boston: Houghton Mifflin.

Noddings, N. (1984). *Caring*. Berkeley, CA: University of California Press.

Noddings, N. (1986). Fidelity in teaching, teacher education, and research for teaching. *Harvard Educational Review*, 56(4), 496–510.

Oakes, J. (1985). *Keeping track: How schools structure inequality*. New Haven, CT: Yale University Press.

O'Conner, T. (1993). Looking back to forward. *Democracy and Education*, 8(2), 9–16.

Ogbu, J. (1988). Class stratification, racial stratification, and schooling. In L. Weis (Ed.), *Class, race, and gender in American education* (pp. 163–182). Albany: State University of New York Press.

Omi, M., & Winant, H. (1994). *Racial formation in the United States: From the 1960s to the 1990s*. New York: Routledge.

Orenstein, P. (1994). *Schoolgirls*. New York: Doubleday.

Pipher, M. (1994). *Reviving Ophelia: Saving the selves of adolescent girls*. New York: Ballantine.

Pocock, J. G. A. (1975). *The Machiavellian moment*. Princeton, NJ: Princeton University Press.

Postman, N. (1995). *The end of education*. New York: Knopf.

Presthus, R. (1979). *The organizational society* (rev. ed.). New York: St. Martin's Press.

Raywid, M. (1993) Finding time for collaboration. *Educational Leadership, 51*, 30–34.

Regan, H. B., & Brooks, G. H. (1995). *Out of women's experience*. Thousand Oaks, CA: Corwin.

Rich, A. (1986). *Blood, bread, and poetry*. New York: Norton.

Rifkin, J. (1995). *The end of work: The decline of the global labor force and the dawn of the post-market economy*. New York: Putnam.

Ritzer, G. (1993). *The McDonaldization of society*. Thousand Oaks, CA: Pine Forge Press.

Robertson, R. (1992). *Globalization: Social theory and global culture*. Newbury Park, CA: Sage.

Rollow, S., & Bryk, A. (1994). *Politics as a lever for organizational change*. Chicago: Center for School Improvement.

Rothman, R. (1996). Linking standards and instruction—HELPS is on the way. *Educational Leadership, 53*(8), 44–46.

Rotundo, A. (1993). *American manhood: Transformations in masculinity from the revolution to the modern era*. New York: Basic Books.

Rowan, B. (1991, April). *The shape of professional communities in schools*. Paper presented at the annual meetings of the American Educational Research Association, Chicago.

Sadker M., & Sadker, D. (1980). Sexism in teacher education texts. *Harvard Educational Review, 50*(1), 36–46.

Sadker M., & Sadker D. (1994). *Failing at fairness*. New York: Scribner.

Sandel, M. J. (1988, February 22). Democrats and community. *The New Republic*, 20–23.

Schmitt, R. (1997). *Introduction to Marx and Engels* (2nd ed.). Boulder, CO: Westview Press.

Scott, W. R. (1992). *Organizations: Rational, natural, and open systems* (3rd ed.). Englewood Cliffs, NJ: Prentice-Hall.

Senge, P. M. (1990). *The fifth discipline*. New York: Doubleday.

Sergiovanni, T. J. (1994). *Building community in schools*. San Francisco: Jossey-Bass.

Shakeshaft, C. (1989). *Women in educational administration*. Newbury Park, CA: Sage.

Shakeshaft, C. (1995). Foreword. In D. Dunlap & P. Schmuck (Eds.), *Women leading in education* (pp. xi–xiv). Albany: State University of New York.

Sleeter, C., & Grant, C. (1993). *Making choices for multicultural education*. Englewood Cliffs, NJ: Merill.

Smith, B. A. (1994). *Teacher quality of work life according to teachers: The case of high schools*. Unpublished doctoral dissertation, University of Minnesota, Minneapolis.

Spaulding, A. M. (1995, April). *A qualitative case study of teacher–student micropolitical interaction: The strategies, goals, and consequences of student resistance*. Paper presented at the American Educational Research Association Annual Conference, San Francisco.

Spring, J. (1972). *Education and the rise of the corporate state*. Boston: Beacon Press.

Spring, J. (1997). *The American school, 1642–1996* (3rd ed.). New York: McGraw–Hill.
Statistical portrait of the nation. (1993, January 26). *The New York Times*, p. A5.
Stiles, L. J., & Dorsey, M. F. (1950). *Democratic teaching in secondary schools*. Philadelphia: Lippincott.
Stone, L. S. (1994). *The education feminism reader*. New York: Routledge.
Strike, K. A. (1993). Professionalism, democracy, and discursive communities: Normative reflections on restructuring. *American Educational Research Journal, 30*(2), 255–275.
Takaki, R. (1993). *A different mirror*. Boston: Back Bay Books.
Tannen, D. (1990). *You just don't understand: Women and men in conversation*. New York: Ballantine.
Task Force on Education of Young Adolescents. (1989). *Turning points: Preparing America's youth for the 21st century*. New York: Carnegie Council on Adolescent Development.
Tom, A. (1984). *Teaching as a moral craft*. New York: Longman.
Tong, R. (1989). *Feminist thought: A comprehensive introduction*. Boulder, CO: Westview Press.
Tozer, S., Violas, P., & Senese. (1995). *School and society* (2nd ed.). New York: McGraw-Hill.
Tyack, D. (1974). *The one best system: A history of American urban education*. Cambridge, MA: Harvard University Press.
Tyack, D., & Hansot, E. (1982). *Managers of virtue*. New York: Basic Books.
Tyack, D., & Hansot, E. (1992). *Learning together: A history of coeducation in American schools*. New Haven, CT: Yale University Press.
United States Government Printing Office. (1994, January). House document 103–177, p. 13.
U.S. Department of Education. (1989). *National Education Longitudinal Study of 1988, Second Follow-up*. Washington DC: U.S. Department of Education, Educational Research and Improvement Office.
Valli, L. (1983). Becoming clerical workers: Business education and the culture of femininity. In M. Apple & L. Weis (Eds.), *Ideology and practice in schooling* (pp. 213–234). Philadelphia: Temple University Press.
Valverde, L. A., & Brown, F. (1988). Influences in leadership development among racial and ethnic minorities. In N. K. Boyan (Ed.), *Handbook of research on educational administration* (pp. 143–158). New York: Longman.
Warren, D. (Ed.); (1989). *American teachers: History of a profession at work*. New York: Macmillan.
Weber, M. (1968). *Economy and society* (3 vols.). New York: Beminster Press.
Weibe, R. (1967). *The search for order*. New York: Hill & Wang.
Weick, K. (1976). Educational organizations as loosely coupled systems. *Administrative Quarterly, 21*, 1–19.
Weis, L. (1988). (Ed.). *Class, race, and gender in American education*. Albany: State University of New York Press.
Weis, L. (1990). *Working class without work: High school dropouts in a de-industrializing economy*. New York: Routledge.
Wexler, P. (1987). *Social analysis of education: After the new sociology*. London: Routledge & Kegan Paul.
Wilbur, G. (1991). *Gender-fair curriculum*. Research report prepared for Wellesley College Research on Women, Wellesley, MA.
Williams, R. (1975). *The long revolution*. Westport, CT: Greenwood Press.
Willis, P. (1977). *Learning to labour*. London: Saxon House.
Wills, G. (1989). *Reagan's America*. New York: Penguin.
Wills, G. (1997). *John Wayne's America: The politics of celebrity*. New York: Simon & Schuster.
Wirt, F., & Kirst, M. (1982). *Schools in conflict*. Berkeley, CA: McCutchan.
Yankelovich, D. (1981). *New rules: Searching for self-fulfillment in a world turned upside down*. New York: Random House.
Zinn, H. (1990). *A people's history of the United States*. New York: Harper & Row.

Author Index

♦♦♦

Italicized parenthetical numbers, following page locators, refer to the number of citations greater than one that an author received on those pages.

Subject Index

◆ ◆ ◆

Bold page numbers indicate definitions.